Metaphysics and Grammar

'William Charlton's thesis that to understand the topics of metaphysics is to understand the grammar of our language sets him radically at odds with most contemporary metaphysics and most contemporary philosophy of language. The interest of his incisive and instructive book lies in the detail of his arguments. This is a book to be reckoned with.'
        Alasdair MacIntyre, Professor of Philosophy Emeritus, University of Notre Dame, USA

'I find it fascinating and full of insights ... this book is always provocative, insightful, and original.'
        Martha Nussbaum, Department of Philosophy and Law School, University of Chicago, USA

'Wonderfully clear and engaging, Charlton's book is the first fully to expound the idea that problems of metaphysics are to be tackled through an understanding of grammatical constructions. Charlton discusses and also goes beyond predecessors such as Wittgenstein, by showing the importance of focussing on a precise notion of grammar, while he also engages with the thought of many living as well as ancient philosophers. Stimulating arguments and a pleasure to read.'
        Alexander Bird, Professor of Philosophy, University of Bristol, UK

'Firmly rejecting current philosophical orthodoxy, with its science-inspired conception of 'research', Charlton's lucid and carefully argued study makes a strong case for thinking the traditional problems of metaphysics are best handled by developing a proper understanding of how language works.'
        John Cottingham, Professorial Research Fellow, Heythrop College, University of London, UK and Professor Emeritus of Philosophy, University of Reading, UK

'This lively and elegantly written book makes important suggestions on how to think about fundamental questions in metaphysics. It is not overly technical, so can be tackled by the interested amateur, but at the same time offers provocative thoughts, from which the professional philosopher could benefit.'
        Jane Heal, Emeritus Professor of Philosophy, University of Cambridge, UK

'William Charlton's study of Metaphysics and Grammar is an original and provoking philosophical enquiry. Written in the clearest of styles, it gently attracts the reader to follow its argument as it successively examines the concepts that have been at the centre of metaphysical reflection during the last two millennia: truth, goodness, existence, change, time, and causation. The book's central thesis is that these most abstract and fundamental concepts are properly understood as corresponding to grammatical constructions of natural language. Although deeply rooted in the history of philosophy (of which Charlton is a peerless expert), the book is eminently philosophical and engages in debates with the most authoritative contemporary philosophers.'
        Paolo Crivelli, Associate Professor of Ancient Philosophy, University of Geneva, Switzerland

Also available from Bloomsbury

Applying Wittgenstein, Rupert Read (edited by Laura Cook)
Contagious Metaphor, Peta Mitchell
Language: Key Concepts in Philosophy, Jose Medina
Metaphysics: An Introduction, Jonathan Tallant
Metaphysics, Alexander Baumgarten (translated and edited by Courtney D. Fugate and John Hymers)
Philosophy of Language, Chris Daly
Philosophy of Language: Key Thinkers, edited by Barry Lee
The Continuum Companion to Metaphysics, edited by Neil A. Manson and Robert W. Barnard
The Continuum Companion to the Philosophy of Language, edited by Manuel Garcia-Carpintero and Max Kolbel

Metaphysics and Grammar

William Charlton

BLOOMSBURY
LONDON • NEW DELHI • NEW YORK • SYDNEY

Bloomsbury Academic
An imprint of Bloomsbury Publishing Plc

50 Bedford Square　　1385 Broadway
London　　　　　　　New York
WC1B 3DP　　　　　　NY 10018
UK　　　　　　　　　USA

www.bloomsbury.com

Bloomsbury is a registered trade mark of Bloomsbury Publishing Plc

First published 2014

© William Charlton 2014

William Charlton has asserted his right under the Copyright, Designs and Patents Act, 1988, to be identified as the Author of this work.

All rights reserved. No part of this publication may be reproduced or transmitted in any form or by any means, electronic or mechanical, including photocopying, recording, or any information storage or retrieval system, without prior permission in writing from the publishers.

No responsibility for loss caused to any individual or organization acting on or refraining from action as a result of the material in this publication can be accepted by Bloomsbury or the author.

British Library Cataloguing-in-Publication Data
A catalogue record for this book is available from the British Library.

ISBN: HB: 978-1-4725-3421-7
PB: 978-1-4725-7930-0
ePDF: 978-1-4725-2887-2
ePub: 978-1-4725-3193-3

Library of Congress Cataloging-in-Publication Data
A catalog record for this book is available from the Library of Congress.

Typeset by Fakenham Prepress Solutions, Fakenham, Norfolk NR21 8NN

Contents

Foreword		vi
1	Introduction	1
2	How Metaphysics Arose	21
3	Grammar and Lexicography	37
4	Wittgenstein and Chomsky on Grammar	47
5	Truth and Predication	69
6	Existence and Quantification	89
7	Goodness, Counsels and Commands	99
8	Change and Tense	117
9	Time and Aspect	127
10	Causation	141
11	Materiality	157
12	Thinking	169
13	Saying	193
14	Conclusion	205
Notes		213
Bibliography		221
Index		229

Foreword

I hope that this book will be found readable by anyone who is interested in the very abstract topics with which it deals and in the efforts of past philosophers to come to grips with them. But it is addressed also to professional academics who will want exact references to the works and authors I discuss. To non-professionals I apologise for peppering my pages with parentheses they can safely ignore. I refer to modern writers (those, roughly speaking, since the late nineteenth century) by name and date. The only exception is Wittgenstein. I refer to his *Blue and Brown Books* by the letters *BB* and the page number, and to his *Philosophical Investigations*, Part 1, and *Philosophical Grammar* by the letters *PI* and *PG* and their entry number. To earlier writers I refer by the titles of their works, and when there is an accepted way of pinpointing passages, as there is for Plato and Aristotle, I avail myself of it. In the case of Hume I give the page in Selby-Bigge's much reprinted editions. The translations are my own except where otherwise attributed.

An earlier version of Chapters 5 and 7 appeared in *Philosophy*, and I am grateful to the editor, Anthony O'Hear, for permission to reuse the material. I also thank Imprint Academic, Exeter, for letting me reuse, in Chapter 2, material that originally appeared in *History of Political Thought*, Volume 6, Issue 1/2. I thank Noam Chomsky for permitting me to quote from his *Problems of Knowledge and Freedom*. Richard King gave me an opportunity to try out ideas that appear in Chapters 2 and 12 at the conference on The Good Life and Conceptions of Life in Greek and Chinese Antiquity, which was held in Glasgow in June 2010. Drafts of several chapters were read to the Newcastle philosophy group, Applied Philosophy, Ideas Section, organized by Mary Midgley and Michael Bavidge; I am much indebted to those present, for their comments and suggestions. Brian McGuinness kindly looked over a draft of my remarks on Wittgenstein, and Jane Heal and Richard Sorabji read early versions of the whole book and made extremely helpful comments. Caroline Bowes Lyon allowed me to consult her about recent work in cognitive science. Anne Jacobson let me see drafts of unpublished work. Ian Ground and Jane O'Grady directed me to relevant material I should otherwise have overlooked. I owe much to anonymous publishers' readers who pointed out weaknesses and omissions; and in the last five years all my friends who have any interest in philosophy or foreign languages have endured being consulted by me on this project.

1

Introduction

Truth, existence, goodness, time, causation, language, thought: these are central topics of philosophy. There are many things we think true, but what is truth? Scientists tell us what animals, vegetables and minerals exist, but they won't tell us what existence is. The difference between existing and not existing could hardly be more obvious or more important, but when we try to put it into words it slips away from us. History tells us what events have taken place; but what is it for an event to take place? Historians of ideas say what various people have thought, but what is thinking? All kinds of people clamour to tell us what is right and what is wrong; but what is it to *be* right or wrong?

Only philosophers address these questions. They tackle other questions too. Moral philosophers today discuss the ethics of abortion, infanticide, euthanasia. Political philosophers consider what systems of government or constitutional arrangements are just, and what rights societies should recognize and sanction. But these are questions about which many people have plenty to say, whereas questions like those I formulated in my first paragraph seem to be peculiar to philosophers.

And very peculiar they seem in themselves, when we look at them without a prejudice in their favour. We may wonder if they make sense, if they are proper English. 'What time is it?' is a normal question; 'What is time?' is not. Try asking it to the woman next to you on the bus, and even if she is a philosopher she will wonder if she has heard correctly: 'How do you mean, "What is time?"' If you are a stranger and a man, she may suspect you of some improper purpose. Similarly with 'What did he think?' and 'What is thinking?', with 'What caused the crash?' and 'What is causing?', with 'What would it be good to do?' and 'What is being good?' We have to bury our heads in the sand of 24 centuries of philosophical literature to blind ourselves to their oddity.

I call them 'metaphysical'. The word has a bad sound, which Hume at the end of his *Enquiry Concerning the Principles of Morals* exploited in reply to an imagined objector:

All this is metaphysics, you cry. That is enough; there needs nothing more to give a strong presumption of falsehood. Yes, reply I, here are metaphysics surely; but they are all on your side, who advance an abstruse hypothesis, which can never be made intelligible, nor quadrate with any particular instance or illustration. (*Enquiries*, p. 289.)

A. J. Ayer, who professed himself a follower of Hume, defined a metaphysical sentence as one 'which purports to express a genuine proposition, but does, in fact, express neither a tautology nor an empirical hypothesis', and on the basis of this definition he declared 'we are justified in concluding that all metaphysical assertions are nonsensical' (1936, p. 41). Without going so far as that, Alan White argued that metaphysics typically ends in postulating 'the existence of entities undreamt of by our ordinary thinking' (among which, writing in the 1980s, he included God; *qualia* and Fregean 'thoughts' might have been better examples) (1987, p. 200). R. G. Collingwood, in contrast, defined metaphysics as the study of what he called 'absolute presuppositions' (1939), and argued that every systematic study has such presuppositions, and makes assumptions that cannot be shown to be true within the discipline. In fact the word metaphysics means very little. It comes from the Greek for 'after physics' and was first applied to certain writings by Aristotle perhaps for no reason except that in some collection of his works they came after the treatises on 'physics', a word which at that time covered all studies of natural phenomena. Aristotle's 'metaphysical' writings do however deal with such topics as being, becoming, existence, number and causation, and today 'metaphysics' is commonly used as a label for the part of philosophy that deals with the topics I have listed.[1] I simply follow that practice.

No less odd than the questions metaphysicians ask is their claim to be better able to answer them than other people. They promise to tell us more than ordinary adults know about truth, goodness, time, causation and the rest. Is that credible? What possible investigations could extend human knowledge about these things? In the last 50 years universities, at least in some English-speaking countries, have come to be seen as places not for higher education, but for research. Funding has been tied to extending human knowledge as distinct from just handing it on, and philosophers in university posts now speak of themselves as engaged in research. Empirical research can certainly help us to argue for or against changes in the laws concerning matters about which all societies have laws or customs – sex, death, citizenship, penal practice, the appointment of officers and so forth. By reading in libraries we can learn what philosophers in the past have said about things like truth, existence and goodness. But what kind of research can give us fresh knowledge about those things themselves?

That question, at least, can be answered fairly easily. Philosophy has always been regarded as an arts subject, and that part of philosophy which deals with these topics is an art rather than a science. Research has no more place in it than it has in poetry or painting. It is legitimate for a novelist or a playwright who wants to set a story in the past or in a remote location to do some historical or geographical research, but nobody suggests that Homer or Shakespeare did that. Pure mathematics too is traditionally classed as an arts subject, and although mathematicians may talk of discovering properties of numbers and figures – not ordinary numbers and figures known to everyone, but the special ones known only to themselves, like those that appear in Marcus du Sautoy's *A Mathematician's Journey Through Symmetry* (2008) – these numbers and figures are not to be found in the physical world, and the mathematicians themselves have the creative project of constructing proofs. The fascination of metaphysical questions is, in fact, not unlike that of obstinate problems in pure mathematics. Why are the prime numbers distributed as they are through the series of natural numbers, the series 1, 2, 3 …? Surely there ought to be a pattern, but no one has ever found out what it is. The primes get rarer as we progress along the series, but they still seem to be scattered at random. Why is the diameter of a circle incommensurable with the circumference? There is a proof of that, but it is extremely long and complicated;[2] surely there must be a simple explanation. Christian Goldbach (1690–1764) conjectured that every even number greater than three is the sum of two primes. That proposition is so simple that either it should be easy to prove it true or it should be easy to find a counter-example; but no proof or counter-example has yet been found. The mathematician considers things highly abstract – the series of natural numbers, the straight line and the circle, which seem both basic and independent of us, yet which baffle our intelligence; and so does the metaphysician.

If metaphysics is an art (something readers of its recent literature may be surprised to learn) it does not have to proceed by research. But how does it, or should it, proceed? And why should metaphysicians know more about its topics than anyone else? That is what I hope to explain in this book. Let me give an outline of my argument. It will probably sound obscure in parts, and when not obscure, highly questionable. But a work of metaphysics is not like a detective novel or a suspense story; from the start the reader needs all the help the author can provide, including an honest statement of where the argument is going.

Sentences are constructed out of words. That is true of all human languages. The words we use, or most of them, words like 'elephant', 'crimson', 'running', 'trumping', 'noun', 'arrogant', signify things that exist or might exist and are investigated by experts of various kinds: the zoologist, the physicist, the athletics trainer, the dedicated card-player, the grammarian, the clinical psychologist, or, in a different way, by the painter or the psychological novelist. The constructions we use have meaning too, but in a different way from these words. Sometimes when we speak we make a statement; sometimes we give advice or make a request; sometimes we explain how something was caused or prevented; sometimes we say why someone did or didn't do something. These are different forms of speech, different, we might say, linguistic acts. The constructions we use determine which of them we perform: using those constructions *is* asserting or counselling or explaining. And in determining this they are expressive of the topics of metaphysics.

At the base of all human language lie two grammatical distinctions which cut across one another: the simplest sentences are either indicative or non-indicative, and either predicative or existential. Examples of indicative sentences are 'That wine is red' and 'There are mosquitoes here', and the former is predicative, the latter existential. Examples of non-indicative sentences are 'Run!' and 'If only there were some water!' and again (though this is less obvious and may need arguing) the first is predicative, the second existential. Truth, I shall argue, is what is expressed by indicative constructions, so anyone who understands indicative constructions has the concept of truth; goodness or rightness is expressed by non-indicative, so anyone who understands these constructions has the notion of goodness; and existence, obviously, is expressed by existential constructions, though that sounds too simple, so instead of existential constructions I shall speak of constructions in which we quantify: the simplest sentences are those in which we either predicate something or quantify something.

The ideas of truth, goodness and existence are the most abstract and fundamental we have. They are bound up with the possibility of language. Less abstract are those of the most general features of the world of which we speak. This is a world in which we act. We have ideas of it as something apart from us, as that in which we act, and we also have ideas of ourselves as acting in it. As a world in which we act it is one in which changes take place over time and are caused. Change, time and causation characterize the physical aspect of the world. As agents acting in this world we desire some changes and are averse to others. Our preferences have reasons. And our action is for the purpose of bringing about changes we desire and preventing changes to which we are averse. Acting for reasons and purposes characterizes the psychological aspect of us as agents in the world.

In Chapters 8 and 9 I show how the change, temporal relations and time itself are expressed by grammar: by verbs of doing and becoming, and by tense and aspect. (The difference between 'The leaves are turning yellow' and 'The leaves were turning yellow' is one of tense, while that between 'They were turning yellow' and 'They turned yellow' is one of aspect.) The concept of time, I argue, depends on a distinction which is created by grammar, the distinction between a change that takes place and its taking place. In Chapters 10 and 11 I show how causation is expressed in such grammatical devices as transitive and intransitive uses of verbs (as in 'The Sun melted the butter' and 'The butter melted') and what grammarians call 'voice'. (The voice is 'active' in 'Ahab killed a whale' and 'passive' in 'Ahab was killed by a whale'.)

In Chapter 12 and 13 I argue that the constructions we use in interpreting our behaviour, including our utterances, in terms of reasons and purposes, express the psychological side of our being, that they give us our ideas of consciousness, belief, desire, feeling and meaning.

All this may sound absurd. 'Truth', 'existence', 'goodness', 'think' and the rest are English words, and it is natural to suppose that truth, existence and goodness are the things they signify. It is natural, I mean, to suppose that, like 'elephant', 'breathing' and 'arrogance', they signify things that exist or might exist and can be investigated. Investigation might reveal that, like 'centaur', 'witchcraft' or 'phlogiston' they signify things that don't exist; but either they are words for things that are real, or they are words for things mistakenly believed to be real. I shall argue that they are neither. The supposition that they must be one or the other leads to philosophy that is either naive or sceptical. Some philosophers have made out that existence is a special kind of activity in which things engage, time a special kind of process that goes on, goodness a special property that can attach to actions, states of affairs or persons; that thinking a process in the way drinking and shrinking are processes, but one that is non-physical. Others have said that time and change are illusions, that nothing is objectively good or bad, that nothing really causes anything, or that mental states and processes are simply physical processes and states of the nervous system. I shall argue that the words which seem to signify the topics of metaphysics apply primarily not to things about which we think and speak but to our speech and thought about such things; they are words about words, second-order words, though they can also be used to give our speech a certain form.

If I am right, how are metaphysical topics to be investigated? How can we extend our knowledge of things expressed by grammar? In a way we cannot extend it. Children may extend it by learning new constructions, learning how to speak of the past and the future, how to explain changes that take place in the world and purposive human behaviour, but an ordinary adult already knows what truth, existence and the rest are. 'What is time?' Augustine asked. 'If you don't ask me, I know, but if you ask me I do not know' (*Confessions* 11.14). The same could be said of all the other topics of metaphysics. We know what they are because we understand the constructions that express them; we cannot say what they are, because we do not know that understanding these constructions constitutes knowing what they are. We think that something further is required, but we cannot say what. Dr Johnson spoke of 'the anfractuosities of the human mind', using a word that suggests 'a deep bay, full of inlets and caverns' (R. A. Knox, 1958, p. 90). Among the deepest anfractuosities are thinking true, thinking real, thinking good, thinking something to be the causing of change, or intentional or conscious. The metaphysician must persuade us that we do conceive them as he or she claims; make us say 'Yes, that's what I thought but I couldn't put it into words.' Pope's description of true wit fits good metaphysics:

> Something whose truth convinced at once we find,
> That gives us back the image of our mind (*Essay on Criticism* 297–300)

That calls for the perceptivity of the psychological novelist together with a debater's ability to anticipate and parry objections – a tall order.

The task attracts philosophers as certain subjects, the human figure, for example, or horses, attract representational painters. Constable, it seems, longs to put down on canvas what he sees in leafy trees, which is different from what Poussin saw and Monet was going to see. Cezanne returns more than once to the Montaigne Sainte-Victoire, as if he wants to get it clear, or try out a new treatment of it. That is how metaphysicians feel about existence, goodness and thought, though these abstract topics are perhaps less like leafy trees or the human figure than deserts. They may be compared to the strangely shaped mountains of the north west of Scotland, which have no trees on them and seem never to have been brought into the use of human beings; or to the gigantic rock formations of southern Utah that have brilliant colours and fantastic shapes, but are almost wholly bare even of vegetation. To spend hours pondering upon existence, truth or time is like walking in these alien landscapes.[3]

I am saying that the topics of metaphysics are things expressed not by words but by grammatical constructions. This claim is, I believe, novel. Philosophers, at least since the Middle Ages, have paid little attention to grammar. Descartes and Leibniz toyed with the idea of a universal grammar,[4] but say nothing about the grammar of languages in which they wrote. Richard Gaskin recently edited a collection of papers entitled *Grammar in Early Twentieth-Century Philosophy* and says at the outset:

> What is the philosophical significance of grammar? No period in the history of philosophy provides a richer source of materials for the consideration of this question than the period running from the end of the nineteenth century to the Second World War. (2001, p. i.)

Philosophers of that period, however, did not distinguish sharply between the study of grammatical constructions and lexicography, and said little about the former. Wittgenstein often used the word 'grammar' for any kind of study of words. Gaskin does not himself define grammar, and only one of his contributors, Alex Oliver, makes use of the work of grammarians; the rest just settle down to problems in the philosophy of language without any special regard for the way in which sentences are constructed. Some twentieth-century philosophers seem to imagine that language could exist without grammatical constructions.[5] Bede Rundle, indeed, in *Grammar in Philosophy* (1979) talks about constructions not only in English but in a wide range of languages. He does not, however, offer any general account of how grammatical constructions have meaning. He gives only two of his 480 pages (pp. 412–14) to discussion of how meaning attaches to different parts of speech and says:

> It is sometimes said that indications of tense and number, for instance, have merely grammatical meaning. However, whatever that means, it remains true that at one level the pattern of explanation is as for other elements of language.

It is surprising he does not think it worthwhile to ask *what* 'grammatical meaning' means or discuss the distinction drawn by pre-Enlightenment philosophers between categorematic and syncategorematic terms. A few philosophers, for instance Zeno Vendler (1957) and Anthony Galton (1987), have noticed the grammatical phenomenon known as 'aspect', but they have not considered using it, as I shall, to explain the nature of time or the distinctions between being and becoming and belief and desire.[6]

A novel claim is liable to be misunderstood or, if understood, vigorously resisted. I shall first try to dispose of some misunderstandings, and then consider some sources of resistance.

First, the word 'grammar' itself may be misunderstood. It comes from the Greek *grammatike*, which means just literacy, the ability to read and write. In England it came to be used for 'the science of speaking correctly'. That is how it is defined in *Todd's Johnson's Dictionary* in 1818, the year of Cobbett's *Grammar of the English Language*, and this usage lingered on. 'I've grammar and spelling for two and blood and behaviour for twenty' sings Lord Tolloller in *Iolanthe* (1882). Noam Chomsky (1965) counts as the grammar of a language a complete description of it comprising rules of syntax for constructing sentences out of components, phonological rules for pronouncing and writing these components, and semantic rules giving the meaning of components. Traditionally, however, a distinction has been drawn between lexicography, which is listing the words in a language and saying what they mean, and grammar in a narrow sense, which is giving rules for the construction of sentences out of words. It is this narrower notion which the 1956 *Shorter Oxford English Dictionary* tries to capture when it defines grammar as 'that department of the study of language which deals with the inflexional forms, or their equivalents, and with the rules of employing them correctly'; and it is grammar in this restricted sense which I wish to connect with the topics of metaphysics.

Grammar needs to be distinguished from two other studies concerned with language, the philosophy of language and linguistics. Grammar is always the grammar of some particular language like English or French, just as a word is always a word in some particular language. Linguistics is the study of language generally; it is an attempt to say what is common to all languages, and to find rules for the construction of sentences that underlie all languages. The philosophy of language, which I am here taking to be part of metaphysics, deals with concepts which, both in grammar and in linguistics, are taken for granted; it deals with saying, meaning, speech and so forth. There is some overlap between these disciplines, but anyone can see that there is a difference between the grammarian's question 'How do you make statements in French?', the linguist's 'How do you make statements in any language?' and the philosopher's 'What is it to make a statement?'.

Unfortunately the notion that there is a correct way of speaking has been thought to buttress class distinctions, and British educationalists after 1945 therefore discouraged the teaching of grammar in state schools. As the result of this well-intentioned but ill-conceived policy many people come to study philosophy without knowing any of the technical terms of grammar in the narrow sense at all. Expressions like 'indefinite article', 'demonstrative pronoun', 'pluperfect subjunctive' and the dictionary's 'inflexional form' seem to belong to a terrifying alien language. It may be helpful, therefore, if I say right now a word about the term 'inflexion' or, as I prefer to spell it, 'inflection', which will appear often in what follows. An inflection is a modification of a word like adding an 's' to the end to indicate plurality. We say 'one bird' but 'several birds'. This is called an 'inflection of number'. English is not rich in inflections, but we also have an 'inflection of tense' that indicates something's belonging to the past: we say 'kill, *killed*', 'think, *thought*', 'drink, *drank*', and an 'inflection of person' which we use in saying that something was done by an individual other than ourselves or the person we are addressing: we say: 'I drink, you drink, he *drinks*.' Latin, which is a very highly inflected language, uses inflections where English uses other grammatical devices (the Dictionary's 'equivalents') such as prepositions like 'of', 'by', 'for' and so called 'auxiliary' verbs 'have' and 'will'.

Grammar being the study of how sentences in a given language are constructed, I do not pretend that metaphysics is part of grammar, or that grammarians know better than anyone else what truth, goodness or thought is. Grammarians have technical concepts of their own that they use in formulating their rules, concepts of subject and predicate, noun and verb and so on. These they can or should define. But the concepts of metaphysics are not among them. Grammarians use concepts of time, causation, belief, purpose and so on without analysing them rather as the rest of us do all the time – but with this difference, that we use them in thinking about natural phenomena, human behaviour and practical problems, whereas they use them in thinking that certain constructions express time or causation or belief or purpose. It is not the business of grammarians to say how metaphysical concepts work, but it is the business of metaphysicians to say how grammar works.

The claim that metaphysical concepts are expressed by grammar may sound similar at first to what is called the 'Sapir–Whorf Hypothesis'. In the 1930s Benjamin Lee Whorf, a disciple of Edward Sapir, put forward the idea that the grammar of a language determines the metaphysics of the society that uses it. The Hopi Indians of Arizona, for instance, have a different concept of time (he says) from Europeans. Their verbs do not have past, present and future tenses, but instead differentiate what is actual or objectively real from what is desired, intended or in other ways subjective or in the making. As a result, they do not have our concepts of past, present and future, or even our distinction between time and space (Whorf 1991, pp. 47–64). Whorf did not discuss in detail any metaphysical topic other than time, but he suggests that a society's grammar determines its concepts of action (pp. 72, 80), causation (pp. 80, 81) and number (pp. 139–40). The suggestion is not that a language's grammar imposes metaphysical theories or analyses on the people who use it; Whorf recognizes that only philosophers are prepared to say what time, causation and number are. Rather the grammar of a society determines what topics its philosophers, if any should arise, will offer theories of.

Whorf was not a professional academic and never gave a full, systematic exposition of his hypothesis. Perhaps that is why it has been treated with less respect than I think it deserves. It has some affinity with my thesis, but the two are different and, in fact, opposed. Whorf believed that grammar determines how we think about the world, what formal concepts we apply to it. We Europeans think physical nature is characterized by change, time and causation; if we had a different grammar we wouldn't. I believe that all human societies have the same forms of thought, that everywhere people think that things exist or occur, that things are good or bad, that changes are brought about and prevented, sometimes for purposes. Different grammars are different systems for expressing the same forms of thought. When thought is expressed in words grammar divides it into statements, orders and explanations, and it is from these different forms of speech that we take our ideas of different forms of thought. At most our grammar shapes our thinking about our *thought* about the world.

It is commonly said today that during the twentieth century philosophy in English-speaking countries took a 'linguistic turn', which proved to be a blind alley and brought the discipline into disrepute. My claim that words like 'truth' and 'goodness' have a primary use in describing forms of speech may sound like a reversion to a discredited way of philosophizing, or perhaps a survival of it. What exactly was this linguistic turn? It is sometimes traced back to Gottlob Frege, who in 1879 published a paper with the subtitle 'A formalized Language of pure Thought modelled upon the Language of Arithmetic' (1952, p. 1). Some philosophers were attracted by the idea of such a language. Others, like A. J. Ayer (1936), used Kantian distinctions between analytic and synthetic judgements and between what can be known by experience and what can be known independently of experience to give a definition of meaning which would rule out as meaningless certain classes of indicative sentence: sentences purporting to express statements about God, rightness and wrongness and about beauty. This definition of meaning is now discredited, and many writers who accepted the description 'analytical philosopher' had no wish either to model all language on that of arithmetic or to dismiss metaphysics, theology, ethics and aesthetics as nonsensical. They simply thought that the main business of philosophy is to analyse certain concepts, to say, that is, how we conceive certain things or what we take them to be, and that the best way to do this is to take our way of speaking about them as a guide. As an account of philosophy in general that is too narrow: logicians and moral and political philosophers do far more than analyse concepts and ways in which we use words. But if we want to discuss things like existence or time or goodness it is only common sense to ask how we conceive them, and in such enquiries we ignore language at our peril. What brought philosophy into popular disrepute was an irritating manner some philosophers had of parrying substantial questions by saying 'It all depends on what you mean by the word "so-and-so",' or engaging in prolonged discussions of trivial English idioms – something that was well parodied by Tom Stoppard.

Many twentieth-century philosophers did work with a picture that goes back to Aristotle of three levels or tiers of reality, a verbal level of words that vary from one society to another, a conceptual level of ideas symbolized by these words, which are much the same for everyone, and a physical level of things of which the ideas are non-physical representations:

> Spoken words are symbols (*sumbola*) of things produced in the mind (*pathêmata en têi psukhêi*), and written words of those that are spoken. And as written letters are not the same everywhere, so spoken words are not the same either; but the things of which these words are primarily signs, the things in the mind, are the same for everyone, and the things [in reality] of which these are likenesses are the same too. (*De Interpretatione* 16a3–8)[7]

These six lines were written not as a formal account but as part of an informal introduction to a treatise on language; nevertheless they have had enormous influence on European philosophy. It can be seen to this day. In 'modern linguistics', we are told by Marc C. Hauser, Noam Chomsky and W. Tecumseh Fitch, the word 'language' is used, not for languages like 'English, Navaho, etc.', but 'to refer to an internal component of the mind/brain (sometimes called "internal language")' (2002, p. 1570). I do not rely on this Aristotelian picture, on the Kantian distinctions[8] or on a belief that arithmetic will serve as a model for all thought. I follow one twentieth-century thinker, Wittgenstein, in arguing that a principal source of bad metaphysics is misunderstanding of how language works; and I draw a distinction which was not recognized in the twentieth century between ideas expressed by words for things, and ideas expressed by constructions. Analysing the latter is quite different from analysing ideas expressed by words that work by signifying things, and proceeds by examining a different way in which words function, namely by determining forms of speech.

My enterprise may encounter resistance from two directions. Questions about truth, existence, goodness, time, causation and mind seem to be the deepest that engage the human intellect. It may feel disappointing to be told that they are questions simply about words or thoughts. Timothy Williamson (2007) says 'Philosophy is in no deep sense a linguistic or conceptual inquiry' (p. 21, cf. p. 211). Taking concepts as 'something like mental or semantic representations', he says they constitute 'only a small fraction of mind-independent reality' (pp. 30, 14). 'Many epistemologists study knowledge, not just the ordinary concept of knowledge. Metaphysicians who study the nature of identity over time ask how things persist, not how we think or say they persist.' 'Contemporary metaphysics studies substances and essences, universals and particulars, space and time, possibility and necessity' (pp. 211, 19).

If we ask how we are to study these latter chunks of mind-independent reality he tells us (chapter 6) to use thought experiments like the one that Edmund Gettier devised to show that knowledge is something more than justified true belief. Gettier (1963) imagined a situation in which a person has a belief which is true and justified but does not *know*. We might suppose that this exercise of imagination can shed light only on how we *conceive* knowledge or how we are prepared to use the *word* 'know'. But Williamson argues that at the heart of this procedure is a counterfactual conditional, 'If you had a true belief in the Gettier situation you wouldn't have knowledge', and claims that this is no more about concepts or words than 'If you had worn thicker underwear you wouldn't have hypothermia.'

He takes the question 'Was Mars always either dry or not dry?' as philosophical, or 'at least protophilosophical in character' (2007, p. 24), and holds, rightly, that it is about the planet Mars. He also says that a good philosophical account of vagueness would enable us to answer it. But vagueness is a property of language and thought. (A person who thinks or speaks vaguely might be called 'a vague person' but only a philosopher would call an object with indeterminate boundaries like a mountain 'a vague object'.) I am not qualified to pronounce on planets, but suppose we are on a walk together, and after a period of silence you pop out the question 'Is Utah dry?' I might respond by asking 'Do you mean dry as against wet or dry as against permitting the sale of alcohol?' That is a question about the sense in which you are using the word 'dry'. If you say 'Dry as against allowing the sale of drink', I can answer your question: 'Parts are dry and parts not.' If, however, you say 'Dry as against wet', I should seek further clarification: 'Why are you asking? What have you got in mind?' My reason would be that 'dry' and 'wet', like 'large' and 'small' and 'loud' and 'soft', are relative terms of a particular kind. Things are called dry or wet in relation to some norm, perhaps to an average, or perhaps to what is best for some purpose. Do you want to know whether the rainfall in Utah is above or below average, or whether the climate is too dry for growing rice, or not too wet for a pleasant walking holiday? Here I am not uncertain about the sense in which you are using the word, but about the purpose for which you are using it in that sense. Williamson does not draw such distinctions, but I think a philosopher might just as well draw them as take Williamson's line and invoke three-valued and fuzzy logics.

Saying 'Philosophers shouldn't study just our concepts of knowledge and the rest; they should study the things themselves', involves both a mistake and a confusion. The mistake I have already identified. It is to suppose that words like 'know', 'think', 'true', 'exist', and 'good' do actually signify things in the same way as 'snow', 'blink', 'blue', 'insist' and 'blood'. The confusion is between two ways of studying representations. 'Zoologists', someone might say, 'don't just study pictures of elephants; they study elephants themselves.' But there are two ways of studying pictures of elephants. You can examine the pigments, the paper, the canvas that the artists employed, and weigh individual canvases, measure frescoes. Or you can see how elephants are represented. You might do that for various purposes. An art historian might compare different styles of representation. If, however, elephants should become extinct, future zoologists might have to work out their anatomy and ways of behaving from how they are represented in surviving pictures. Analytical philosophers who supposed truth, existence and the rest are realities signified by words in the same way as natural substances, qualities and modes of locomotion, still thought they have to be studied through the ways in which we think and speak about them; Williamson reproves them as though they advocated examining words in the way pictures are examined by removals men or analytical chemists.

Another philosopher who bids us study things directly and not through language is John Heil (2003). The idea that 'we must start with language and work our way outwards', he says (p. viii), 'is responsible for the sterile nature of much contemporary analytical philosophy'. The antidote is ontology, which he doesn't define but seems to conceive as the study of the things in the world that make true assertions true (*ibid.*). That sounds a good project, but what, then, distinguishes the ontologist from the historian, the natural scientist and other academics? From Plato onwards philosophers have drawn distinctions between things that 'make assertions true' which are quite different from the distinctions drawn by chemists between elements, by zoologists between species of animal, by musicologists between sounds. They have distinguished substances from qualities and relations, changes from states of affairs and so forth, labelling these categories by taking words from ordinary language but giving them technical, philosophical senses. Ontology deals with the basis of these distinctions, which is debatable. Do daffodils differ from the colour yellow and the process of growth in what they are or in how they are spoken of? Heil himself arrives at two basic types of thing, which he calls 'objects' and 'properties', and argues that properties are '"particularized" ways particular objects are' (pp. 126–7),[9] but he starts (chapter 3) from the grammatical notion of a predicate-phrase like 'is red' (p. 27). His complaint against sterile analytical philosophers is that they accept (often unconsciously) what he calls the 'Picture Theory'. The 'core idea' of this theory, he tells us, is 'that the character of reality can be *read off* our linguistic representations of reality' (pp. 6, 23, 189). He does not explain this further, but what he means is that they think the surface grammar of sentences like 'That tomato is red' is a sure guide to the kinds of thing that make such sentences true and mirrors the structure of reality. That philosophers (and not just 'analytical' philosophers) think this and go astray in consequence is precisely the complaint Wittgenstein makes in his later writings. So far Heil and that leading 'linguistic' philosopher are in step. The remedy, however, is not to avoid language altogether like an unclean thing; if we do that we shall never explain how we mean to use words like 'object', 'property', 'quality' and 'disposition'. Rather we should study language more closely and see how the structure of reality is in fact expressed.

A different source of opposition to my theory may be found in cognitive science. In order to interact with the world as we do, driving cars, touch-typing, carrying on conversations, we need muscular skills and skills at recognizing things by sight and hearing under varying circumstances. Cognitive scientists ask *how* we do these things. They identify the physiological processes involved in controlling our limbs and perceiving. George Lakoff and Mark Johnson (1999) claim that this work shows how metaphysical questions arise and how to deal with them. Williamson denies that we should study our concepts of time, existence and the rest, but holds, nevertheless, that we can do metaphysics without leaving our armchairs. They disagree on both points. To analyse the concepts we must team up with neurologists and conduct (presumably painless) experiments on student volunteers. Stimulations of sense-organs produce neural states, which are 'the neural mechanisms that give rise to concepts'; these states are in fact 'embodiments of concepts' and shape or determine them (pp. 36–7). The concepts of metaphysics are formed out of these primal concepts by composition and transference comparable to the transference of words in metaphor. Cognitive science reveals that they are accumulations of concepts borrowed from various sources, mutually inconsistent but each with its uses. Time, for example, is conceived as motion, and that in two incompatible ways, and also as a kind of substance (pp. 52, 139–48); existence is 'presence in a bounded region around a deictic center' (p. 205) It is futile, they infer, to seek clear and coherent accounts of metaphysical topics. We must just acknowledge the inconsistencies and use whatever account suits us on each occasion. I grant that if such brain processes did not occur we should not have the metaphysical concepts we have, and it is interesting to know just what their sources are. But we can certainly argue that some conceptions are wrong and misleading; and I do not see how any neurological discovery could make it impossible ever to arrive at an account of something like time or existence that is completely unimpeachable. Someone enamoured of empirical methods might wait and see.

In a literary metaphor you transfer a word which applies to one thing to another to which it is known not to apply. This normally has the effect of bringing our ideas of the things to which it does apply, what Lakoff and Johnson call the 'source', into interaction with our thought about the thing to which we apply it, the 'target'. It may make us look for analogies between the two. Reading Shakespeare's lines:

> When to the sessions of sweet silent thought
> I summon up remembrance of things past ...

we are led to conceiving thinking at leisure about past experiences on the model of a judicial sitting to which people may be summoned as witnesses. When we read:

> Then let not winter's ragged hand deface
> In thee thy summer, ere thou be distilled:
> Make sweet some vial

We think of the person addressed *as* a flower without thinking he *is* a flower. So much is a commonplace of literary theory. Many philosophers, including Wittgenstein, have remarked that people unconsciously conceive time on the model of movement, the mind on the model of the body, thought on the model of seeing, and other metaphysical topics by transferring to them concepts obtained through our sensori-motor system. Cognitive scientists may identify neural processes underlying or matching these ways of thinking. I do not think it follows that some physical necessity obliges us to think as we do. Wittgenstein said that we model the mind on the body and thinking on bodily movements partly because we use the same grammatical constructions in speaking of both. The same might be suggested about time, that it is our grammar that leads us to conceive it as we do.

A poet assumes we have some knowledge of the targets, memory, beautiful youths, old age and so forth, independently of the sources – sittings of magistrates, flowers, the succession of the seasons. If we had no conception of the topics of metaphysics, how could we transfer other concepts to them? Lakoff and Johnson sometimes speak of a non-metaphorical conceptual 'skeleton' or of 'literal' concepts (1999, pp. 128, 134). We have a literal concept of the mind as 'what thinks, perceives, believes, reasons, imagines, and wills' (p. 266), that is, as the subject of mental activities. We also have a literal conception of causation as 'a determining factor for a situation'. The word 'determine' here sounds metaphorical, but we are told that a factor is determining if, in its absence, 'we could not conclude that the situation existed' (p. 177). They may not realize it, but Lakoff and Johnson are here drawing upon the grammatical notions of a subject and a counterfactual conditional.

Talk of interaction between modes of thought is itself metaphorical, and students of literature do not ask what it is to think of one thing as a model for another. Lakoff and Johnson probably think that an explanation of this can be given in terms of interacting neurological networks, and that this interaction is inevitable. I should prefer to say that thinking metaphorically is a matter of *comparing* source and target, that comparison is a form of intelligence, and that although inclinations to misconceive things like existence, time and thought may be unavoidable, at least by speakers of European languages, they can be resisted.

The philosophers I have mentioned are agreed that attention to language was a wrong turn for philosophy; has it found the right way now? Williamson is remarkably optimistic:

> He says: In many areas of philosophy we know much more in 2007 than was known in 1957; much more was known in 1957 than in 1907; and much more was known in 1907 than was known in 1857. (Williamson 2007, pp. 279–80)

And he gives *truth* as something about which far more is known.

This progress, if it is real, has not been made without cost. In 1957 philosophical books and articles were largely intelligible to educated non-philosophers. We have arrived today at a situation like that which existed in the Greek-speaking world under Justinian and in Western Europe in the later middle ages: there are plenty of experts, but they write chiefly for one another according to very strict rules. The arguments are intricate and tortuous, and are expected to take note of every relevant point made in the ever expanding literature. This description applies equally to Simplicius's commentaries on Aristotle,[10] to commentaries on the Sentences of Peter the Lombard, and to our contemporary quarterly *Mind*. The new knowledge about truth is:

the result of technical work by philosophical and mathematical logicians. ... on how close a predicate in a language can come to satisfying a full disquotational scheme for that very language without incurring semantic paradoxes. (Williamson 2007, pp. 281–2; this from someone who condemns 'the linguistic turn')

It is as though philosophers forget what ordinary language is like when they sit down to write. Williamson gives 'Was Mars always either uninhabited or not dry?' as an example of 'a recognizably *unphilosophical* question' (p. 25, my emphasis). And here is what he says (pp. 64–5) about logical truth:

In one good sense, sentences of the form 'P if and only if actually P' are logical truths, and therefore Frege-analytic, because true in every model (Davies and Humberstone 1980, Kaplan 1989). Nevertheless they can express contingent truths on the same reading; it is not necessary for me to be my actual height. Although we could add a modal qualification to the definition of logical truth in order to exclude such examples, by requiring logical truths to be true at every world in every model, this mixing together of the modal dimension with the world dimension is bad taxonomy; perspicuous basic notions keep such different dimensions separate.

But is it really credible that philosophers today have a better knowledge of what truth is than ordinary people 50 or even 2,000 years ago? Philosophy, I repeat, is more like the arts than the sciences.

Can writers today tell us more about human life than Shakespeare or Homer? Do artists today know more about how to represent the human figure than Degas, Michelangelo or Praxiteles? Styles of representation change, but do not necessarily improve. It may be that some artists today try to please only professional teachers or critics, and care nothing about what ordinary people think about their work, but that does not justify philosophers in taking a similar stand. In fact they write as they do because they conceive philosophizing as a form of research, and hope to make advances in philosophy like those in science that are presented in the magazine *Nature*. I quote Williamson again since as Wykeham Professor at Oxford he has had responsibility for many graduate students:

It must be sensible for the bulk of our research effort to be concentrated in areas where our current methods make progress more likely. (2007, p. 287)

Philosophers ought to ask themselves if it is worthwhile to devote their lives to writing what not only is as unreadable, but also goes out of date as quickly, as scientific research. A professor whom I shall not name said to me a few years ago that he did not think it was possible any longer for someone who had taken the Oxford classics course taken by Isaiah Berlin, Gilbert Ryle, A. J. Ayer, Bernard Williams and other twentieth-century philosophers to have a career teaching philosophy, because the expertise now needed in logic and the philosophy of language could not be acquired by anyone also studying ancient literature and history. That is no ground for complacency. Metaphysics withered in the past because it became too professional, and it could well perish from the same disease today. Although its topics seem abstract and irrelevant to practical life, although it may seem to have value only as a kind of idle recreation like walking in deserts or, as Hume says, 'bringing home half a dozen woodcocks or plovers, after having employed several hours in hunting after them' (*Treatise* 2.3. 10; p. 452), if it is to flourish it must be capable of attracting amateurs. It revived in the seventeenth century because Descartes wrote, as he put it, so that 'even women' might understand something of what he said.[11] By the nineteenth, thanks to the professionalism of Kant and Hegel, in Continental universities it had retreated into what Peacock called 'transcendental darkness',[12] but it came to receive new life in England from the lucid and stylish English of Bertrand Russell, and from an intelligent re-reading of Plato and Aristotle. So long as metaphysics can engage the general reader, there remains open a channel through which it can feed and fertilise, if only subliminally, our understanding of ourselves and our place in the universe; it can work in our culture like wine in a sauce: you may not taste the wine, but it makes the whole dish better. This will not happen if new original works freeze off the general reader, and if no one will interpret or criticize the classic works of the past.

What follows is intended to be an original work; but I shall not refer to every recent work that touches on the same topics; I couldn't if I tried, and if I did the result would be intolerable to non-professionals. I shall refer to selected works by Wittgenstein and Chomsky which I think it imperative to discuss if you are examining the relations between metaphysics and grammar; I shall quote from eminent past philosophers when I think this will help to make clear what ideas and positions I am considering; and I shall be as colloquial as the somewhat crabbed nature of the subject matter and of those dedicated to it allows. To borrow the motto of the Scrope family, *devant si je le puis*. I do not expect to achieve a real page-turner, but my project is to demystify metaphysics, and that is a literary no less than a philosophical ambition.

Before constructive work can start, however, some preliminaries are necessary. Orwell says in *Nineteen Eighty-Four* that those who control the past control the future. No philosopher works without what is now called a 'narrative', a story about the history of the subject, how it started, how it progressed, who were the good guys and who the bad. I think many philosophers working today are hampered by narratives that are unhistorical. In Chapter 2 I say how, in Europe at least, metaphysics began. I show that it arose in tandem with grammar, and I have further reasons for this historical section. The philosophers of classical Greece were artists as great, in their peculiar way, as the poets and sculptors. The work of Plato and Aristotle has hardly dated more than that of Aeschylus or Phidias. They avoid errors into which more recent philosophers, ignorant of their work, have fallen, and Horace's words:

> *Vos exemplaria Graeca*
> *Nocturna versate manu, versate diurna*[13]

are advice to philosophers no less than to poets.

I must also explain more fully than I did just now what grammar is and how it differs from lexicography.

2

How Metaphysics Arose

Our word 'philosophy' comes from the Greek *philosophia*, but *philosophia* did not mean what is done by departments of philosophy in modern universities. It meant love of *sophia*, and although *sophia* is commonly translated 'wisdom', it expresses a slightly different and less daunting concept. The word was originally applied to outstanding technical skill and artistry,[1] and came to be used for any knowledge deeper or more exact or more elusive than what was needed for immediate practical purposes. A desire for this kind of knowledge is likely, Aristotle says (*Metaphysics A* 981a25–b25), to arise in any society in which the necessities of life are provided in sufficient abundance or with enough ease for people to have leisure. That was the situation in the Greek cities of Ionia, on the Aegean coast of Asia Minor, in the sixth century BC. The richest of them was Miletus, then a sea-port, though now, thanks to the silting up of the river Meander, totally landlocked and little more than an archaeological site. There arose among its citizens curiosity about natural phenomena which went beyond practical needs. Thales is said to have predicted the solar eclipse of 585 BC, and to have had theories about magnetism and the nature of matter. His younger contemporary and possibly kinsman Anaximander wrote a treatise concerning 'nature', which apparently covered astronomy and zoology. These pioneers were followed by Anaximines, also of Miletus, and men in other Ionian cities, notably Heraclitus of Ephesus and Xenophanes of Colophon.

These individuals are commonly called 'Presocratic philosophers', and if 'philosopher' is used in the ancient Greek sense, the phrase is correct. They did not tackle the topics of metaphysics. They have also, however, been called 'scientists – and great scientists at that' (Barnes 1982, p. 52). That seems to me doubtful. The scientific attitude is hard to define, and it has been questioned, for instance by G. E. R. Lloyd (1980, 1983), whether it existed in antiquity at all. What wells up spontaneously in the human mind is random speculation in which scientific, philosophical and theological problems are blended into a homogeneous perplexity. It is this that fills the pages of Hermann Diels's great compilation of the Fragments of the Presocratics, as it fills what Joseph Needham calls 'the almost limitless caverns of Chinese scientific history'.

Before any progress can be made, either in the sciences or in any other academic discipline, people must distinguish questions which can be answered by empirical investigation from questions which must be tackled in other ways. And these different kinds of question do not formulate themselves naturally. An academic language must be created. The earliest of Diels's fragments is by Anaximander, and it runs:

> From whatever things there is coming to be, into those same things there is passing away; for they indict each other and make reparation for injustice according to the order of time. (Diels 12 B 1)

Xenophanes wrote not in prose but in poetry, in the metre used by Homer; and so did two of the most influential thinkers of the fifth century BC, Parmenides and Empedocles. Their language, even when they are in mid-exposition, is poetic. Here is Parmenides on astronomy:

> The narrower rings [of the cosmos] are filled with unmixed fire, and those after these with night, and with these goes a burst of flame. In the middle of these is the divine female being who controls everything; for everywhere she is the source of painful birth and mixture, sending female to mix with male and contrariwise male with female. (Diels 28 B 12. See also B 8, where Parmenides speaks of logical necessity as 'justice')

And here is Empedocles on the descent of man:

> Come now, and hear how fire, in being separated, sent up nocturnal shoots of men and often-weeping women: for my story is not far from the mark or foolish. First undifferentiated forms of earth arose, having a share of both water and shape [*eidei*; possibly meaning 'heat']. For fire sent them up, wishing to come to its like; but they did not yet exhibit the lovely structure of limbs, nor voice such as is the customary organ of men. (Diels 31 B 62)

We can echo Plato's comment: 'Each of them seems like someone telling a story to children.' (*Sophist* 242c8–90).

It is also necessary to establish general principles of sound reasoning, and reasoning of different kinds. Primitive or uninstructed men can reason adequately about practical problems and technical contrivances, but they go astray on abstract issues and matters of principle and they are at a loss to differentiate valid from invalid patterns of inference. Anyone who doubts this might try the following inferences on a person who has not studied logic:

1 Anyone who is pro-Russian is anti-American. You're anti-American. So you must be pro-Russian.
2 Anyone who is pro-Russian is anti-American. I'm not anti-American. So I can't be pro-Russian.
3 Anyone who is pro-Russian is anti-American. I'm not pro-Russian. So I'm not anti-American.

It is my experience that university applicants have great difficulty in saying which, if any, of these inferences is valid and which not. And uncertainty about such matters is not confined to university applicants. The following Lewis Carroll statement was once tried on a number of Cambridge men:

> Angles that are greater than the same angle are greater than one another.

A good number held it to be a self-evident truth.

A third requirement for the existence of academic disciplines is that there should be institutions harbouring their pursuit. People seeking *sophia* either about nature or about anything else that is studied in modern universities, such as history, languages or foreign institutions, need places in which they can study and teach, places where books and specimens can be preserved and experiments conducted, and, embarrassing as it is to say this, endowments. It has to be apparent that a life of pursuing knowledge for its own sake is a practical possibility. Although there were people who studied the heavens and readers of books in ancient Egypt and China their *sophia* was too integral a part of the life of a priest or a government official to be what we should call scholarship or science today.

The threefold task of distinguishing different kinds of question, introducing rigour into language and reasoning, and setting up institutions of higher education, was done by three individuals, Socrates (469–399 BC), Plato (c. 429–347 BC) and Aristotle (384–322 BC). Socrates and Plato were Athenians and knew each other well. Aristotle's father was lived in northern Greece, but Aristotle came to Athens at the age of 17 to study under Plato, and remained in Athens (though with trips elsewhere) until the year before his death. These developments, then, took place in Athens, at that time an independent city-state.

Aristophanes in his comedy *The Clouds* (423 BC) shows Socrates as running a school in which research is carried out in natural science and grammar. Research is not at all the same thing as simple observation. Observation consists in noting with interest what is presented before one's eyes. Gilbert White's

Natural History of Selborne is a paradigm of observation. Research is systematic; it requires a theory that is to be tested and refined, and a programme for making observations and measurements. The Ionians did no research and little enough observation. Aristophanes attributes to Socrates a programme for discovering 'how many of its own feet a flea can jump. ... He dipped a flea's feet in wax, and when it cooled, with the sandals so formed he measured the space' (*Clouds* 145–52). This is meant to be funny and we need not suppose that Socrates really did what Aristophanes says. Nevertheless Aristophanes was writing for people to whom Socrates was a familiar figure. His audience would have known whether Socrates had a school or not, and if he had not had a school at all, or conducted any sort of research, the joke would have fallen flat. If he had such a school, it was probably the first. Lovers of *sophia* outside Athens in the fifth century BC seem to have liked roving in a way that prevented them from establishing research institutes; and if such institutes had existed there would have been a word for them, and Aristophanes need not have invented the joke-name *phrontisterion*, 'thinking-chamber' on the model of *bouleuterion*, 'council chamber'.

Whatever the truth about Socrates, Plato certainly set up a school. It was based on an existing institution. In the fifth century BC there were informal dining clubs of a kind we today would reckon partly literary and partly religious; they were called 'guilds (*thiasoi*) of the Muses'. Plato's institution, which he funded himself, had premises in the part of Athens called the Academy, and sheltered studies in mathematics and astronomy by Archytas and Eudoxus as well as discussions and lectures we should now call 'philosophical'. The physiological passages in the *Timaeus*, such as the theory of respiration at *Timaeus* 79–80, suggest that there may also have been some medical research.

At Plato's death the premises passed to his nephew Speusippus, and Aristotle, who had been teaching there, set up his own school in what was called the Lyceum. We know a fair amount about how it was organized. There was a library, a museum (literally a temple of the Muses), which served not only to house specimens of animals, plants and minerals but also as a forerunner of the college chapel, rooms in which lectures were given according to a fixed timetable and collegiate meals. By the time of Aristotle's death Athens had two institutions in which we can discern all the features of a modern university. Not only have the Academy and the Lyceum given their names to the vocabulary of education, but every institute of tertiary education in the world today is descended from them.

So much for what is called 'infrastructure'; what of the other requirements for academic study? In Athens the whole citizen population assembled to pass laws and take decisions on such important issues as whether to form alliances and whether to go to war; and day to day administrative functions, including trials at law, were carried out by groups of citizens selected by lot. Dubious arguments must have been employed daily and important-sounding words like 'justice' flung about without anyone's trying to say what they meant. Socrates, Aristotle tells us (*Metaphysics M* 1078b 27–9), made a practice of looking for general definitions of words like 'justice', 'virtue' and 'knowledge'; he also introduced a form of inductive argument.

Perhaps these sound modest contributions that someone was bound to make if democracy went on long enough.[2] The first involves recognizing the difference between two ways of answering a question of the form 'What is so-and-so?' – we can give examples or offer a general account. But obvious as this distinction looks, there is no evidence that it was grasped by any Presocratic thinker. In a number of his dialogues Plato shows Socrates having to work hard to explain it. 'What is courage?' Socrates asks Laches, a distinguished soldier. 'That's easy', Laches replies. 'It's keeping your position in the battle line and thrusting against the enemy.' 'Ah,' says Socrates, 'but that's the courage of a heavy infantryman. There's also the courage of cavalrymen, and courage at sea, courage in sickness, courage in politics. I was asking what is the same in all these cases. Do you understand?' 'Not very well', Laches admits. So Socrates takes a simpler case: there's quickness in running, and quickness in playing a musical instrument, and quickness in learning; 'But if I was asked "What is that thing which in all these cases you call 'quickness'", I should say "It is the power to accomplish a lot in a short time."' (*Laches* 190e–192b) Plato envisages the same difficulty with addressing the questions 'What is virtue?' and 'What is knowledge?' – people offer a list of virtues or kinds of knowledge – and he deploys the same strategy in the *Meno* (72c–75b) and *Theaetetus* (146a–147c).

Socrates's type of inductive argument is used repeatedly by Plato. In *Republic* 1 341b–343 he uses it to refute the cynical view that being good at governing is simply skill at accumulating power and wealth for oneself; other examples can be found at *Euthyphro* 13 and *Protagoras* 311–12. Argument from particular cases to a general principle is sometimes thought to be a peculiarity of science, but Socrates used it to analyse concepts that come up in ethical and political discussions, and whereas in science it is risky – it does not follow, because all the swans you have seen are white, that swans *must* be white – it is a sound technique in debates in ethics and politics which turn on conceptual claims.

Plato's dialogues bring out the difficulty that Athenians had in grasping the simplest logical principles. In *Euthyphro* 12 Euthyphro is unable to understand the difference between saying 'Everything holy is right' and saying 'Everything right is holy'. Socrates tries to explain it by pointing out the difference between 'Where there is reverence there is fear' and 'Where there is fear there is reverence', and Euthyphro has to struggle with this too. The Academy provided teaching on argumentation, for which Aristotle became responsible. His *Rhetoric*, *Topics* and *Refutations* (or the first drafts of these works) were probably composed at the Academy during Plato's lifetime, and give a fair idea of what was taught there. The *Topics* begins:

> The objective of this work is to find a method by which we may be able to reason about any topic that is put before us from generally accepted premises, and, when we put forward an account of our own, avoid contradicting ourselves. (*Topics* 1 100a18–21)

Aristotle proceeds to describe four 'tools' for providing ourselves with reasonings: finding statements to put forward, distinguishing different things to which a word is applied, finding differences and studying similarities (*Topics* 1 105a21–5). He claims that his treatise is useful for training or practice, for intercourse with other people – he probably has especially in mind political life in a democracy – and for the kinds of knowledge called *sophia* (*Topics* 1 101a25–8). To us this seems obvious, but he tells us that practically nothing had been written on the subject of reasoning before him (*Refutations* 184b1–2).

The teaching in the *Topics* and *Refutations* is by itself enough to bring rigour into ethical and political debate and turn studies of natural phenomena into academic disciplines; but logic proper, the systematic study of validity in reasoning, depends on using variables. By a 'variable' I mean a letter or other sign which stands for any object of a given type. Mathematicians use letters as variables for numbers; they say that the square of $(a + b)$ is equal to $a^2 + 2ab + b^2$, and here a and b stand for any two numbers you care to take. So far as we know, Aristotle was the first person to introduce variables of any kind. Although people before him produced proofs of mathematical theorems, and probably used letters in doing geometry, there is no evidence that they used algebraic variables. Aristotle not only uses letters for quantities, for instance in his *Physics* 6, but, more important, in his *Prior Analytics* he introduced variables in formulating patterns of inference. He says, for instance, 'If A is predicated of all B and B of all C, then A must necessarily be predicated of all C' (*Prior Analytics* 1 25b37–9). Here the letters stand for what are called the 'terms' of a proposition, for things we talk about like men and circles, and qualities we attribute to them like being viviparous or white. Later logicians introduced variables for propositions but the first step, introducing variables at all, was the most important. Without variables there can be no systematic formal logic, and without logic, no proof that an argument is or is not valid. Indeed, in a society without variables there can hardly be a clear conception of what it is for an argument to be valid. For a valid argument is not just one the conclusion of which is true. It is one the conclusion of which follows from the premises. A conclusion follows only if the form of the argument ensures that if the premises are true the conclusion is true. Without variables how can anyone say what the form of any argument is?

Besides laying the foundations of logic, Plato and Aristotle distinguished different types of question. Plato shows that we recognize three completely different types of explanation (*Phaedo* 96a–100c).[3] First, we appeal to the material components of things and their causal powers. For instance I can say: 'I am sitting here because I am composed of flesh and bones and sinews, and the sinews can stretch and contract, and the bones are hard and jointed, so that when the sinews contract my legs bend.' Secondly we appeal to an agent's reasons or purpose. I might say: 'I am sitting here in order to talk to my friends.' And finally we appeal to definitions. For instance I can say that there are two pieces of wood here, not because somebody divided a stick, or added a second stick to one that was already there, but because they satisfy the definition of two. Plato probably used this last example because explanations in mathematics depend on definitions. If we want to explain why the square on the hypotenuse of a right-angled triangle is equal to the sum of the squares on the other two sides, we give a proof which rests on the definition of a right-angled triangle. But he was taking a risk because numbers are extremely hard to define. Frege was the first person to define the numbers zero, one and two, and he did so only at the end of the nineteenth century. More mundane examples, however, will illustrate Plato's idea. I might say 'He's my brother-in-law because he's married to my sister.' Your brother-in-law is defined as a man who is either your wife's brother or your sister's husband. Or 'He was imprisoned unjustly because he had done nothing wrong': it is contrary to the definition of justice to imprison innocent people.

Plato's distinction between these three types of explanation is the basis for the distinction between three types of enquiry. First there are the physical sciences. Physical scientists (I argue in Chapters 10 and 11) explain how things affect one another in terms of their material. Secondly historians, and also people engaged in making or enforcing laws, are concerned in one way or another with purposes and human motivation. Historians ask for what purpose nations went to war; in law-courts it is important to show not only that a person did or did not do some deed but whether it was done intentionally or accidentally. And thirdly we have formal logic and mathematics, where explaining something is giving a deductive proof of it from definitions.

Williamson mentions possibility and necessity as topics of modern metaphysics (2007, p. 19). Logicians today use the notion of a possible world to construct a single logical system that can be applied to all statements of possibility and necessity, but a metaphysician, as distinct from a logician, needs a different notion for each of Plato's types of enquiry. Explanation in terms of materials brings out physical, that is to say causal, necessity. Explanation by deductive proofs from definitions shows logical necessity. And explanation in terms of human purposes has to do with practical or rational necessity.

How did these three men come to do all this? How did their conception of an academic discipline arise and take the form it did? Whereas in the sixth century BC people were seeking *sophia* concerning nature, in the fifth language became the subject of keen enquiry. Protagoras of Abdera, who was born c. 485 BC, divided sentences into prayers, questions, answers and orders, and noticed that nouns have gender.[4] Prodicus of Ceos and Cratylus, contemporaries of Protagoras or slightly younger, were interested in the origin of words and their variants between different speakers. Cratylus was an Athenian and Plato is said to have studied under him; the other two, though they came from other Greek cities, both visited Athens and appear to have been well known to Socrates. Aristophanes (*Clouds* 659–90) attributes to Socrates a preoccupation with the gender of nouns which he may have derived from Protagoras. Plato and Aristotle were keenly interested in language and made important advances in grammar. Metaphysics and grammar were hatched, like Helen and Clytemnestra, from the same egg at the same time.

On the face of it, the study of any actual language comprises two parts: we have to compile a dictionary of the language and a grammar. In the dictionary we list the words that belong to it and say what they mean; in the grammar we say how sentences of different kinds are constructed out of these words. Protagoras's division of sentences in prayers, questions, answers and orders was a seminal achievement, but we do not know what criteria he used, or whether he explained how sentences of these kinds are constructed. Nor do we know whether Cratylus or Prodicus, who are recorded only as being interested in words, drew any grammatical distinctions between words. We do not know, for instance, if they distinguished between nouns and verbs, though it seems unlikely that they did, since in their time the one Greek word *onoma* was used for both.[5] Plato, however, does distinguish nouns and verbs, or rather he distinguishes nouns and what are called 'finite parts' of verbs, linguistic items like 'walks' and 'walked' rather than infinitives like 'to walk'. Plato's distinction is more important philosophically than a mere distinction between noun and verb; as he says, a noun and an item like 'walks' are basic elements we must put together to say something true or false (*Sophist* 261d–262d). A finite part of a verb has a kind of incompleteness; it needs to be completed by another item, a noun or subject, to form something complete.[6] Plato also distinguishes adjectives which admit of comparatives and superlatives ('hot', 'hotter', 'hottest') and take adverbs of degree ('slightly', 'very') from adjectives that do not, like 'equal' and 'double' (*Philebus* 25c–e; that 'equal' admits of comparatives is an Orwellian grammatical joke); he distinguishes relative terms, like 'other' and 'master', from non-relative, like 'lion' or 'triangular' (*Parmenides* 133c–d; *Sophist* 255c–d); and he recognizes that verbs have tense (*Timaeus* 37e; words inspired, perhaps, by Parmenides, Diels 18 B 8, line 5) and verbs and nouns both have number (*Sophist* 237d). Aristotle develops these points, defining nouns and verbs and introducing the grammatical terms 'inflection' (*ptôsis*, De Interpretatione 16b1, 16b17), and 'connective' (*sundesmos*, Poetics 1456b21). If you had asked Plato and Aristotle what they were doing in all this, they would have said that they were pursuing *sophia* concerning language.

It may be noticed that Plato's distinctions do not leave an obvious place for philosophy. Philosophers are neither scientists nor historians nor mathematicians, though they are expected to know a bit of logic. They do not try to say why anything happened or why anything is as it is. As I said earlier, philosophy is akin to the arts, and *sophia* covers the arts. The works of Shakespeare may enlighten, but they do not explain, nor do those of Bach or Monet. Plato sometimes uses the word 'dialectic' for what we call 'philosophy', but never arrives at a clear and definitive account of what dialectic is. The word means 'to do with speech', and so does the word *logikos* which Aristotle sometimes uses in this context.[7] Plato and Aristotle might have thought that in the more abstract parts of philosophy, those we today count as metaphysical, they were artists in words, 'giving back the image of our mind'.

Their work, however, was not motivated by an interest in the grammar of Greek for its own sake. Plato's prime purpose in his *Sophist* was to explain how truth and falsehood can get into language. And he wanted to do that, not out of interest in truth for its own sake, but because he wanted to say that some teaching is false, and had to meet arguments purporting to show that it is impossible to speak falsely. This led him to recognize that sentences have a grammatical structure, and grammatical phenomena like inflections, verbs of being and becoming, and demonstratives then forced themselves on his attention. The meaning of 'to be' and 'is not' is discussed in *Sophist* 243b8 and 243d9–e2; demonstratives are mentioned in *Theaetetus* 157b and *Timaeus* 49d–e. Earlier Greeks had been literate; they had used written signs to represent these linguistic items; but they need not have thought about them. People speak in sentences, not in single words, and while a sentence has to be analysed phonetically to be written, it does not have to be analysed grammatically. The Greeks of Plato's day did not, in writing, put spaces between words.

Plato's grammatical analyses not only provided him with an account of truth; they opened up the whole field of metaphysics. Once we see how sentences are constructed questions arise both about the ordinary words which are joined together and inflected, and about the connectives and inflections.

Ordinary words like 'lion', 'run', 'sit' and 'yellow' are words for things that are studied in various disciplines like zoology and physiology. The subject of these sciences is not the meaning of words, but a grasp of the meaning of certain words is a grasp of the subject-matter of science. But this can seem puzzling. If zoologists are not trying to tell about this or that particular elephant but about elephants generally or whatever it is that 'elephant' is a word for, we may wonder what kind of thing this is. This is the metaphysical problem called 'the problem of universals', and gets off the ground once we recognize the class of linguistic items that are expressions for things that there are.

Furthermore, the things that these expressions signify are different in kind. The word 'elephant' signifies an animal, 'green' a colour and 'swim' a mode of locomotion. All these things are found in the world, but animals are a different kind of thing from colours and ways of moving are different from both. Today we are inclined to think that the world consists primarily of material objects like elephants and guns and substances like water and air, things themselves composed of atoms or particles. This, however, is thanks chiefly to Aristotle. Early Greek enquirers into nature who lived before the advent of grammar seem not to have distinguished objects like elephants from qualities like heat; they were prepared to think that the world consists of hot and cold or dense and rare. 'Material object' and 'quality' are not, like 'elephant' and 'hydrogen', scientific terms. They belong to philosophy. Plato introduced the word 'quality' (*poiotês*, *Theaetetus* 182a) and Aristotle distinguished objects and materials (labelling both 'substances', *ousiai*), from qualities, quantities (the word 'quantity', *posotês*, was probably his coinage), and other things for which we have words or phrases, and argued at considerable length that 'substances' are the primary objects for academic study. It is not clear how far our view of a world of material objects is shared even today by societies acquainted with Western science but uninfluenced by Greek philosophy.

Besides verbs of doing like 'cut' and 'run', languages contain what grammarians call verbs of being and becoming, verbs of saying and thinking like our 'assert', 'believe' and 'want', adjectives of quantity like 'all' and 'no', prepositions and conjunctions like 'for', 'of' and 'if', particles like 'not', and inflections of mood, tense, number and case. Once these linguistic items are noticed, it becomes a question what they mean or in what way they have meaning. What is the meaning of 'is'? of 'think'? of the imperative mood or the subjunctive? These are either straightforward metaphysical questions, or linguistic versions of the questions 'What is being?', 'What is thinking?' and the other traditional problems of metaphysics.

Plato asks what thinking is in *Sophist* 263d–e and *Philebus* 38b–39c; Aristotle asks this in *De Anima* 3 429a12–15. We may think that any reflective person would stumble on the question 'What is thought?' But look at how the verb 'to think' was used in that last sentence. 'We may think that' could be replaced by the single word 'surely'. Or in 'Will the President be re-elected? What do you think?' 'What do you think?' could be replaced by a reiterated '*Will* he?' As for being, Plato says of the Presocratics:

> When one of them says that many things, or one, or two, *are or have come to be or come to be*, or speaks of hot mixed with cold, or somewhere else posits 'separations' and 'mixtures', do you, by God, understand them? (*Sophist* 243b, cf. 244a)

It is doubtful if this complaint would have occurred to anyone who did not analyse sentences grammatically.

Socrates died before Plato had drawn the crucial distinction between nouns and verbs, and may have had no interest in purely metaphysical questions – he bequeathed none, at least, to Xenophon. Plato and Aristotle were interested in them, but why? They certainly have a charm for a certain kind of mind, and Plato and Aristotle doubtless possessed that kind of mind and enjoyed thinking about them for their own sake. But for both of them the pursuit of these questions was subordinate to other concerns. Aristotle appears to have wanted to do systematic zoology and chemistry, and that programme requires a metaphysics that gives a central place in the world to animals, plants and natural substances. In the nine years between 332 and 323 BC Alexander was planting internally autonomous cities throughout what had formerly been the

Persian empire, and another aim of Aristotle was to give constitutional guidance to these projects; hence his collection of existing Greek constitutions and his theoretical treatises on ethics and politics. He states clearly in the first chapter of *Nicomachean Ethics* 1 (1094a28–9) that this is a work of political theory. Plato was not satisfied with analysing concepts like courage and justice and working out what forms of reasoning are valid. Living before Philip and Alexander of Macedon had shown that there was no future for the wholly autonomous city state; he wanted to bring about political change. He believed that the ideal constitution would be one in which the offices of a state were held by the people with best qualifications, rather than, as in Athens, by any fool on whom the lot might fall. This sounds to us good sense; there is nothing that modern liberals want less than election by lot, unless it is legislation by referendum. But anyone who takes this view ought to say what the best qualifications are. Plato, like Aristotle, was interested in natural science, though unlike Aristotle he preferred the physical to the biological sciences, and cherished the dream that physics might be reducible to mathematics. It is not surprising, then, that he thought that the best qualification for holding office in a state is higher education, and offers the rather feeble justification that office-holders need to know some arithmetic and generals and admirals need to know some astronomy (*Republic* 7 525b, 527d). We today think that the more important the office, the less science and mathematics the holders need to know – that sort of expertise can be delegated to boffins of lower rank. However Plato did not suggest that offices should be filled by competitive examination in science and mathematics; more reasonably, he thought that a few people should be chosen by ballot, and they should appoint everyone else (*Laws* 6 752–6, *Statesman* 305–9), discerning their fitness by virtue of their own more liberal higher education.

Plato's political views are now universally accepted throughout the Western world, though he is rarely given credit for them. Nor is it often noticed that they go with a view of human nature which too we take for granted. Every rational activity from hunting and gardening to waging war and doing physics involves reasoning, measuring, counting, calculating, evaluating and comparing, but people engaged in these activities do not often notice they are doing these things. Plato called attention to them. Not only did he think that excellence at them is a prime qualification for political office – that we want political leaders with brains. They are, he claimed, the best things we do, and that within us which is responsible for them, the intellect or mind, is the best thing in us. We are, above all else, intelligent beings, and Socrates dissatisfied is better than a pig satisfied. It is because we accept Plato's view of human nature that Western philosophers today give so much attention to that part of metaphysics which is called the philosophy of mind. In Eastern civilizations there is no glorification of the pig – that was left to Plutarch in *Gryllus* (a dialogue between Odysseus and a pig, *Moralia* 985–92) – but nor is there quite the same view of us as beings with minds. In Chapter 12 I shall discuss the notions of belief and desire which play a leading part in modern Western philosophy; east of Constantinople I am not sure that to this day people readily think of themselves as having beliefs. Anglophone philosophers use 'belief' and 'desire' as generic terms to cover a variety of things: on the belief side, positive and negative opinions, surmises, pieces of knowledge, perceptions; on the side of desire, positive and negative feelings, attitudes, wishes, violent longings, mild preferences. Sages elsewhere may not have this taxonomy. And we expect moral, political and religious practices and customs to have associated beliefs. Asking people from other societies 'What are your beliefs?' may meet with the same blank response as would 'What is the case?' if it were asked in London or New York.

Let me summarize what I have said so far. In any society in which there is leisure, *philosophia* in the original sense of desire for knowledge which goes beyond what is needed for practical purposes is likely to arise. But it is unlikely to generate academic disciplines unless three conditions are satisfied. First someone distinguishes different kinds of question, moral, philosophical in our sense, scientific, and so on. Secondly, someone introduces rigour into diction and argumentation. Thirdly, someone sets up institutes of higher education where people can spend their lives pursuing *philosophia*. These conditions were satisfied, and so far we know, satisfied only, in classical Greece. The work was done by three individuals who knew each other, who shared a view of its value, and whose working lives spanned a period of 100 years in which each built on his predecessor's achievements. Perhaps it was statistically unlikely that such a trio should appear in the same society but spaced in time over a century: the genetic odds may have been against its occurring wherever there is civilization. However that may be, not only were these Greeks endowed with outstanding intellectual and organizational gifts, not only did they have politics and economics on their side, being financially independent and living in a society not too unfavourable to their projects, but they had a language which (unlike, for example, Mandarin Chinese) was rich in inflections of mood, tense and number and other grammatical devices, and they were interested in the grammatical structure of sentences. They were, of course, literate, but literacy alone would not have been enough; they also needed basic grammatical concepts – which, indeed, they had to make for themselves rather as early craftsmen must have made tools for themselves. In the arts, the making of tools and innovation cannot be separated.

Before leaving classical antiquity I should issue a warning. Until quite recently a rather different account of ancient philosophy was sometimes given. Wherever (it was said) the curtain of history rises, it reveals men kept in ignorance by the repressive force of religion. Lucretius put it well when he said 'Human life lay on the ground foul to see, weighed down under religious fear.'[8] From this dark force salvation could come only from science. But when the first shoots of science poked up in ancient Greece, they were systematically blighted by Socrates, Plato and Aristotle. Socrates introduced the retrograde, animistic notion of purpose in nature (Olsen 1978, pp. 179–99). Aristotle taught that 'the whole cosmos with all it contains is the result of previous planning', and constructed his mechanics on the 'supposition of an "intelligent nature" functioning by deliberate design' (Sambursky 1956, pp. 81, 84). Worst of all was Plato. Implacably hostile to any kind of empirical research, he taught that the only realities were non-material Forms or Ideas of entities like Equality, Largeness and Beauty existing in a world of their own beyond space and time, accessible only to pure intellectual intuition.

This 'narrative' is now discredited. It is gently satirized in the section headings of Jonathan Barnes's *The Presocratic Philosophers* (1982), and details have been attacked by various writers, including me (1985, 1995). Lakoff and Johnson offer a fresh version of it (1999, pp. 346–90), but on their own admission this is based 'not on traditional historical or textual scholarship, but something new: the cognitive science of early metaphysics' (p. 350). Traditional historical and textual scholarship would have saved them from some errors. The treatment of Plato is particularly unfair. In several places Plato does criticize people who rely simply upon their eyes and ears to inform them about natural phenomena (*Timaeus* 91d; *Republic* 7 529–31), but he is not inviting his readers to substitute pure speculation for empirical research; rather he is exhorting them to substitute empirical research for casual observation. Comparable remarks can be found in ancient writers who are commended as favourable to empirical science like Empedocles (Diels 31 B 17, line 21: 'Look with the mind instead of sitting staring with the eyes'), Anaxagoras (Diels 59 B 21) and Democritus (Diels 68 B 11). It is ironical that Plato should be saddled with a bizarre, extravagant theory of transcendent Ideas such as the Large, the Small, the Equal and the Good, when he was the most rationalistic and down to earth of thinkers. His critics seem unable to think themselves into the world he had to contend with. Typical Athenians of his day were like Anytus, whom he portrays as holding that any upper-class Athenian citizen is capable of giving young men all the education they require. Anytus has a horror of such travelling searchers after *sophia* as Protagoras and Prodicus, although on his own admission he has never met one (*Meno* 92b–e). Plato's portraits of Callicles and Thrasymachus in his *Gorgias* and *Republic* 1 show us more intelligent fifth-century enemies of academic study, and in the fourth century BC they found a spokesman in Isocrates. Isocrates attacks an educational package consisting of mathematics, physical science and training in argument; he particularly warns young men against immersing themselves in the writings of 'the old sophists' such as Parmenides, Empedocles and Gorgias; and he counsels them, instead, since certain knowledge about practical affairs is unobtainable, to qualify themselves to give advice that will be right for the most part, especially on matters of concern to the whole of Greece (*Antidosis* 46–7; 260–71). This programme is hardly rich in precise detail, but no doubt he thought his own works good specimens of the kind of advice he had in mind. In the struggle between Isocrates's conception of tertiary education and Plato's, Plato was so completely successful that now Isocrates is remembered only by classical scholars.

3

Grammar and Lexicography

I said just now that to give a full description of a language we must do two distinct things. One is to make a list of the words in it and say what each means; that is what we call 'lexicography'. The other is to say how, out of these words, we can construct sentences of various kinds, statements, commands, questions, expressions of desire and so forth; and that is grammar. Lexicographers do not, strictly speaking, need any special technical terms, though in practice they borrow some from grammar. But grammarians do need a special vocabulary: they need words for the various kinds of sentence and for the various 'parts of speech', as they call the constituents out of which sentences are constructed. Indeed the words 'word' and 'sentence' themselves are technical terms taken from grammar. Grammar begins with the recognition that statements, orders and the rest are not simple wholes, lumps of speech like lumps of butter, but constructions out of components like apple pies or at least like loaves of bread. A loaf of bread is not just a quantity of bread but a quantity of bread in a definite shape, and a one-word command like 'Go!' is not just a monosyllabic sign for a kind of action but a sign in what is called 'the imperative mood'.

The explanation I have just given of the distinction between grammar and lexicography is certainly too simple; it cannot stand without qualifications. But strange as it may seem, many philosophers today think it totally misconceived. There is, they claim, no interesting difference between lexicography and grammar, since both are concerned with the meaning of words. Before I tackle this radical view, let me provide my rough account with some qualifications.

First, 'word' is not simply a grammatical term. It is used in different situations, and it can express slightly different conceptions. As a compositor making up a page of type I should treat '1984' as one word, and 'nineteen eighty-four' as two, or possibly three; from one point of view 'tomorrow and tomorrow and tomorrow' contains two words, from another five.[1]

Next, I spoke of words in a language, but not every word we use is a word in some language. Every sentence is a sentence in some language, but a sentence in English may contain a word that is not an English word. It may contain nonsense words like 'runcible' and 'brillig', and these are hardly English words. So called 'proper names' like 'Caesar' and 'Rome' are not words in a language. The sentence 'Caesar was killed in Rome' contains five words, but 'Caesar' and 'Rome' are not *English* words; they do not belong to the vocabulary of English. Latin lexicons contain proper names that appear in classical texts, but that does not make them Latin words. I do not think it is a rule of any language that anything is the proper name of anything, not even a phrase like 'The General Theory of Relativity'. Grammar allows us to use proper names in constructing sentences, and in inflected languages grammar tells us how to inflect them. The English use 'Rome' as the name of a city the ancient Romans called 'Roma'. But this is a fact about the English people and the ancient Romans, not about the English language and Latin, whereas it is a fact about English and Latin that English-speakers use the word 'horse' for the animal for which Latin-speakers use the word 'equus'. Similarly I think it is a fact about the English that in pain they say 'Ouch!' Interjections are not words in a language; *otototototoi* appears often in Greek tragedies, but it is not a Greek word.

These qualifications are of minor importance. What is crucial from a philosophical standpoint is this. There are words which definitely belong to the vocabulary of a language and which are listed in it, but the meaning of which belongs primarily not to lexicography but to grammar. Medieval writers called them 'syncategorematic' words. Ockham says 'they do not signify things distinct from the categorematic words [he meant words that signify things we predicate, like 'gallop' and 'green' and (he thought) 'horse']. … but added to other words they make them signify something, or stand for things in a special way, or perform some other function' (*Summa Logicae* 1.4). Examples in English are 'the', 'not' and 'than'.

In carpentry and building we distinguish between the materials out of which an object is made, and any materials *with* which the object is made out of these materials. Chippendale made chairs out of pieces of wood with glue. The glue contributed to the weight of the finished chair, but its function was more like that of a joint than that of a piece of wood. A modern artist, in contrast, might make a chair out of glue. Similarly Palladio built houses out of stone with cement, but *we* sometimes make buildings out of cement. Now consider the sentence: 'The pen is not mightier than the sword': although 'the', 'not' and 'than' are constituents, they (and 'is') are analogous to glue in a Chippendale chair.

The role they play is the same as that of inflections and word order. Unlike 'pen' and 'sword' they must be mentioned in the grammar of English. We mention 'not' in giving the rules for negative statements, for saying that one thing is not another or that something is not the case. We mention 'than' in giving the rules for making comparisons. In English we say one thing is greater or less than another by using 'than'; in Latin we can do the same by using a case-inflection.

The grammar of an inflected language is sometimes subdivided into two parts, called 'accidence' and 'syntax'. Accidence tells us what the inflections are, and syntax says what they mean, and how sentences, clauses and phrases are constructed. The concept of grammar with which I shall be concerned in what follows is that of syntax.

Some writers today use 'syntax' in contrast with 'semantics' for the physical structure of written and spoken signs, as contrasted with their meaning. We give the syntax of a sentence simply by giving the order of the words in it, and saying how they come to have that order and any modifications of shape or sound they may have, without any mention of their meaning. So far as the grammarian is concerned, the sentence might have nothing to do with language at all; it might be an arrangement of bricks or flowers. All questions of meaning belong to semantics. Chomsky in *Syntactic Structures* declared 'Grammar is autonomous and independent of meaning' (1957, p. 17); it 'is best formulated as a self-contained study independent of semantics' (p. 106). Chomsky himself, however, argues at some length that syntactic structure is not a physical property of a sentence. The basic elements out of which ordinary sentences are constructed, he says, are not sounds or visible signs but purely theoretical entities, 'phrase markers' (1965, p. 17), with an internal structure, and the construction of a sentence is explained in terms of operations on these entities. Moreover, it will appear in Chapter 4 that syntax even as Chomsky conceives it is not as independent of meaning as the remarks quoted just now suggest. Here I give warning that I myself am not using 'syntax' in a physicalistic manner. Rather I follow the great Latin grammarian Henry John Roby who said: 'I have regarded syntax not as being a synthesis of rules for the formation of sentences, but as an analytical statement of the meaning and use of the inflexions and parts of speech' (1903, p. xix).

Rules of syntax, as I understand the term, do not tell us how to form sentences that will be merely structures of written marks or spoken sounds. They tell us how to *say* things, how to perform definite linguistic acts. There are acts which can be performed only in a game, like trumping and castling. You castle in chess, by complying with the rules of chess, and you trump in bridge and whist, by complying with the rules of those games. By a 'linguistic act' I mean an act that is performed in a language in compliance with the rules of the language. Saying something true or false, asking a question, advising, ordering, forbidding, explaining one thing by another are such acts, and learning the grammar of a language is learning how to perform them in that language. Rules of syntax give the meaning of constructions in that they tell us what acts we perform when we comply with them.[2]

That is different from the way in which lexicographers tell us the meaning of words. Lexicography has rules, but its rules tell us that words in a language are words for certain things; it is a rule of English lexicography that 'refute' is a word for proving something false, and we break it if we use it for simply saying something is false.

I have been using expressions like 'signify', 'stand for', 'be a word for', and non-philosophers use these interchangeably. Words, however, that (unlike 'the', 'not' and 'than') are agreed to be words *for* things are used in sentences of two kinds: sentences in which we predicate one thing of another, like 'Mars is red' and 'Atalanta ran', and sentences in which we quantify something, like 'Mars has two moons' and 'There is no wine'. One way in which a word for something has meaning is by being a word for something we predicate when we use it; a second is by being a word for something we quantify. 'Red' and 'run' are words for things we predicate, and 'moon' and 'wine' are words for things we quantify. In general adjectives of quality and verbs for things we do are words for things we predicate, whereas common nouns are words for things we quantify. To grasp the meaning of a word for something we quantify is to know what we quantify in using it. To grasp the meaning of a word for something we predicate is to know what we predicate in using it. To mark the difference we may say that grasping the meaning of a word for something we quantify is knowing what it *stands for*, while grasping the meaning of a word for something we predicate is knowing what it *signifies*.

The distinction looks obvious. But in English we can use words for things we quantify as complements of 'to be' – we can say 'That's a planet' – so we may think they are also words for things we predicate and have meaning in the same way as 'red' and 'run', that in fact they have both kinds of meaning. Moreover things we predicate, qualities, kinds of action and so on, can also be quantified, though we use different expressions when predicating and when quantifying – in the first case, as I said, adjectives and verbs, in the second abstract expressions like 'sphericality', 'shade of blue', 'kind of motion'. And sentences in which we quantify are grammatically of subject-predicate form. In 'Dodos used to exist but don't now', 'exist' is grammatically a predicate-expression and may be thought to be a word for something we predicate; and in 'Mars has two moons' 'has two moons' is a predicate-expression and 'has' may be thought to signify a relationship. I tackle these complications in Chapters 5 and 6.

My distinction between knowing what a word signifies and knowing what it stands for has some affinity with Frege's distinction between grasping the 'sense' of an expression – he says a word 'expresses its sense' (Frege 1952, p. 61) – and grasping its reference, that is, knowing to what it refers. There are, however, two differences. The same linguistic item cannot have both of my kinds of meaning, whereas it can have both of Frege's; and my distinction is applied only to single words like 'red' and 'tiger' whereas Frege's is extended to proper names like 'Leningrad', to referring phrases like 'the author of *Waverley*' and to whole sentences. I think this has generated confusion and prevented philosophers from seeing a simple point about word-meaning.

Lexicographic rules are grammatical only in the Lord Tolloller sense of 'grammar'. The difference between the ways in which grammar and lexicography explain meaning is reflected in our use of the word 'express'. We may say with Frege that a word expresses what we predicate in using it. In this way 'crimson' expresses a colour, 'honest' a trait of character. But we also talk of expressing denial, command, interrogation, and we express these things by constructions. In English we express denial by inserting 'not'; we express interrogation by inverting the order of subject and verb ('Is Mars red' in place of 'Mars is red') or by using an interrogative particle like 'who', 'which' or 'where'; and in Latin we express command by the inflections of the imperative mood. Latin rather perversely translates 'You are going' by *is* and 'Go!' by *i*. These constructions do not signify denial, command and the rest by being expressions *for* them, but they may be said to be expressive *of* them. They are expressive of them in that using them *is* denying, commanding or asking a question.³ And the same goes for the words grammar requires us to use in these constructions, like 'not': they have meaning in the same way. 'Not' is expressive of denial; using it is denying. I mean, of course, using it as part of the construction of a simple indicative sentence, since we also use it in other constructions, in prohibitions, in conditional clauses and so on, and then we are not denying. I discuss this in Chapter 5, where also I distinguish between denying one thing *of* another ('It is false *of* the Sun that it moves'), and denying absolutely ('It is not the case that the Sun moves').

Language is also called 'expressive' in other ways. Poetry is praised for being expressive and emotions like rage and erotic desire can be expressed (and not merely betrayed) in speech. In general poetic and rhetorical expressiveness is a matter of what I below call 'practical' meaning, the aptitude of a speech to affect the state of mind of someone who understands the words and constructions. There are literary devices for doing this but they belong to rhetoric, not grammar. In some societies, however, there are customary ways of expressing gratitude or respect in words. In these societies expressing gratitude or respect is a kind of social act, performed by complying with rules that are rather social than grammatical or rhetorical, but they may require grammatical forms. In Latin there are 'polite' forms of imperative, in Spanish and other languages, polite forms of address. In the Marquesas, I was told in 1978, 'on tutoie tout le monde'; I think this is not a grammatical rule which distinguishes Marquesan French from metropolitan French; the Marquesans speak the same language as the Parisians, but it is not their custom to use the 'polite' form 'vous'.

Although grammatical and lexicographical rules are different in character, they are not independent. Their interrelations are quite complicated. In the first place, they have to be used together. We can use a word as a password, or to make someone blush, without using it in a construction. But I cannot use 'yellow' *for* a colour or 'shirt' *for* a garment without using it in a construction and making a statement or giving an order or performing some other linguistic act.

Secondly, dictionaries contain grammatical information. In the case of some words a lexicographer may simply give a synonym or an equivalent in another language ('babi = pig' I learn from a small Indonesian–English lexicon). But, as I say, there are words the meaning of which can be explained only by giving the constructions to which they contribute. Dictionaries also usually say what part of speech a word is, whether it is a noun, a verb, an adverb or what. Parts of speech differ grammatically. In highly inflected languages nouns decline and verbs conjugate, while adverbs and prepositions do neither, though some adverbs have comparatives. Pronouns can be subjects and objects; prepositions cannot. Dictionaries also tell us what constructions words take. Harrap says that in French 'jouer' ('verb, to play') takes the preposition 'à' with a word for a game, and 'de' with a word for a musical instrument (Mansion, ed., 1961, p. 346), and an English lexicographer might say that we play *at* chess but *upon* the flute. Of course, the fact that dictionaries contain grammatical information does not show that the information is not really grammatical, or that giving the meaning of words in a language is not a different task from saying how sentences in it are constructed.

Thirdly, there are words, I mentioned 'the', 'not' and 'than', the meaning of which can be explained only by giving the constructions to which they contribute. Though they have meaning in a different way from words like 'wine' and 'red', the fact that a word has meaning through contributing to a construction is a piece of lexicographical or semantic information. That sounds, perhaps, like a riddle, but I hope that a couple of not uncontroversial examples will not only make it clear, but also show its importance for what I shall be arguing.

The sentences 'That wine is good' and 'Is that wine good?' differ not in the words used but in their construction, and the difference in meaning between them arises from the difference in construction. The sentences 'That wine is red' and 'That wine is white' differ not in construction but only in the words used, and their difference in meaning arises from the difference in meaning of the words used: 'red' and 'white' signify different things, different colours. The sentences 'That wine is red' and 'That wine is good' are the same in construction, and their difference in meaning too arises from the difference in meaning of the words used as complements, 'red' and 'good'. But 'red' and 'good' do not *signify* different things. Rather 'red' signifies something, a certain colour, while 'good' has meaning in that using it in this construction is not describing something or saying that anything is true of anything, but recommending something for some (unspecified) purpose. The difference in meaning between 'red' and 'good', I shall be arguing, lies not in the things they signify but in the way they have meaning.

Similarly the sentences 'Tom Bowling's friends were many' and 'Tom Bowling's friends were true-hearted' have the same construction; they differ in meaning because 'many' and 'true-hearted' differ in meaning. Those two words, however, do not signify different things. 'True-hearted' signifies a trait of character; 'many' has meaning in that using it is quantifying, comparing in number with an unstated norm.

We can sometimes show that words have meaning in different ways by appeals to grammar. People sometimes talk of 'surface' grammar and 'deep' grammar, and a grammatical argument to show that words have meaning in different ways could be classed as an appeal to deep grammar.[4] In the examples given, 'That wine is red' and 'That wine is good' have the same surface grammar, but if we point out that it is grammatically correct to say 'It is good that …' but not 'It is red that …' we are indicating a difference in deep grammar. We are also peering into deep grammar if we show that 'many' and 'true-hearted' have meaning in different ways by pointing out that it is correct to say 'Each of his friends was true-hearted', but not 'Each of his friends was many.'

Finally, there are words of two kinds which do not themselves have meaning by contributing to grammatical constructions – they signify things there are – but the meaning of which is explained, at least partly, by referring to grammar.

Grammatical terms themselves form one kind. 'Word' and 'sentence' signify signs with which grammatical rules deal. 'Inflection' signifies an operation with grammatical significance. 'Noun', 'adjective', 'verb' and 'preposition' signify words that play certain grammatical roles, and so do the phrases that signify their subclasses, like 'relative pronoun', 'interrogative adjective'. When we get to subclasses, however, like common nouns and collective nouns, adjectives of quality and adjectives of quantity, it is not immediately clear whether distinctions are based on grammatical considerations or on considerations about the things signified by words in the subclass. In the past grammarians tried to define nouns, adverbs and the rest by the kinds of thing they signify. Chomsky (1965, pp. 94–5, 164–70) introduces the notion of a grammatical lexicon. Whereas an ordinary lexicon contains the words in a language and tells us their meanings, his grammatical lexicon contains items that can be turned into words by phonetic rules, and tells us to what grammatical category each belongs and in which constructions it can be used – everything except its meaning.

The second group of tricky words consists of general terms used by philosophers, like 'object', 'material', 'quality', 'shape', 'power', 'emotion', 'mode of action'. Whereas grammarians classify sentence-components, philosophers from Plato onwards have tried to classify things that exist. Plato divides 'all the things that now exist in the whole universe into two or rather three groups' (*Philebus* 23c 4–5). Aristotle's categories – substances, qualities, relations, actions, etc., – are kinds of thing 'said without combination' (*Categories* 1b25–7), that is, things signified by sentence-components: the word 'combination' (*sumplokê*, literally 'weaving together') is taken from the passage (*Sophist* 262c–d) in which Plato says that speech depends on weaving together two sorts of expression. The things that exist coincide on the whole with the things for which there are expressions, and we may wonder whether it is better to classify them by the ways they are expressed and come into language, or by the ways in which they exist and come into reality. Aristotle puts in different classes things signified by words we use to answer questions introduced by the different interrogatives *ti, poion, poson, pou,* and *pote*. (*Ti, pou* and *pote* translate the English 'What?' 'Where?' and 'When?' *Poson* translates the French *Combien*, and *poion* is roughly equivalent to 'What's it like?') These interrogatives will be mentioned by grammarians; but answers to the questions they introduce need not differ in surface grammar; consider 'We got there in three ships' and 'We got there in three weeks'. Distinguishing qualities from substances, Aristotle says that words for qualities have comparatives whereas words for substances don't (*Categories* 3b33–4, 10b26–7). That is a grammatical point. On the other hand in distinguishing varieties of quality he considers whether the word is applied because the thing signified is more or less long-lasting, or because it has a physical power, or because it has been affected in some way (*Categories* 8b28–9, 9a14–19, 9b9–11). These are considerations about the things signified themselves, though the notions of duration, physical power and being affected may be partly grammatical. Grammarians and philosophers have different objectives, there is no exact match between the philosopher's categories and the grammarian's, and there is room for debate about how far particular classificatory terms used by philosophers can be defined in grammatical terms.

Some of the disputed questions will be taken up below. I consider grammatical differences between processes and events in Chapter 9, between countable objects and measurable materials in Chapters 6 and 11, and between inanimate objects and living organisms in Chapters 5 and 12. What I wish to emphasize here is that the interrelations between grammar and lexicography go no way to invalidating the general distinction between the two, or the specific distinction between the kind of meaning that attaches to grammatical constructions and the kind that attaches to most of the words that appear in lexicons. Typical lexicon words are words for things, and signify the things they are words for. Constructions are constructions for performing linguistic acts of various kinds, and have meaning in that using them is performing those acts. But there are words, I have pointed out, which, though they appear in lexicons, have meaning in the same way as constructions; a word of this kind is not a word *for* anything, but using it is part of using a construction. I said that though such a word does not signify anything, it is expressive of something, and I distinguished this kind of expressiveness, which is necessary for saying anything at all, from the kind of expressiveness sought by poets and public speakers, which is helpful for influencing a reader's or a hearer's state of mind in a particular way. It is in the light of these distinctions, and with the aid of these concepts of expressiveness and of the meaning of a grammatical construction, that I shall tackle the traditional problems of metaphysics.

Many philosophers today just ignore the distinction between grammar and lexicography. Some want to attach truth and falsehood to sentences while treating the sentences as if they had no grammatical structure, so the distinction is irrelevant to their interests. Wittgenstein has been credited with an explicit rejection of the traditional distinction between grammar and lexicography. Chomsky, apparently, is at the opposite end of the spectrum from Wittgenstein. Not only does he distinguish sharply between syntax and semantics; he says that grammar has nothing to do with meaning whatever. In the next chapter I shall defend a degree of autonomy for grammar greater than was allowed by the later Wittgenstein,[5] but less than is claimed by the early Chomsky.

4

Wittgenstein and Chomsky on Grammar

Medieval education generally started with grammar, and medieval philosophers began their studies from grammatical works, Aristotle's *Categories* and *De Interpretatione*, Porphyry's *Introduction* to the *Categories* and Boethius's *Commentary* on Porphyry. It was different in the age of the Enlightenment. Descartes was taken to have proved that the only things of which we have direct and certain knowledge are our own mental states and mental activities. Locke, Berkeley, Hutcheson, Hume, Adam Smith, Kant, Mill, Russell, G. E. Moore, the youthful A. J. Ayer and practically every other philosopher in Europe and America concentrated upon these. Wittgenstein brought grammar back onto the philosophical stage. I shall refer to his *Philosophical Grammar* (1932–4/1978) by *PG* and entry number, to his *Blue and Brown Books* (1933–4/1956) by *BB* and page, and to his *Philosophical Investigations* Part 1 (1945/1958) by *PI* and entry number. In his lectures in 1933–4, now known as *The Blue Book*, he made the arresting statement that many, if not all, philosophical problems arise from 'grammatical misunderstandings' (*BB*, pp. 8, 9, 16). 'Philosophy as we use the word', he says, 'is a fight against the fascination which forms of expression exert upon us' (*BB*, p. 27), and his later work makes it clear that the forms of expression he has in mind are not poetic or slangy or archaic forms, fascinating as those may be, but grammatical forms. 'Grammatical illusions' produce 'superstitions' (*PI* 110). 'We do not command a clear view of our use of words; our grammar is lacking in perspicuity' (*PI* 122). Problems arise 'through a misinterpretation of our forms of language' (*PI* 111), and are to be solved 'by looking into the workings of our language, and that in such a way as to make us recognise those workings: *in despite of* an urge to misunderstand them' (*PI* 109). At the end of the *Blue Book* he says: 'In these investigations we were concerned with the grammar of those words which describe what we called "mental activities", seeing, hearing, feeling etc.' (*BB*, p. 70). The effect of his investigations was to show that the mental states and activities on which philosophers from Descartes onwards had been concentrating were largely illusory.

Not only, however, did Wittgenstein not advocate a return to medieval thought; he did not connect philosophy and grammar in the way I do here. His use of the words 'grammar' and 'grammatical' is in fact misleading. Sometimes he uses them in their usual sense, and he does claim that grammar in that sense has caused philosophers to make disastrous assumptions. But far more often what he calls 'grammar' is what would ordinarily be considered lexicography, even if it is lexicography pursued in an idiosyncratic way. Let me document these points.

First, his use of grammar in the sense in which it is distinct from lexicography. He claims that the grammatical form of certain words leads us astray. 'We try to find a substance for a substantive' (*BB*, p. 1). By a 'substantive' he means a noun like 'cat' or 'milk' or a phrase like 'the thing you said' or a pronoun like 'I' or 'they'. The word 'time', for instance (*BB*, p. 6), is a noun like 'thyme' or 'lime' and since 'thyme' and 'lime' signify substances, we think that 'time' too must signify a sort of substance, perhaps something like slowly flowing lava. Similarly when we see a phrase like 'object of thought' we ask questions about objects of thought like our questions about fires, or thieves (*BB*, p. 31). Something similar happens with verbs. 'Think', 'mean', 'expect' are grammatically similar (only up to a point, but Wittgenstein ignores this) to 'write', 'speak' and 'shoot' (*BB*, pp. 7, 35), which signify bodily actions; 'believe', 'wish' and 'will' have inflections like 'cut', 'chew' and 'run'; so we are inclined 'to interpret them analogously' and think they stand for activities which differ from writing, shooting and the rest only in being mental or 'aetherial' rather than bodily (*BB*, p. 47).

The tenses of verbs too can create illusions. The present tense in 'He is capable of ...', 'He is able to ...', 'He can ...', 'suggests that the phrases are descriptions of states that exist at the moment at which we speak' (*BB*, p. 117); that is, it suggests that skills and abilities are states of mind analogous to physical or bodily states – for when I say 'You have mumps' or 'you are obese' I say that you are in a certain bodily condition right now. In the sentence 'When I said "Add 1 each time" I meant you to write 101 after 100,' 'the past tense of the verb "to mean" suggests that a particular act of meaning had been performed' (*BB*, p. 142), that is, we think it reports a mental act of meaning simultaneous with the vocal utterance 'Add 1 each time.'

Wittgenstein must, I think, have in mind mistakes arising from grammatical similarities in the well known passage:

> How does the philosophical problem about mental processes and states and about behaviourism arise? – The first step is the one that altogether escapes notice. We talk of processes and states and leave their nature undecided. Sometime perhaps we shall know more about them – we think. But that is just what commits us to a particular way of looking at the matter. For we have a definite concept of what it means to know a process better. (The decisive movement in the conjuring trick has been made, and it was the very one that we thought quite innocent.) (*PI* 308)

Words like 'remember' and 'pain' are grammatically similar to words for physical processes and states like 'dismember' and 'malaria' (at least in German: the German for 'He is in pain' is 'Er *hat* Schmerzen').

Wittgenstein does not claim that grammatical similarities are the only source of philosophical error; other sources are given at *BB*, pp. 17, 36, 44, 46, 70 and *PI* 593. But he thinks them an important one. He also uses grammatical concepts to explain how philosophers have come to believe that the only things of which we have certain knowledge are things of which non-philosophers have never heard, like sense-data. In the *Blue Book* he distinguishes a transitive and an intransitive use of words like 'fear' (*BB*, p. 22). We can say 'Europa felt afraid of the bull in front of her' or simply 'Europa felt afraid', meaning she was in a jittery state. Wittgenstein calls the first use 'transitive' because it attributes to Europa an emotion directed to a definite object. It is like 'Europa patted the bull' where 'patted' is a transitive verb with a grammatical object 'the bull'. In the second case we attribute to Europa only a sort of mood, and Wittgenstein says the words are used intransitively because they are used without an object, like 'giggled' in 'Europa giggled'. Wittgenstein says that when we encounter an intransitive case we are inclined to treat it as transitive and conjure up a fictitious object, something of which we are aware as we can be aware of a bull in front of us, but which, unlike the bull, we cannot describe. In the *Brown Book* he says that words like 'particular' and 'peculiar' have analogous uses (*BB*, pp. 158–60). They can introduce a precise specification: 'I want you to paint the walls a particular shade of green – this one, here in the colour chart,' or 'This soap is not odourless, it has a particular smell, that of sandalwood.' But they can also be used simply to express a sort of emphasis. 'I say "This face gives me a particular impression which I can't describe." The latter sentence may mean something like: "This face gives me a strong impression."' 'I say "This soap has a *peculiar* smell" – "peculiar" here stands for some such expression as "out of the ordinary", "uncommon", "striking".' Locke had declared that 'What *perception* is, everyone will know better by reflecting on what he does himself, when he sees, hears, feels etc., or thinks, than by any discourse of mine' (*Essay* 2. 9. 2). He also says that if anyone wants to know what willing is, he must 'reflect on what he himself does when he wills' (*Essay* 2. 21. 15). Later philosophers have thought it obvious that there are sensations of colour which are known only to people with sight and which cannot be put into words, that red, for example has a peculiar 'feel' or 'comes to us in a particular way'. Wittgenstein suggests that when we try to look into ourselves and see what happens when we think or choose or see something red we have experiences which are particular in the intransitive sense but construe them as transitive but, so to speak, reflexive (*BB*, pp. 160, 174). Just as aestheticians like to say that a truly great or expressive work of art expresses *itself*, and nothing else, so these experiences seem to be experiences of themselves.

The notions of a transitive verb and a reflexive pronoun are genuine grammatical notions, and although grammarians would not apply their distinction to 'particular' as Wittgenstein does in these places, their distinction inspired him to give a brilliant diagnosis of the genesis of belief in Locke's 'simple ideas of sense and reflection', Hume's 'impressions and ideas', Russell's 'sensations' and the 'sense-contents' of Ayer's *Language Truth and Logic* (1936).

In these places Wittgenstein is making use of grammar in the ordinary sense, though he is not saying, as I shall, that things like thought and desire are expressed by the grammar of sentences, or that philosophers are led astray by confusing words which belong to grammar with words that belong to vocabulary. But most often when Wittgenstein uses the words 'grammar' and 'grammatical' he uses them in ways that are all his own and that have been the subject of some debate. His style of writing leaves even those who have studied him most carefully uncertain how to interpret him. One of the leading experts on his work, Gordon Baker, had a radically different understanding of it at different times in his life.[1]

In the past there was talk of logical syntax, but that phrase might mean more things than one. Formal logic deals with the forms of propositions, and represents these in logical formulae like $P \rightarrow Q$. Logicians have rules for constructing such formulae, rules that exclude formulae like $P \rightarrow Q \rightarrow$ as ill-formed. These might aptly be called rules of 'logical syntax'. Rules of ordinary grammar forbid constructing sentences like 'He conquered if he came if he.' They do not, however, forbid ambiguity in logical form. English allows 'Everything I formerly believed might have been false' which is ambiguous in scope. A philosopher might dream of a language with a grammar that ensured that no sentence in it was ambiguous, that in every statement the logical form was clear. Such a grammar could be called 'logical syntax' and Wittgenstein could have had the idea of such a grammar when writing the *Tractatus*, not, however, when writing the *Investigations*.

Ordinary grammar forbids combining certain linguistic items. Not only can we not have a sentence consisting solely of nouns like 'Men lions'; we should not say 'Dr Johnson refuted that matter is unreal' or 'Every children should be taught to read.' 'That' clauses must be preceded by verbs of saying or thinking; 'every' must be followed by a singular noun. Philosophers offer classifications of things there are; they put them into categories. As one linguistic item may fail to fit with another, so it seems that items in some categories will not fit with others. Colours cannot be predicated of numbers; physical actions can be performed only upon physical objects. Ryle gives the name 'category mistake' to bringing together in speech items in categories that do not fit together, for instance saying 'Numbers above 100 are red' or 'Let's make war on time.' Philosophers discussing these matters usually concentrate on indicative sentences, but some of the best examples occur in imperative or optative sentences, as in Shakespeare's *Sonnets*. Category mistakes do not, like invalid reasoning, offend against the rules of formal logic, nor are they blatantly self-contradictory, but they involve impossibilities that are in some way logical. Classifications like Aristotle's *Categories* were once said to belong to 'material' logic. Some readers of Wittgenstein, Edward Witherspoon (2000) argues – he refers particularly to Carnap (1956) and Baker and Hacker (1985) – have attributed to him the idea of a grammar consisting of rules that prevent category mistakes. It is hard, however, to find Wittgenstein using this idea in any of his work, and if Witherspoon is right, he actually rejected it.

If, when Wittgenstein isn't using 'grammar' in the usual way, he is using it neither for rules to make clear logical form nor for rules to prevent category mistakes, how *is* he using it? 'The characteristic of a metaphysical question', he says, is 'that we express an unclarity about the grammar of words in the *form* of a scientific question' (*BB*, p. 35). That is, we take what are really grammatical questions and statements to be questions and statements about reality. He describes the following as grammatical statements: 'We know the motives of our actions' (*BB*, p. 15), 'I know what I wish' (*BB*, p. 30), 'The room has length' (*BB*, p. 30; similarly, *PG* 83; *PI* 251), 'I and another person cannot both have the same pain' (*BB*, p. 54), 'Thinking is an incorporeal process' (*PI* 339), 'An order orders its own execution' [and therefore something that doesn't yet exist] (*PI* 458).

These are not grammatical statements in the ordinary sense of 'grammatical', and still less is '3 x 18 inches won't go into 3 feet' (*BB*, p. 56). Some people would say that they express 'logical' or 'conceptual' truths. Wittgenstein thinks that they are statements about words, that they are true because of the meanings of the words used. That makes them more lexicographical than grammatical. 'A yard is 36 inches' is a straightforward piece of lexicography, given in the *Shorter Oxford English Dictionary*. If Wittgenstein calls these utterances 'grammatical' it is because he thinks giving the grammar of a word includes explaining its meaning. 'To explain my criterion for another person's having toothache', he says, 'is to give a grammatical explanation about the word "toothache" and, in this sense, an explanation concerning the meaning of the word "toothache"' (*BB*, p. 24; *PI* 572). He also says: 'Asking whether and how a proposition can be verified is only a particular way of asking "How d'you mean?" The answer is a contribution to the grammar of the proposition' (*PI* 353). The puzzle about how time can be measured which Augustine raised in his *Confessions* Book 11 is to be solved, we are told, by:

> comparing what we mean by 'measurement' (the grammar of the word 'measurement') when applied to a distance on a travelling band with the grammar of that word when applied to time. (*BB*, p. 26)

Wittgenstein himself explains what we mean by 'measurement' as applied to time by describing ways in which people might learn to give measurements of time (*BB*, pp. 104–8). We here see two idiosyncratic Wittgensteinian uses of 'grammar', slightly different from each other, and both widely different from the ordinary use.

First, he calls any statement which he takes to be really about the meaning of words a '*grammatical statement*'. Thus he says that Augustine's puzzlement 'about the grammar of the word "time" arises from what one might call apparent contradictions in that grammar' (*BB*, p. 26). What appear contradictory are the statements 'We measure time' and 'Only a durationless instant is ever present'. These are what Aristotle would call 'generally accepted opinions', *endoxa*, about time, but Wittgenstein holds that, properly understood, they express decisions about how we use the words 'time', 'instant' and 'present'. His phrase 'the grammar of the word "time"' designates the set of what other philosophers might call our 'intuitions' about time, or the things we take to be true and perhaps logically necessary.

Secondly, Wittgenstein believes that the right way to *investigate the grammar* of a word or phrase is to think up circumstances in which it can be used correctly. He is probably operating with this conception of grammar when he says 'the grammar of a word seems to suggest the "necessity" of a certain intermediary step, although in fact the word is used in cases in which there is no such intermediary step. Thus we are inclined to say "A man *must* understand an order before he obeys it"' (*BB*, p. 130; cf. *BB*, p. 50; *PI* 431–3). This, he says, leads us to conjure up spurious mental acts of understanding that get performed whenever we obey an order or a rule (*BB*, pp. 141–3), or read a sentence (*BB*, p. 151), or spurious acts of willing that we perform whenever we do something on purpose (*BB*, p. 150). There is nothing in the grammar, in the strict sense, of 'obey' or 'read', or of words we use for intentional action, to conjure up these illusory internal acts; but when we think of certain cases where we obey an order or a rule, or read something, or do something demanding, we find in these cases a process of coming to understand or of steeling our resolution, and we imagine there must be something similar in all.

In the *Philosophical Investigations* we read:

When we look into ourselves as we do philosophy we often get such a picture. A full-blown pictorial representation of our grammar. Not facts; but as it were illustrated turns of speech. (*PI* 295)

This passage is arresting because it tempts us to hope that we might look into ourselves and see a full-blown pictorial representation of the Ablative Absolute, but that is not what Wittgenstein has in mind. He has just been considering the utterance 'I know what pain is only from my own case.' This utterance is in fact, he tells us, 'grammatical': it means 'We do not allow "pain" to fill the gap in "I can feel his …".' 'Pulse' is all right in this gap, but not 'pain'. But if we do not realize that this is a linguistic rule we have adopted, the words 'I know what pain is only from my own case' may conjure up a picture of a real situation in which it might seem natural to say 'I know only from my own case': being locked up in a windowless room in solitary confinement. 'Methinks', says Locke, 'the understanding is not much unlike a closet wholly shut from light …' (*Essay* 2.11.17).

It is similar when Wittgenstein speaks of grammar in connection with descriptions of the visual field (*BB*, pp. 8–9, 63–4), the tactile sensations of water-diviners (*BB*, pp. 9–10^2) and appearances (*BB*, pp. 70–1). He says we do not know the meaning of the sentences 'The visual field is in the brain', 'I feel in my hands that water is three feet below the ground' or of the phrases 'the geometrical eye', 'the sense-datum of a tree', until situations have been described to us in which someone uttering the words would be said to speak truly. He himself presents us with such descriptions, and armed with them we are supposed to recognize that visual fields and ploughed fields, 'geometrical' eyes and physical eyes, sense-data of trees and real trees, differ from one another not as railway engines differ from railway carriages, but rather as railway engines differ from railway accidents and railway laws (*BB*, pp. 64). They belong to what Aristotle called different 'kinds of thing that is', *genê tou ontos*. Wittgenstein says 'Grammar tells us what kind of object anything is' (*PI* 373). In *Philosophical Grammar* he surmises that 'in ordinary grammar one might well distinguish "shape words", "colour words", "sound words", "substance words" as different parts of speech' (*PG 25*). By 'ordinary grammar' he means what is ordinarily taken to be grammar, but he does not (as Chomsky might) offer genuinely grammatical criteria for distinguishing words for shapes from words for colours, let alone adjectives of quality from adjectives of quantity, and when he says that the different kinds have 'different grammatical structures' (*BB*, p. 19), I think he has in mind the kind of situations which give meaning to statements concerning them. However it may be with shapes and colours, the situation in which we can say 'He really saw the tree' (the tree, for example, which eminent dendrologists later described as unique) is quite different from the situation (discussing a hallucination, or the art of Monet) in which we say 'He saw the sense-datum of a tree'.

In *PI* 398–401 Wittgenstein gives the 'grammar' of the phrase 'the visual room' (roughly speaking, the room as seen from where we are) in much the way in which (in *BB*, 63–4) he gave the 'grammar' for 'the geometrical eye'. He first thinks up circumstances in which we can talk of a 'visual room'. He then says 'You have a new conception [sc. the visual room] and interpret it as seeing a new object. You interpret a grammatical movement made by yourself as a quasi-physical phenomenon.' In what way is your movement grammatical? Not in the same way as shifting from the past to the historic present, or from indirect to direct speech. Many people would say simply that using the phrase 'visual room' and descriptions that fit it ('the lines of the bookshelves converge') is a new way of talking about the room, describing it as an artist would paint it. They could still then make Wittgenstein's point: we are liable to misconstrue a new way of describing an object as a description of a new sort of object. Wittgenstein calls the change in our way of speaking a 'grammatical' movement, either because he is prepared to use the word 'grammatical' to cover any difference whatever in ways of speaking, or because the two ways of speaking have different grammars in his special sense. Different circumstances justify saying that the lines of the bookshelves converge in the visual room, and saying they converge in the real room. The first remark would be a tip to an artist, the second a reproach to the carpenter.

* * *

That completes my argument that Wittgenstein uses 'grammar' and 'grammatical' in a way peculiar to himself. I am not the first person to say that. G. P. Baker and P. M. S. Hacker (1985, p. 56) observe that Moore charged Wittgenstein with using these words in a special sense; and they argue that he was right to repudiate the charge and say that there is no firm line between grammar in the ordinary sense and the linguistic investigations he calls 'grammatical'. In a later work Baker says that he [Baker] leaves 'out of account such vexed questions as whether he [Wittgenstein] himself did not misuse or stretch the term "Grammatik"' (2004, p. 53), but it is clear that on this vexed question at least Baker did not change his mind. He goes on (p. 59) to express sympathy with the idea that by 'our grammar' Wittgenstein means 'our descriptions of word-use (especially, but not exclusively, our compilations of what we call "explanations of what our words mean").'

'Three central points stand out,' say Baker and Hacker. The first is 'philosophical grammar is *concerned with rules for the use of words* (their emphasis) just as ordinary grammar is'. My reply to this is that ordinary grammar is concerned with constructions, and with words only when (like 'not') they belong to constructions. They concede that 'explanations of meaning are ordinarily conceived as belonging not to grammar but to lexicography', but brush this aside: 'Presumably he [Wittgenstein] would have argued that in both cases we are concerned with rules for the use of words' (1985, p. 52 n. 13). Their second and third points are that 'Wittgenstein clearly thought that there was no essential dividing line in the patterns of use of words between so-called "syntax" and "semantics"', and 'Wittgenstein was inclined [they cite *PG* 45] to characterize grammar very generally as all the conditions, the method, necessary for comparing the proposition with reality.' Here they are not defending Wittgenstein against Moore's accusation that he uses 'grammar' in a novel manner, but restating it.

It is true that both in lexicography and in grammar 'we are concerned with rules for the use of words'. But we talk of using words in two ways. We say that English-speakers use 'yellow' for the colour for which French-speakers use *jaune*, and we also say that we use words to perform various linguistic acts, such as making statements, giving orders and offering or asking for explanations. Rules for using words are correspondingly of two kinds. There are rules that tell us what words to use for what, and rules that tell us how to perform the various different linguistic acts. As I said in Chapter 3, these rules complement one another. I cannot use 'yellow' for a colour without using the word in a construction and performing a linguistic act. But it does not follow, because they are complementary, that there is 'no essential dividing line' between them. On the contrary, if I cannot use 'yellow' for a colour or 'shirt' for a shirt without making a statement or giving an order or performing some other linguistic act, then there must be rules for performing such acts different in character from rules saying what is a word for what. Complementarity depends on difference.

In the *Cratylus* (388b, 433d) Plato suggests that words (that is, words like 'man', 'horse', 'swim') are instruments for 'showing' things, and that the relationship of a word to what it shows is like that of a picture to what it depicts (429a).[3] The difference is that while a picture of a horse has a natural likeness to a horse,[4] the word 'horse' does not. In different languages different words show the same thing. A word shows what it shows by convention, a convention embodied in a rule of vocabulary. Merely painting or exhibiting a picture, however, is not saying anything; nor, as Plato points out in *Sophist* 262b–c, is merely uttering words like 'man' and 'runs'. In *Cratylus* 430–1 he suggests that saying that someone is a woman is like showing someone a picture of a woman and saying 'This is your picture.' This explanation is circular, since saying 'This is your picture' or 'This is like you' is itself making a true or false statement. If we want to know how we manage to make true or false statements it will not do to say: 'It's like exhibiting a picture and making a statement about it; you utter a word and say that that word applies to something.' In the *Sophist* Plato recognizes that to say something we must 'weave together' words that 'show' things according to a grammatical rule. The rules for performing different kinds of linguistic act are just as variable between different societies as the rules for 'showing' different kinds of thing, but the two kinds of rule do not merge seamlessly into one another like yellow and orange.

Baker and Hacker try to show that there is no dividing seam by asking us on which side of it we should place the sentences 'The word "north-east" should not be used in the contexts "north-east of the North Pole" or "north-east of the South Pole"' and 'The words "it is true that …" should not be used with an adverb of time.' They admit that grammarians would 'typically contend that the first is not a grammatical rule, that "We are sailing north-east of the North Pole" is grammatically correct'. But they say that this is 'arbitrary'. Take the rule 'The words "north-east of" must be followed by a noun or pronoun in oblique case' [where by a 'pronoun in an oblique case' is meant a word like 'me', 'him' or 'them']. If, as their opponents would say, this is a rule of grammar, so is 'They must be followed by a designation of a place', and so is the further addition 'a place other than the Poles themselves'. This, however, is mere assertion on their part.[5] Whereas 'north-east of they' is plainly ungrammatical, 'north-east of the polar regions' and 'north-east of happiness' are not, and if grammar is invoked to exclude them it will rule out a good deal of lyric poetry. Is it a rule of grammar that 'rearward of' must be followed by a designation of a place? Then Shakespeare wrote ungrammatically when he wrote:

> Do not, when my heart has scaped this sorrow,
> Come in the rearward of a conquered woe. (Sonnet 90)

And Shakespeare's howlers are nothing to those of poets today:

> Rain threads me to a
> clover sea. All roads out
> are signed in shining
> arrows. (Crump 2009, p. 127)

It is a pity Baker and Hacker do not go into the alleged rule about 'it is true that …', since it is philosophically more interesting. I discuss the grammar of temporal constructions in some detail later. For the moment I shall say only this. It certainly seems to be a rule of grammar that adverbial expressions like 'now', 'formerly' and 'next Tuesday' cannot be used with nouns; it is ungrammatical to say 'Several now sheep'. Grammar has nothing, however, against using them with the verb 'to be'; we can say 'There now are several sheep in the field,' 'The clouds formerly were red,' and there is no obvious grammatical objection to 'it is now true that …' or 'it will next Tuesday be true that …'.

In Chapter 3 I pointed out ways in which grammar and lexicography are interrelated, but denied that these abolish the difference between them. Wittgenstein, I think, considered the difference was of no philosophical importance because of views he held but nowhere states about language and meaning.

On the face of it there is a distinction between what, in speaking, I mean to *say*, and what I mean to *achieve by saying this*. We may call the former my 'linguistic' meaning and the latter my 'practical' meaning. There is a corresponding distinction between what I actually say, and its actual aptitude to affect the state of mind of people who grasp what I actually say. We may call these the linguistic and the practical meaning, not of the speaker, but of the speech. Literary critics are concerned with both, with what is actually said in a poem or a story, but still more with the effect it is likely to have on readers who understand what is said.

What I actually say is determined by the words I use and the construction in which I use them. Reading a sentence in a language of which you know the grammar and vocabulary you can work out what anyone uttering it says, what statement is made, what order given, what question asked. If I know English, I normally mean to say what I in fact say. My linguistic meaning and the linguistic meaning of my speech usually coincide, so if you too know English you can be confident about my linguistic meaning. But you may still wonder: 'Why should he want to say *that*?' or 'What could anyone saying *that* hope to achieve?'

The range of practical purposes for which I may make a sound or inscribe letters is unlimited. I might mean to cause an echo, to open a magic casket, to attract an onlooker's attention. But our proximate practical purpose in *saying* something is to cause (or prevent) some change in the state of mind of a person who *understands what we are saying*. We wish to make someone know or think something, to excite or quiet a desire, to preserve or change a feeling, to remove puzzlement or, occasionally, to create it; obfuscation is a possible, if disreputable, practical aim.

In medieval education grammar was followed by rhetoric, and by the 'art of rhetoric' was understood precisely skill at affecting the mental state of someone who understands what you are saying. The aptitude of a sentence to enlighten, confuse or move a reader or listener depends partly on the words and construction, and to that extent it more or less coincides with what Frege called its 'tone' or 'colouring' (1967, pp. 22–3). But it also depends on other things, such as the circumstances and people's expectations, and if you want to know why I say something that at first seems false or impossible, for example that I feel in my hand that the water is three feet under the ground (Wittgenstein, *BB*, p. 9), it may help you to be told circumstances in which anyone saying that would be thought to speak truly or appropriately.

Now this notion of saying seems to me absent from Wittgenstein's later work. He goes straight to the practical purpose an utterance has. For him practical meaning does not presuppose linguistic; it supersedes and supplants it. Wittgenstein urges us to replace talk of meaning by talk of use: 'If we had to name anything which is the life of the sign, we should have to say that it was its *use*' (*BB*, p. 4; *PI* 432). And he does not think of using words as a matter of constructing sentences out of them or, in an inflected language, of inflecting them – he is not speaking of using a noun in the ablative or a verb in the aorist optative. To explain how a word is used *grammatically* is to say what someone using it in that construction *says*. Grammatical rules are rules precisely for the use of words in saying. Wittgenstein believes we can skip grammar and start with rhetoric (though of course it will not be medieval rhetoric if we do). He is interested in the use of words, and of the sentences composed of them, in getting people to think or do things. When he says 'There are *countless* kinds' of sentence (*PI* 23), and hence countless ways of using words, his examples include 'giving orders, and obeying them', 'forming and testing a hypothesis', 'singing catches', 'making a joke' and 'thanking', and, with the exception of giving an order, these are not acts simply of saying; they are acts of saying something for a practical purpose or simply acts of doing something.

If we make practical meaning primary, grammar becomes relatively unimportant. Working with the ideas of training (*PI* 5), drill (*BB*, p. 12) and what we call 'conditioning', Wittgenstein takes the most primitive pieces of speech to have no significant internal structure. In the language-games described in *BB*, pp. 77–9 and *PI* 2 there seems to be no syntax. In the discussion of 'Slab' in *PI* 21–2 he does not mention syntax, and in *PI* 2 (cf. *PI* 19) we are to imagine a language consisting only of orders. For Wittgenstein (as for Jonathan Bennett [1976[6]]) all that is philosophically interesting in language is present before grammar and vocabulary are distinguished. How little importance Wittgenstein attached to grammar is apparent from the way he keeps talking about using sentences (*BB*, pp. 72, 101, 104, 114, 171, 174; *PI* 278). It is natural to talk of using a word; we use it when we utter it or write it in a sentence for the purpose of saying something. We seldom talk of using sentences; and when we do, we have in mind some special practical purpose. In philosophy we use sentences as examples. When Plato used 'Theaetetus is seated' his aim was not that we should believe that Theaetetus was seated, but that we should understand how someone uttering the sentence says something true or false. In a court of law I might use a sentence uttered by someone as evidence. If, however, we do not think that the words in a sentence and the construction make distinct contributions to its meaning, but that it has meaning as a seamless whole, we think of ordinary speech as the use of whole sentences. When Wittgenstein talks of the grammar of a sentence, proposition or statement (*BB*, pp. 9–10, 51, 72), he does not mean its syntax, but rules for using it for practical purposes. Baker shows some recognition of this in *Wittgenstein's Method*. He suggests that when Wittgenstein contrasts 'surface grammar' and 'depth grammar' (*PI* 664), he takes doing 'depth grammar' to be doing such things as investigating 'differences in the ways individual words are integrated into human activity', 'differences in the ways *complete* sentences are *employed*' and engaging in a variety of investigations all, in one way or another, connected with the practical use of words or sentences (2004, pp. 78–9).

Several contributors to *The New Wittgenstein*[7] attribute to Wittgenstein a principle they call the 'context principle' which might seem to justify his strategy. Frege, in the Introduction to his *Foundations of Arithmetic*, formulates the following 'fundamental principle': 'never to ask for the meaning of a word in isolation, but only in the context of a proposition'.[8] There are good reasons for this. I said earlier that to give the meaning of a word is to say what you quantify or predicate when you use it in a sentence. In many languages the same word (or morpheme) may be used as a noun or verb, and if as a noun either as a count-noun or as a mass-noun: for example the English 'fish', 'egg'. A proper name, also, can be used to signify predicates associated with its bearer, as in the unkind 'He is no Adonis.' Wittgenstein, says Witherspoon, extends this principle. 'He comes to think that sentences in isolation do not have senses: sentences have senses in their context of use, in their relations to other sentences, in language-games' (2000, pp. 323–4). So we should never ask the meaning of a sentence in isolation, but only in the part it plays in a particular established practice, like giving orders to builders or, Wittgenstein might say, engaging in communal religious worship.

As I said just now, it seems to me incorrect to speak of using sentences – except in the 'context' of a libel action or a philosophy seminar. I agree that to understand any word we must have some grasp of a construction; we must distinguish indicative from imperative sentences. Making statements and giving orders or advice are social practices in which we engage for practical purposes; but they are *linguistic* practices, practices of *saying*, which do not count as Wittgensteinian language-games. Perhaps they could have grown up only in societies in which there was already cooperative practical activity, but as things are at present, understanding them and, in general, being able to speak the real language of your society, is a prerequisite of taking part in such practices as building projects and religious festivals.

It might be argued that the meaning of simple predicate-terms like 'red' and 'round' depends on what they are applied to. Saying that an apple is red is saying that its skin is red; saying a glass vase is red is saying it is red all through. So to understand 'That's red' we have to know the context in which it is uttered: whether it is a discussion of apples or of glassware. I reply that the word 'red' does not have two meanings, 'red-skinned' and 'red all through', which lexicographers have overlooked. (What would 'red' have meant in 'red all through'?) Rather the context determines on what basis we apply the word. If you say simply 'We bought some red apples' I will take it that you predicate the colour of the apples on the basis of their skin-pigmentation, whereas if you say 'We bought a red glass vase' I take it you predicate the colour of the vase on the basis of the colour of the glass. Conventions used to hold for applying colour-words to human beings. They determine whether the person using the words speaks truly or correctly, but the words are words simply for the colours.

The scholars I am discussing say that Wittgenstein rejects the idea of a species of grammar that would rule out category mistakes. There would be a place for such a grammar only if it were possible to commit a category mistake, and you can commit a category mistake only if you can construct a sentence that makes sense in a way, since we can tell that it brings together items in categories that do not fit together, yet is nonsensical. But the notion of a sentence that makes sense but is nonsensical is incoherent. Either a sentence makes sense, in which case it says something, or it does not make sense, in which case it says nothing. To suppose there can be category mistakes we must suppose that there can be two kinds of nonsense, what Conant calls 'substantial' nonsense, which makes sense of a sort, and 'mere' nonsense, which is gibberish. In fact there is only mere nonsense. Lewis Carroll's 'Once a coincidence was taking a walk with a little accident, and they met an explanation' (*Sylvie and Bruno, Concluded*) is just as much gibberish as 'When and strawberries for' or 'heb xing bi&ng$'.

The issue here is relevant to the question whether the meaning of a sentence is determined by the words and construction. If it is, then sentences which are grammatically correct like Lewis Carroll's have meaning and say something. If they are gibberish the way is open to say that the meaning of a sentence is determined primarily by its place in a language-game, and its only meaning is practical meaning.

The only argument offered to show that category mistakes are impossible depends on the premise that the sentences that appear to contain them are nonsensical. In fact the English word 'nonsense' is a term of disparagement that covers not only gibberish but any kind of tosh. That being so, it is perfectly proper to distinguish at least three kinds of nonsense. An utterance is grammatical nonsense if uttering it is not saying anything. Babbling is grammatical nonsense, and so is making a grammatical mistake like 'His parents is blue-eyed', though making a minor grammatical mistake may not matter for practical purposes, since it is usually clear what you mean to say, and people act as if you had said that. Moreover a writer may deliberately break a grammatical rule in order to make the reader ask why. You talk logical nonsense if what you say is logically objectionable, and there are different ways of being that. Contradicting yourself is objectionable to formal logicians; so is blatantly fallacious reasoning such as Shakespeare often gives to characters for comic effect, and sentences containing category mistakes are objectionable to 'material' logicians or ontologists. Ryle (1971b, p. 174) was prudent to call sentences expressing 'category trespasses' like 'Saturday is in bed' 'absurd' rather than 'nonsensical'. An utterance is factual nonsense if what is said is plainly false or wrong. Counsels and commands as well as orders can be called 'nonsense' in this last way; someone might say that the writings of Marx or Hitler are factual nonsense. The rules of grammar prevent us from mouthing babble; they enable us to talk logical and factual tosh.

If the New Wittgensteinians were right that there is only grammatical nonsense, those who spend good money on books by Carroll and Edward Lear and imagine they find them amusing would be suffering from delusions.[9] A theory with this consequence is a poor ground for extending the context principle from words to sentences, denying that what we say is determined by the words and constructions we use, and holding that all meaning is practical meaning. Wittgenstein's aversion to pure acts of saying, however, seems to me of a piece with his aversion to mental processes. He fears that if there is such an act as *saying* it will have to be an act of *meaning* what is said, and that will be something mental. In Chapters 12 and 13 I suggest that he cannot give a satisfactory account of either thinking or saying because lacks a satisfactory concept of teleological explanation.

* * *

Wittgenstein and Chomsky approach grammar from different directions. Wittgenstein comes from philosophy and wants his study of language to solve problems in the philosophy of mind and the philosophy of language. Chomsky comes from linguistics and wants to discover what all languages have in common, something the later Wittgenstein seems to think a quest for El Dorado. They run the risk, therefore, of being ships that pass in the night. Nevertheless we may say that Chomsky upholds the traditional distinction between grammar and lexicography. 'The meaning of a sentence', he says, 'is based on the meaning of its elementary parts and the manner of their combination' (1965, p. 162; similarly, p. 136). He also accepts, at least in effect, the distinction Wittgenstein rejects between linguistic and practical meaning.

> Although consideration of intended effects avoids some problems, it seems to me that, no matter how fully elaborated, it will at best provide an analysis of successful communication, but not of meaning or the use of language, which need not involve communication or even the attempt to communicate. If I use language to express or clarify my thoughts, with intent to deceive, to avoid an embarrassing silence, or in a dozen other ways, my words will have a strict meaning *and I can very well mean what I say*, but the fullest understanding of

what I intend my audience (if any) to believe or to do might give little or no indication of the meaning of my discourse. (Chomsky 1972, p. 24)

Chomsky formulates rules for constructing sentences out of words which make no mention of the meaning of the words until their inflectional form, if any, and place in the final sentence, have been determined. Following these rules we obtain what might be called sentence-patterns or formulae for sentences, like 'Definite article – count-noun,[10] – verb – number-word – count-noun'. From these we can derive grammatically correct English sentences by substituting arbitrarily chosen nouns, verbs and so on of the varieties specified in the rules from the vocabulary of English. A successful English grammar would be a set of rules which can produce every correct English sentence and will produce no sentence that is incorrect. Over the last 50 years Chomsky has refined the details of his account but he has not changed his opinion that we should regard sentences as built up out of elementary structures of simple components in accordance with rules applied one after another, rather as the objects around us are built up out of atoms and molecules. This idea is almost universally accepted and I consider it a real improvement on earlier grammatical thinking. What I wish to consider here is whether he gives any reasons for saying that meaning cannot be 'assigned directly' to grammatical devices (1957, p. 108). I shall later consider what sort of theory he has of speech generally.

When Chomsky declared in *Syntactic Structures* that grammar is independent of meaning or semantics (1957, p. 17), he was opposing two views in particular. One is that that for a sentence to be grammatically correct is for it to be meaningful, to have 'semantic significance' (1957, pp. 15, 94); the other is that certain grammatical constructions somehow 'correspond' to certain real relations. Neither of them is a view I wish to defend.

Chomsky attacks the first, that to be grammatical is to be meaningful, by saying that the sentence 'Colourless green ideas sleep furiously' (an example made up by Russell) is grammatically correct but nonsensical. His opponents here are evidently identifying being nonsensical with being meaningless or not making sense, and taking it that the function of grammar is to exclude nonsense. These are Wittgensteinian ideas. Wittgenstein urges us to 'understand the connection between grammar and sense and nonsense' (*BB*, p. 65). Sentences are supposed to have meaning as wholes; grammar tells us when they can properly or meaningfully be used, and the function of grammar is to exclude utterances that 'make no sense'. 'To say "This combination of words makes no sense" excludes it from the sphere of language.' (*PI* 499). '"Of course

I know what I wish" can be interpreted as a grammatical statement' since '"Are you sure it is this you wish" ... makes no sense' (*BB*, p. 30).[11]

Chomsky suggests that 'Colourless green ideas sleep furiously' is mildly ungrammatical in that it has an abstract noun as subject, and its verb calls for an animate subject. As he observes, however (anticipating my objection to Baker and Hacker above) we must allow for metaphor and personification (1965, p. 149). In point of fact, the sentence is not only perfectly grammatical but also perfectly meaningful. If you utter our sentence you say something, namely that colourless green ideas sleep furiously. It may be unclear why you should want to say that, since sleeping is an animal function, and ideas are not animals. But we can make a conjecture. Perhaps you are writing a historical poem about our own time, and trying to convey the atmosphere of a period when aggressive members of the Green movement are not actually doing anything but boiling up to some violent demonstration. Haas (1972–3) offers a comparable interpretation of another Russellian example, 'Quadruplicity drinks procrastination'.

Secondly, Chomsky attacks the idea that the grammatical relation *Subject – Verb-phrase* 'corresponds' to the 'structural meaning' *actor – action*, and the grammatical relation *Verb – Noun-phrase* 'corresponds' to the 'structural meaning' *action – goal of action – object of action* (1957, pp. 94, 100). I agree that in a sentence of the form *Subject – Verb-phrase* the verb of the verb-phrase does not have to be a verb of action, and in a verb-phrase of the form *Verb – Noun-phrase* there is no necessity that the noun phrase should either refer to a thing acted upon or else express an objective. But I do not think that the wrongness of these grammatical rules undermines anything I shall say in Chapters 9 and 10 about how causation is expressed grammatically.

It might be thought, however, that Chomsky's method of setting out grammatical rules makes it unnecessary to assign any kind of meaning to grammatical constructions. In traditional grammar, the components of sentences are classified as nouns, pronouns, adjectives, verbs and so on, and these categories are subdivided: nouns, for instance, into common and abstract nouns, pronouns into personal, possessive, demonstrative, interrogative, etc. Traditional grammar also divides inflections into inflections of number, case, person, tense, mood, voice and gender, and for uninflected languages provides rules for expressing what these inflections express. And it employs concepts of specific linguistic acts, making statements, counselling and commanding; explaining in various ways; expressing temporal relations; reporting speech. Equipped with these terms or concepts, traditional grammar then tells us how to perform these various acts in the language being described. Chomsky undertakes to devise a system of rules which will tell us everything a traditional grammar of English will tell us, but in which the traditional concepts and terms are defined purely in terms of their mutual syntactical relations, without any appeal to meaning (1965, pp. 63–4). He further wants his rules to apply up to a point to all languages, in spite of the fact that many languages do not seem to have the same parts of speech as English or even the same minimal range of inflections.

This programme is not ill conceived. When grammarians try to classify parts of speech by what they signify, the results can be embarrassing. Gildersleeve and Lodge, whose *Latin Grammar* was for many years the sheet anchor for Latin beginners, distinguish adverbs, prepositions and adjectives in Latin as follows:

> The *Adverb* shows *circumstances*. The *Preposition* shows *local relation*. The *Adjective* adds a quality to the Substantive: **bonus vir**: a *good* man. (1908, s. 16)

Nouns, adjectives and the rest differ not so much in what they signify as in how they signify, they play different syntactic roles in sentences. But as I said, it is open to debate how far sub-classes of nouns, adjectives and the rest can be defined syntactically without reference to meaning. Chomsky takes *animate* and *human* to be subcategories of nouns (1965, pp. 80–5). These look like semantic terms, and Chomsky does not offer syntactic analyses of them. In Chapter 12 I argue that the notions of life and thought are syntactic in the sense that they are expressed by syntax, but that leaves the adjectives with semantic meaning of a sort.

It is the same with number and tense: can we really give rules for inflections of number and tense without saying what they are inflections for? The rules Chomsky offers for inflections of number in English seem rather artificial. He tells us that a noun with an 's' at the end must be followed by a verb without, and vice versa (1957, p. 64), and armed with this rule we can construct the sentences 'Spies spy' and 'A spy spies'. To give complete rules for inflections of tense and number without saying that they are inflections of *tense* and *number* would be a big undertaking, and Chomsky later seems to acknowledge that the traditional device of setting out the declension of *mensa* and the conjugation of *amo* is, after all, satisfactory:

> I know of no compensating advantage for the modern descriptivist reanalysis of traditional paradigm formulations in terms of morpheme sequences. This seems, therefore, to be an ill-advised theoretical innovation. (1965, p. 174)

Lakoff and Johnson (1999) devote a chapter to attacking Chomsky. Although they do not say categorically that grammatical constructions have meaning

– they prefer to say 'the grammar of a language consists of the highly structured neural connections linking the conceptual and expressive (phonological) aspects of the brain' (p. 498; I think they mean that we are able to speak grammatically because of these connections) – they do say that the tense-inflection of 'worked' in 'John worked' 'expresses the temporal location of the working as past relative to the time of utterance. In other words, a linguistic form is a tense in virtue of what it means' (p. 501).[12] They also give examples to show that the rules for constructing and transforming sentences cannot be formulated without drawing on semantics. Certain main-clause constructions can be used in subordinate clauses after a conjunction that introduces a reason, but not after one that introduces a mere condition. We can say 'I'm leaving because who wants to watch a dull movie' but not 'I'm leaving if who wants to watch a dull movie'. And in a sentence that contains clauses joined by 'and', whether it is possible to operate on one of the conjuncts without the others depends on what is signified in the conjoined clauses. We cannot change 'John ate hamburgers and Bill drank beer' to 'What did John eat and Bill drank beer?' but we can change 'Bill can drink beer and stay sober' to 'What can Bill drink and stay sober?' (pp. 483–92; I have slightly simplified their examples.)

The difficulty of dispensing with semantic considerations becomes most evident when we consider the notion of a sentence. This is fundamental in any grammar, including Chomsky's. His rules are primarily rules for constructing sentences and performing operations on parts of sentences, but he does not tell us what is to count as a sentence. If he allowed himself the notion of a linguistic act, an act such as asserting or ordering, he could say that a sentence is a complete piece of behaviour by which we perform a linguistic act and say something. But in fact the only notion he allows himself is that of a sentence that is grammatical. 'The fundamental aim', he says, 'in the linguistic analysis of a language L, is to separate the *grammatical* sequences which are the sentences of L from the *ungrammatical* sequences which are not sentences of L' (1957, p. 13). He offers two criteria for being grammatical. One is that the sentence should be acceptable to native speakers, where acceptability is to be judged by their observed reactions (1957, pp. 13, 49–53). This criterion can be used for other things besides speech, such as good manners. The use of it, therefore, will not distinguish speaking ungrammatically from pushing through doors ahead of others, eating steak with your fingers, or interrupting the Queen when she is speaking. The other, which Chomsky prefers, is that the sentence be constructed according to grammatical rules. But what makes a rule grammatical? It will not do to say that a grammatical rule is a rule for constructing something which is constructed according to grammatical rules. And even if we have an intuitive idea of a grammatical rule, why should we want to produce something constructed according to grammatical rules unless we have some further idea of what these rules are for, what purpose they have beyond that of producing things constructed according to them? As it stands, Chomsky's theory of grammar is rather like Kant's theory of ethics, according to which the only way of behaving well is to do something because doing it is a rule.

I return in Chapter 13 to the question whether it is possible to construct a grammar without using notions of acts like asserting and ordering, and there suggest that it is because he is unwilling to draw on such notions that Chomsky feels it necessary to postulate linguistic universals.

So much for preliminaries. In the next three chapters I discuss truth, existence and goodness, which medieval philosophers called 'transcendent' not because (like God, perhaps) they lie outside the spatio-temporal world and are somehow superior to it, but because they are not confined to any one of the pigeon-holes – objects, qualities, actions and so on – into which philosophers sort its contents, but apply in all.

5

Truth and Predication

The first metaphysical topic to be tackled in Europe was probably truth. Plato addresses it in three dialogues, the *Cratylus*, the *Theaetetus* and the *Sophist*. He does not actually ask 'What is truth?'[1] His aim was to meet sceptical or sophistic difficulties about the possibility of saying anything false. His explanation, however, of how we can speak falsely, provides sufficient conditions for a statement's being true, and explains how both truth and falsehood get into language. Plato is not followed by metaphysicians today, but I shall argue that his theory was on the right lines.

Today philosophers do ask what truth is, and give surprisingly different answers. The American Pragmatists revived an idea Plato attributes to Protagoras (*Theaetetus* 166–7), that strictly speaking there is no such thing as truth, but we count beliefs as true if they are useful or healthy, and false if they are the opposite (James 1916, p. 58, endorsed by Lakoff and Johnson 1999, p. 109). Frege claimed that truth and falsehood are things designated by sentences: that they stand to sentences as a particular human being stands to the name 'Kepler' or the number six to the phrase 'The double of 3' (1952, p. 63). The idea is that just as 'the double of' signifies the function the value of which, for the argument three, is the number six, so '*is* the double of 3' signifies a function the value of which, for the argument six, is truth. This theory still has defenders (Mendelsohn 2001). Michael Dummett (1958–9), trying to improve on it, suggested that a statement is true if we are justified in asserting it. One might have thought it was the other way round.

The natural supposition is that for a statement to be true is for it to correspond to reality or to the facts. When, however, we try to say precisely what it is to which a true statement corresponds, and what precisely the correspondence consists in, we get stuck. We are inclined to think of statements as being like images and say that a statement is true if it is an accurate representation of something real. The trouble with this line of thought, as I said on page 56, is that a picture is not true or false in itself; what is true or false is the statement that it is a good or bad likeness. How statements can be true or false, how truth and falsehood can attach to statements, is a deep mystery because they cannot (dentures notwithstanding) attach to anything physical.

The words 'true' and 'false' are sometimes used by themselves, as when we say 'The statement that Caesar was stabbed is true'. Grammarians call this using the words 'absolutely'. But they can also be used with 'of', as in 'It is true *of* the younger Cato that he committed suicide, but false *of* the older.' In grammar this use is called 'relative'.[2] Philosophers in recent years have concentrated on the absolute use. Dummett explains truth *of* something in terms of absolute truth: 'A one-place predicate is, then, true of a given individual just in case the sentence which results from inserting a name of that individual in the argument-place (gap) of the predicate is true' (1973, p. 11. For example, it is true *of* the Moon that it is spherical if and only if it is true *that* the Moon is spherical). When philosophers today speak of 'the truth predicate' they mean 'true' used absolutely in sentences like 'That Mars is red is true' or 'The sentence "Mars is red" is true'.

Timothy Williamson (2000, p. 280), telling us how much more we know about truth than did our predecessors did, speaks of disquotation. That word arises from the thought (which goes back to Alfred Tarski's 1944 paper 'The semantic concept of truth') that the sentence 'Caesar was stabbed' is true if and only if Caesar was stabbed. The same holds, apparently, for any indicative sentence; we can say what it is for it to be true by removing the quotation marks around it. Let S be any sentence; then the sentence 'S' is true if and only if S. Or, to put it differently, since it is true *that Caesar was stabbed* if and only if Caesar was stabbed, let p stand for any proposition: it is true that p if and only if p.

In fact, we cannot arrive at a general account of truth in this way. We are trying to say 'A reported speech is true if and only if … [*and then that speech, no longer reported but simply made directly*].' No such sentence is possible in English or any other language. The sentence beginning 'A reported speech is true if and only if' breaks off ungrammatically. But if we give the name 'T sentence' to sentences like 'That Caesar was stabbed is true if and only if Caesar was stabbed' then we can say that any predicate term is a 'truth predicate' or signifies truth if it 'makes all T sentences true' (Davidson 1990, p. 65), or if applying it to a sentence is equivalent to uttering the sentence, or if there is 'complete cognitive equivalence between Tp and p' (Blackburn 2010, p. 3, following Horwich 2000). On this view 'true' does not signify any property, relational or intrinsic, of reported speeches, but using it serves to turn a reported speech into that speech itself; it removes, so to speak, the quotation marks around it. Many English-speaking philosophers[3] take this line, and it is called holding a 'deflationary' or 'redundancy' theory of truth. Others say that different sorts of statement, logical, physical, ethical, historical and so on, are true in different ways, and some Continental writers seem to think that objective truth is a complete will o' the wisp.

Modern discussions start from the assumption that the things which are true or false and which non-philosophers require to correspond to reality are more or less static entities. Either they are sentences constructed out of words, or (see Sainsbury and Tye 2011, pp. 101–24) they are mental representations constructed out of ideas or concepts. Either way they are conceived as *things*. In fact what is true or false and corresponds or fails to correspond to reality is not a sort of thing but a sort of act, an act of saying or thinking.

To put this point differently, we try to explain the meaning of 'true' and 'false', and since 'true' is an adjective like 'blue', we think it signifies something predicable of statements and beliefs; we ought, instead, to consider the meaning of 'truly' and 'falsely', which are adverbs like 'quickly' or 'deliberately' signifying manners in the which something is done. If we ask 'What it is to speak truly?' we can arrive at an account of truth that shows both how it is different for different kinds of statements, and how simple statements of two basic kinds correspond or fail to correspond to reality

It is hard to avoid the assumption that truth and falsehood attach primarily to static entities, because we certainly say things that are true or false. If I say something true it seems to follow that there is something which is true and said by me. Certainly if I wear something blue there is something, perhaps a sweater, which is blue and worn by me. But as Wittgenstein warns us (*BB*, pp. 7, 36 and 70), we should be wary of reasoning like this. Things present misleading appearances, for instance the top of a cylinder like an oil drum is said (at least by philosophers who have an axe to grind) to appear elliptical rather than circular when viewed from the side. The axe-grinding philosophers infer that there is something that really is elliptical and is presented by the top of the drum; this elliptical reality does not exist in physical space, but it exists in the minds of those to whom it is presented. Versions of this argument can be found in Russell (1912, Chapter 1) and Ayer (1964, Chapter 1). It is unsound. 'The top presents an elliptical appearance' means: 'The top presents an appearance of being elliptical', not: 'The top presents an appearance which is elliptical.'

If there really were things which are true or false and said by us, it would be easy to say how truth and falsehood come into language. They are transmitted to our language from the things said, rather as a germ can be transmitted to you from the person you sit next to, or a colour transmitted to your white handkerchief from the ripe cherries you wrap in it. But it is a desperate move to model truth and falsehood on micro-organisms or physical properties. And what are these 'things' we say? They appear to be entities known only to philosophers; certainly they are not known to natural scientists. Philosophers call them 'thoughts' or 'propositions' but using words for them which are in common use is not enough to make them respectable. The difficulty is particularly acute over false things. We can certainly construct 'that' clauses which will serve as subjects to 'is false'. 'That Caesar died in his bed is false', I can say, or 'That 7 + 5 = 11 is false.' But it is extremely awkward to say 'There is such a thing as that Caesar died in his bed', or 'There is such a thing as that the sum of 7 and 5 is 11.' 'That Caesar was assassinated', we may say, 'is a historical event'; but that he died in his bed is not a historical event; at best it is a non-event, and history does not contain non-events as well as events. Similarly that the sum of 7 and 5 is 12 may be a mathematical truth, but that the sum is 11 is not a mathematical truth; it is an untruth and mathematics does not contain untruths as well as truths.

When 'is true' and 'is false' are used as predicates to 'that' clauses, they are equivalent to 'is the case' and 'is not the case', phrases in which the words 'the case' simply smooth away the awkwardness English-speakers feel in using the verb 'to be' by itself. That being so, saying that there are things that are not the case seems to be saying that there are things that are not, or simply that there are things that there aren't; and that sounds self-contradictory. This point was made by Plato and his predecessors, and led Plato to the sort of theory I am about to recommend.

Instead of 'is the case' and 'is not the case' we sometimes use 'is a fact' and 'is not a fact'. Will the word 'fact' help us out of our difficulties? Can we say that a statement is true if it states a fact that exists and it is false if it states a fact that does not exist? That seems to be a step backward, since how can there exist facts that do not exist?

Clauses like 'that Caesar died in his bed' certainly express things that are true or false. But they do not express entities known only to philosophers; what they express is what is known to grammarians as 'indirect speech', *oratio obliqua*. They do not get us out of language and thought into a metaphysical reality from which language and thought can borrow truth and falsehood; their truth or falsehood is simply that of the statements or beliefs they report. 'Philosophy', says Wittgenstein (*PI* 109), 'is a battle against the bewitchment of our intelligence by means of language'. Phrases like 'say something true' and 'put forward something as true' bewitch us into thinking that there are things which are true or false independently of being put forward or said. As a counter-charm I recommend the phrases 'speak truly' and 'speak falsely' (which correspond to single words in Greek, *alêtheuein* and *pseudesthai*). That Caesar died in his bed is false, if saying that Caesar died in his bed is speaking falsely.

* * *

There is no real mystery about how truth and falsehood can get into language. That is exactly what grammar tells us. The grammar of any language tells us how in that language we can refer to things and make true and false statements, or give good and bad advice, concerning them. Plato starts his account of how truth and falsehood get into language by considering indicative sentences consisting of a noun and a predicate-phrase, and I shall do likewise. (I consider existential statements in Chapter 6 and imperatives in Chapter 7.)

Suppose I say 'The Moon is spherical', and you say 'The Moon is not spherical'. Then I say that the Moon *is* something you say it *is not*; I say it *has* something you say it *lacks*, namely spherical shape; I *assert* of it something you *deny* of it. In these cases I speak truly, I make a true statement, if the Moon is what I say it is, if it has the property I say it has, if what I assert of it is true of it. If that condition is fulfilled, *you* make a false statement. On the other hand if the Moon is not what I say it is, if it lacks the property I say it has, if what I assert of it is false, then my statement is false and yours is true.

This needs qualifying in the way indicated above (p. 60). What it is to speak truly when we predicate one thing of another may depend on the context. The context, however, does not determine either the meaning of the words used or the meaning of the predicative construction; it is only when these are understood that the context can be taken into account.

I here offer sufficient conditions for making a true or false statement. They are not necessary conditions: we can speak truly or falsely without saying that anything is or is not anything, notably in saying things exist. But if we say that something is something, and it indeed *is* that thing, then we speak truly.

In this basic theory of truth I do three things which are not as innocent as they may look. In the first place I explain making a true statement in terms of something's being true *of* something. Secondly I distinguish between predicates – not, that is, predicate-expressions like 'spherical' but things predicated like spherical shape – and the things *of which* they are predicated, like the Moon. And thirdly I count saying that something is something and saying it is not something as alternative modes of predication. Let me take these questionable moves in turn.

First, I explain absolute truth in terms of relative. Plato and Aristotle did this, and that strategy persisted at least till 1960 when W. V. O. Quine said: 'Predication joins a general term and a singular term to form a sentence *that is true or false according as the general term is true or false of the object, if any, to which the singular term, refers*' (p. 96, my emphasis). Today, however, as I said, philosophers deal with absolute truth directly. Corresponding to the absolute and relative use of 'true' and 'false' there are absolute and relative uses of the verbs 'assert' and 'deny'. I can deny of the asteroid Icarus that it is spherical or simply deny absolutely that Icarus is spherical. Plato and Aristotle, though they do not point out that verbs of saying are used in two ways, do speak of asserting and denying one thing of another; they use compound verbs, *kataphanai* and *apophanai*, the literal meaning of which is 'to say of' and 'to say from'. Philosophers today, in contrast, following Frege, consider only the absolute use of 'assert' and 'deny'. But though they do not speak of asserting or denying one thing of another, they use similar constructions in analysing sentences containing the words 'all', 'some' and 'no'. They would say that 'All planets are spherical' is equivalent to 'There is nothing that is a planet and that is not spherical.' Sentences containing 'nothing such that' or 'something such that' have to have clauses beginning with a pronoun, not a noun like 'Theaetetus', 'man' or 'quadruplicity'. An advantage of the traditional strategy is that the notion of asserting one thing *of* another is considerably clearer than the notion of asserting *tout court*.

Next, I distinguish between the things *of which* we say that they *are or are not something*, and the things we say that they *are* or *aren't*. There is nothing fishy about the things of which we say that they are spherical or seated or yellow; those are things we all know like planets and people and materials. But what about the things we say they are, the properties we say they have or lack, the things we predicate of them as true or false of them? Are they any more respectable than entities which are true or false absolutely? Or are they too things known only to philosophers, metaphysical entities distinct both from mental representations and from things investigated by scientists? Are they not *universals*, the bugbear of medieval philosophy?

I reply that they are not known only to philosophers. Spherical shape is known to geometers; the colour red is known to physicists; drinking, which Russell predicated of quadruplicity in 'Quadruplicity drinks procrastination', is known to physiologists. As I said earlier, to grasp the meaning of predicate-expressions is precisely to grasp the subject matter of academic disciplines like the natural sciences. The knowledge we seek in the sciences is knowledge of the things expressed by general words, and not simply of the individuals designated by proper names.

Are predicates, then, abstract objects like the seated position and sphericality? In English we have at least three different phrases for the linguistic act I call 'predicating': these are 'saying that one thing is or is not another', 'saying that something is had or lacked, or is or isn't done, by something', and 'saying that something is true or false of something'. Corresponding to these, we have three different sorts of linguistic item which may be said to express predicates: we have ordinary adjectives and verbs like 'spherical', 'drink' which signify what something is asserted or denied to be or do; 'that' clauses introduced by a pronoun like 'that it is spherical' which are used in reported speech to express what we say is true or false of something; and abstract nouns or phrases like 'sphericality', 'the seated position' which signify the things we say something has or lacks. No doubt other languages have different phrases for predicating and different grammatical forms for expressing what is predicated. But if the linguistic act of predicating is the same, the things predicated are the same, whatever grammatical form we use, and they are not chimerical or known only to philosophers. Or those that *are* known only to philosophers are things like mental and moral qualities in which philosophers have made an honest corner.

It is true that qualities, bodily postures and predicates generally are not separate in reality from the things of which we predicate them. They are separated from them only in language: we have separate words for them. In the sentence 'Mars is round' the word 'round' is separate from the word 'Mars'. But that does not make them spurious; there really is such a shape as spherical shape, such a posture as the sitting position and so forth. Predicates give rise to perplexity, and to what is called the 'problem of universals', only if we suppose they are just like subjects, just like concrete objects except that they are abstract, and ask about them the same sort of questions we ask about the Moon or water. We are led to do this by reflecting on utterances like 'There are things I am that you aren't' and thinking that to *be* something is to stand in some sort of relation to what you *are*. F. H. Bradley did just that in *Appearance and Reality* (1902, chapter 2). Since the question whether a linguistic item signifies a relation bears on the central thesis of this book and will recur in later chapters, let me linger on this point.

Plato (*Sophist* 255c12–13) and Aristotle (*Categories* 1b29–2a2) distinguished things that something can be said to be 'all by itself' or *tout court* from things that something can be said to 'in relation to something', *pros ti*. A cherry is red or round 'by itself', whereas it is similar *to* something else and larger, or other, *than* something else. So they recognized a class of things signified by predicate-expressions which a thing is 'to something', and the test for belonging to this class was grammatical: the expression signifying it needs to be supplemented by a referring expression. They did not count prepositions as predicate expressions but as connectives, and Aristotle speaks of them as non-signifying, *asêma* (*Poetics* 1456b38–1457a2), though he did not think them wholly meaningless. He takes prepositions like 'in' to combine with referring expressions like 'the Lyceum' to signify *where* something is, and that a phrase like 'the year before last', which contains a preposition of time, signifies *when* something happened.

The ancient notion was taken over by Western medieval philosophers. Ockham speaks of a class of things signified by words that 'so signify what they signify that they cannot be used to say something true unless there is added to them another word in a prepositional phrase [in Latin, 'in an oblique case']' (*Summa Logicae* 1.49). He too denies that prepositions signify things (*Summa Logicae* 1.4); he counts them as syncategorematic terms. The Greek phrase *pros ti*, however, which I translate 'in relation to something', was rendered in Latin by the noun *relatio*. The class of things which the Greeks labelled 'things said in relation to something' became the class of relations. Words like 'similar', 'equal', and 'larger', and also words like 'father', 'son', 'servant' and 'master' were said to signify relations, and relations were said to have foundations. The relation of father to son is founded on a causal act, begetting; similarity and equality are founded upon the properties similar things have 'all by themselves'. Philosophers, Ockham reports, disagree about whether relations exist in reality (that is, not just in thought and language), independently of their foundations, a question that could hardly have been formulated by anyone who could rely only on the Greek phrase. And the word 'relation' also enables us speak of different kinds of relation: causal, social, economic, and also spatial and temporal. Russell (1912, chapter 8) treated prepositions like 'in' as predicate terms signifying spatial relations, and spatial relations as properties not of single objects but of pairs or larger sets.

There is room for debate whether we do better to take prepositions of place and time as signifying predicates in this way, or as having meaning through contributing to constructions; and the same applies to other groups of words. Russell took 'similar', 'equal', and 'larger' to signify relations, but they are used in comparing things, something Plato considered an important type of intellectual act (*Protagoras* 357a–b; *Theaetetus* 186a–b; *Philebus* 55d–e). In the phrase 'larger than' the ending '-er' and the word 'than' have meaning in that using them is comparing. The same could be said about 'similar', 'equal' and 'double'. Plato counts 'same' and 'other' as relational terms, but he also groups sameness and otherness with existence. Instead of saying that 'same' and 'other' signify relations in which one thing can stand to another or to itself, we can recognize linguistic acts of identifying and differentiating, and say that 'same' and 'other' are syntactic words used in performing these acts. Identity is often taken as a metaphysical topic, and can be dealt with in the same way as the topics on which I concentrate in this book. C. J. F. Williams (1992) denies that identity is a relation and in *What is identity* (1989) he argues, in effect, that it is what is expressed by reflexive pronouns like 'himself'.

The word 'relation', unlike *pros ti,* suggests something that exists between two things, some kind, even, of connection. When we ask if there is a real relation between two things I think we are asking whether the foundation of the relation is not just something real but something that connects the related things. Causal action does connect a father with his children, or their coming into being, and entering into a contract connects a husband and wife or an employer and an employee. That makes the relations seem real; they are independent of language and thought, though not of the laws of biology or society. A stretch of time may be said to connect earlier and later events, and a stretch of space (I shall argue we do better to say 'a possible movement') connects objects that are at a distance from one another. That justifies saying that spatial and temporal relations are real. On the other hand nothing in the same way connects things that are similar or equal; they are connected only by us in speech and thought when we compare them. That is a reason for saying that 'similar' and 'equal' when used with referring expressions are syncategorematic terms. Besides being used with referring expressions they are used in such sentences as 'His head was like a coconut.' In this we do not refer to any particular coconut, but predicate of the head an unspecified property characteristic (or commonly thought characteristic) of coconuts. Here too 'like' contributes to a construction: not a construction for comparing things, but a construction for predicating unspecified properties.

'Is' is not completed by a referring expression in 'The Earth is spherical', nor is 'became' in 'Balbus became an architect', or 'has' in 'Caesar has ambition' or 'Anne has a cold'. There is no question, then, of their signifying relations. It is significant that languages which, like Polynesian languages, have no verbs of being or becoming, have no verbs of having either. Verbs of having can be used with a referring expression, as in 'Sebastian has a sister.' But in this case 'have' is used to quantify, as is *avoir* in *il y a*. We are saying that there is someone who stands to Sebastian as a sister, and the relationship is signified by 'sister', not 'has'. Our verbs of having do other jobs besides quantifying. We say 'I have to go', 'I have caught a salmon', and there are idioms like the good humoured 'Ah, you had me there', and the slightly lewd 'have a woman'. Polynesians say these things in other ways.

Having a property is not standing in a relation to that property. Nor is being an instance standing in a relation to what is instantiated. If I said 'There has never been a philosopher king' you might reply 'Marcus Aurelius was an instance of a philosopher king.' But this is simply an emphatic way of saying 'Marcus Aurelius *was* both a philosopher and a king.' 'Instance' is not a word like 'cousin' and does not signify a relationship. Nor is *doing* something standing in a relation to what you *do* – to walk is not to stand in a relation to walking.

To deny that 'is' or 'has' signifies an act or relationship is as much as to say that there is no such thing in reality as being or having. Philosophers have said not only that there is such a thing as being, but that it is the main subject of metaphysics. Martin Heidegger's magnum opus is entitled *Being and Time*, *Sein und Zeit*; Jean-Paul Sartre's is *Being and Nothingness*, *L'être et le néant*; and Jacques Maritain gives as the subtitle of his *Preface to Metaphysics*, *Seven Lectures on Being*. The verb 'to be', they think, even when used predicatively in a sentence like 'Mars is spherical', means something, and it is part of the metaphysician's job to investigate whatever it may be that it means. They derive the idea that this calls for study from Plato and Aristotle. Heidegger begins his book by quoting a passage in which a character in Plato's *Sophist* (244a) makes an imaginary appeal to Presocratic philosophers: 'Since we are at a loss, please make clear to us what you are trying to signify when you say "being". It is clear that you have known this all along, and we thought we did, but now we are at a loss.' Maritain says the object of metaphysics is *ens inquantum ens*, 'being as such', which is a translation of Aristotle's *to on hêi on* (*Metaphysics* Γ 1003a21). Plato and Aristotle did distinguish the predicative use of the verb 'to be', *einai*, from its 'absolute' use where it expresses existence, and they thought it their business to study both uses. That is not, however, to say that they thought that there is anything in reality which it signifies in either use.

Even if there is no such thing as being, there is an important difference between being something and not being it, and philosophers might be asked to explain that difference. Now you do not have to be a philosopher to know the difference between being spherical and not being spherical. Anyone who knows what spherical shape is knows that. Equally anyone who knows what flying is knows the difference between flying and not flying. But it is not part of knowing what a sphere is to have a general idea of the difference between being and not being, nor is it part of being an aeroplane pilot to have a general idea of the difference between doing something and not doing it. The rules for predicating, however, are general. To grasp them is to know what it is in general to say that something is or is not something or does or does not do something. If we grasp this, we must have a general idea of the difference between being something and not being it, between doing something and not doing it.

We use 'true' and 'false' with 'of' to distinguish two forms of predication. Things I predicate of you, whether they are things that you can *be* or *have* or *do*, are things I predicate as true or false of you. Plato did not use 'true' and 'false' in this way. To explain the difference between speaking truly and speaking falsely he made do with the verb 'to be', and talked of being '*concerning*', *peri*, something. He wrote 'Saying things which *are not* concerning you as *being* is speaking falsely' (*Sophist* 263b–d). This is awkward, and it is easier to say: 'Saying things that are *false* concerning you as *true* is speaking falsely.' To have a general idea of being true or false of something is to know what is expressed by the constructions of affirmative and negative predication. And that is not an achievement in philosophy but a first step in learning to speak.

But now I must address the third dubious move in my basic theory of truth. Are there really these two forms of predication?[4] Would it not be more economical to recognize just one, saying that something *is* something. Then we can treat saying 'Theaetetus is not seated' as asserting of Theaetetus that he *has* the negative property of not being seated. Aristotle (*De Interpretatione* 19b19–20a1) and P. F. Strawson (1974, p. 6) countenance negative predicates, but they are far more problematic than positive predicates. Artists as well as physiotherapists study the seated posture, but no one studies the non-seated posture. We might try to define the property of not being seated as that property which belongs to all those things, and only to those things, which are not seated. But no property known to non-philosophers is common and peculiar to the members of this vast class, and how is the class to be defined? If the things that are not seated are the things to which the property of not being seated belongs, then the definition of that negative property is circular. If they are the things to which the property of being seated *does not* belong, the things that *lack* that property and *are not* seated, then we must recognize saying that things lack properties as an alternative to saying they have them.

Frege argued that denial is not an alternative to assertion, that they are not two different forms of speech. His argument, however, which I shall consider in a moment, relates not to asserting and denying one thing of another, but to asserting and denying 'absolutely' or *sans phrase*. Hence it does not tell against the basic theory.

* * *

The basic theory tells us that I speak truly, or make a statement that is true, if I assert of something what is true of it or deny of it what is false of it. It permits 'true' to be used absolutely, but it does not imply that when used absolutely as in 'The statement he made is true' it signifies a property of what some philosophers call 'propositions' and Frege called 'thoughts'. It is like 'ridiculous' or 'novel'. As some of the things you say are ridiculous if anyone saying some of the things you say speaks ridiculously, so some of the things you say are true if anyone saying some of the things you say speaks truly. The basic theory does not stop anyone from saying: 'It is true that p if and only if p.' But that 'T sentence' tells us nothing about what it is to speak truly. The basic theory does tell us what it is to speak truly in constructing a simple indicative subject–predicate sentence. In Chapter 6 I shall argue that it can be extended to simple existential sentences like 'There are elephants here', and to sentences like 'All elephants eat grass' (though there are other ways of dealing with sentences that contain 'all'), and in Chapter 8 I extend it to sentences with verbs of becoming and sentences with verbs in past and future tenses. But the basic theory certainly does not cover the statements we make by performing certain grammatical operations on simple sentences: prefixing them with words like 'It is not the case that', 'it is possible that', 'Galileo said that' or linking them with conjunctions like 'if' and 'or'.

In the case of simple predicative sentences, what it is to speak truly is fixed, in a way, by nature. It is a matter of human convention what shape is signified by the word 'spherical', but not what it is for that shape to be had by something. Similarly the meaning of 'elephant' is fixed by convention, but what it is for elephants to be present is a matter to be ascertained by hunters or zoologists. When, however, we get beyond simple sentences, what it is to speak truly seems to be determined largely by convention or custom.

Suppose I say: 'If Theaetetus is seated, he is tired.' There is no such property as being tired if you are seated; science, at least, recognizes no conditional properties of that kind. Therefore it is not sufficient for my speaking truly that Theaetetus has this property, nor sufficient for my speaking falsely that he lacks it. I certainly speak falsely if he *is* seated but is *not* tired. Hence a formal logician might say it is sufficient for my speaking truly that one or the other of these conditions should not be fulfilled, that either he is not seated, or he is tired. But in an ordinary conversation you might think that if Theaetetus is not seated, the question of truth doesn't arise, and I might be thought to have spoken falsely if he is tired and seated, but not seated *because* he is tired. 'If he is seated, he is tired' would be understood as 'If he is seated, it's because he's tired.' In ordinary conversation the conjunction 'if' is often used to express an explanatory relationship, somewhat as 'and' is often used to express a temporal relationship. Saying 'He opened the window and entered the room' is different from saying 'He entered the room and opened the window.' In these cases, then, conditions for speaking truly or falsely are determined by the conventions governing the conjunctions.

I shall not go into the use of 'it is possible that' and 'it is necessary that' but only plead that we distinguish logical, physical and practical possibility and necessity. I think in considering what it is to speak truly when we use these words we do better to hold fast to these distinctions than to rely on formal logicians who treat all kinds of necessity and possibility in the same way, for example by speaking of possible worlds. But I must say something about 'it is not the case that'.

If Socrates says 'Theaetetus is flying' and Theodorus retorts 'Theaetetus is not flying' Theodorus denies of Theaetetus what Socrates asserts of him. If instead of 'Theaetetus is not flying' Theodorus says 'It is not the case that Theaetetus is flying' (or 'it is not true' or 'it is false'), he denies absolutely what Socrates asserts absolutely. Frege argued that denying absolutely is not a form of speech alternative to asserting absolutely. Rather, in denying absolutely what Socrates asserts, Theodorus asserts something other than what Socrates asserts: he asserts its negation. What is meant here by 'a negation'? I considered the suggestion that in 'Theaetetus is not flying' we assert of him the negative property of not flying, and said that if this is that property, whatever it may be, which belongs to everything to which the property of being seated does not belong, then it may be objected that there is no such property. A similar objection may be made, if anyone says that the negation of what is asserted in 'Theaetetus is seated' is that thing, whatever it may be, which is true absolutely if that Theaetetus is seated is false. There is nothing which is true if and only if it is not the case that Theaetetus is seated; as there are no negative properties, so there are no negative truths, though there are negative ways of speaking. Saying that something is not the case is speaking negatively, but it is too simple to say in speaking negatively we speak truly if we put forward a negative truth.

A person who says 'It is not the case that Theaetetus is flying' certainly speaks truly if it is false of Theaetetus that he is flying. But suppose Hamlet says 'My father's ghost is flying over the ramparts' and either there are no ghosts at all, or at least there is no ghost of his father. In that case we might say to him 'It is not the case that your father's ghost is flying over the ramparts', not because it is false of his father's ghost that he is flying over the ramparts but because there is no such ghost for this to be true or false of. Putting 'it is not the case' before a predicative sentence is speaking truly, not only if the predication is false, but if any of the referring expressions in it does not refer.

Frege is right, however, that saying something is not the case is not an alternative to absolute asserting. 'An assertion', he says, is 'the manifestation' of a 'judgement' (1967, p. 22) and 'Judging, we may say, is acknowledging the truth of something' (1952, p. 126 n.). What he calls 'asserting' is in fact simply stating. It contrasts not with denying absolutely but with counselling or commanding. Whenever we say anything true or false, even when we say 'It is false of Theaetetus that he is seated' or 'It is not the case that Theaetetus is seated' we express something as true absolutely; we profess to be speaking truly, just as (to anticipate Chapter 7) when we say 'It would be wrong to sit down' we profess to be advising rightly. But as Frege says,

> We do not have to use the word 'true' for this. And even when we do use it, the real assertive force lies, not in it, but in the form of the indicative sentence. ... We have no particular clause in the indicative sentence which corresponds to the assertion, that something is being asserted lies rather in the form of the indicative. (1967, p. 22)

It is not improper to say 'I am speaking truly' or 'I am telling a tissue of lies', but only if you are referring to some further speech, perhaps to what you have just said. But that we are now speaking truly, that we are now making a statement, is not part of what we say, but is expressed by the indicative form of construction.

We have here the source of 'T-sentences' like 'The sentence "Snow is white" is true if and only if snow is white,' of the project of 'disquotation' and of the idea that the 'truth predicate is redundant'. It is redundant because what it signifies, namely absolute truth, is what is expressed by the indicative syntax. On the other hand the notion of truth *sans phrase* is not vacuous, because what is expressed by the indicative mood is different, as we shall see, from what is expressed by non-indicative moods.

Unfortunately Frege failed to hold on to the insight that truth is expressed by grammar. He denied that using an indicative construction is sufficient for assertion, on the ground that actors on the stage and novelists construct indicative sentences but do not really assert. They express true or false things in words, they say things that are true or false, but they do not really put them forward *as* true; they only *appear* to be asserting. I argued that absolute truth belongs primarily not to things said but to acts of saying. If that is right, the distinction between saying something true or false and putting something forward as true is extremely elusive. What is it really to assert? Dummett (1973, pp. 3, 295–363) tried to help Frege out by appealing to social convention. Complying with grammatical rules is enough for saying something true or false, but we assert only if we use an indicative construction in circumstances in which, or in a situation in which, according to the customs of our society, we can be reproached if what we say is not true.[5]

There is no need for such an expedient. The distinction between saying something true or false and making an assertion is introduced to deal with exceptional cases, acting on the stage or giving an example in philosophy. It is always risky to base a general theory on exceptional cases, and we do not have to appeal to social conventions to deal with these rogue speakers. Austin (1962b, pp. 70–1) observed: 'A definite sense attaches to the assertion that something is real, a real such-and-such, only in the light of a specific way in which it might be, or might have been, not real.' Just as there is nothing additional an object has to be, in order to be real, but a duck or a door is real unless there is something that stops it from being real – being a decoy duck, say, or a trompe l'oeil door – so there is nothing additional that makes saying something true or false asserting. When confronted with exceptional cases, instead of bringing in social conventions we may recall the distinction between linguistic and practical purpose. Usually when we use an indicative construction we want our hearers to believe what we say, and our hearers think that that is our purpose. But when we say something obviously false our hearers doubt if that is our purpose and try to attribute a different purpose to us. If in a lecture I construct the sentence 'Snow is red' my hearers think my purpose is not to get them to believe this but to illustrate some point about predication or truth. A theatre audience thinks the actors are trying to represent characters caught up in some tragedy or comedy, and when an actor says 'The queen, my lord, is dead' they think he is asserting something which will be true only if it is true of the queen that she is dead, not in order that we may believe this of her, but in order to play the part of Seyton saying something in order that Macbeth may believe it. The actor does this by himself making the assertion he represents Seyton as making.

Let me sum up this account of truth in language. I take the fundamental notions to be those of being true or false of something. These are not notions of properties of anything: this relative sort of truth is neither an intrinsic nor a relational property. Absolute truth is expressed by the indicative form of speech. Using the indicative is saying you are speaking truly, and in general, grasping the meaning of indicative constructions is knowing what absolute truth is. But since indicative form can supervene on many different constructions – predicative, quantifying, hypothetical, and so forth – there is no one thing which it is to speak truly. What it is to speak truly varies with the construction used. In simple constructions it is determined by the nature of the things which the words used signify. In constructions with conjunctions and locutions like 'it is not the case that', it is determined partly by convention and custom, but the conditions for speaking truly are still conditions for objective truth because the basic theory holds for the simple sentences out of which the complex or compound sentences are constructed.

* * *

We use the word 'true' not only of statements but of beliefs or thoughts; can the basic theory be applied to thought? Plato felt able to apply it without modification. For he held that thinking is talking silently to oneself (*Sophist* 263e–264a; *Philebus* 39a). That cannot be right, since we sometimes say things that we don't believe, but we cannot believe things we don't believe. Nevertheless verbs of saying and thinking have the same grammar. We have 'absolute' beliefs, like the belief that Theaetetus is seated, and we can believe something *of* or *concerning* something, believe of Theaetetus, but not of Socrates, that he is seated. Moreover the constructions for reporting beliefs are the same as those for reporting statements. That being so, here is a simple theory of true and false belief. To believe true of something what is true of it, and to believe false of something what is false of it, is to believe truly. To believe false of something what is true of it, or true of something what is false of it, is to believe falsely. As there are two forms of speech, saying one thing to be true of a second and saying it to be false of it, so there are two forms of thought, thinking one thing true of a second, and thinking it false of it.

What of beliefs that something is not the case? In the way in which all stating or asserting is saying to be true, so all believing, including the belief that something is not the case, is believing to be true. All belief, we might say, aspires to truth as does all assertion. If I believe it not to be the case that

Theaetetus is flying to New York, I believe truly, perhaps, if either it is false of him that he is flying to New York, or he no longer exists, having died of wounds in 369 BC.

Philosophers often call belief a 'propositional attitude'. That invites us to conceive it on the model of taking up a bodily attitude towards a person or state of affairs. The question then arises whether believing something not to be the case is adopting a different attitude from that of simple belief. Frege is sometimes thought to have shown that it is not. There is only one attitude we can take up when we think something to be true, but there are different things towards which we can adopt it, and when we think it true that something is not the case we adopt that attitude towards something negative, a negative proposition or a 'thought' that is a negation. An assumption of this is that there are propositions, true or false *things*, for us to adopt attitudes towards.

I raised some doubts about propositions at the beginning of this chapter, and in Chapter 12 I offer an alternative to conceiving belief as a mental attitude. As saying something to be true is not just exhibiting a kind of representation that is already true or false, so thinking something to be true is not just confronting something that is already true or false. When we make a statement its truth or falsehood arises from the construction of our sentence, and this construction determines our statement's logical form. As a statement of negative form arises from a negative construction, the grammatical operation of negating, so, I hold, a belief that something is not the case arises from the way in which we think about the same things that enter into our thought when we believe that it is the case. Does Frege show that this is a mistake?

He asks us (1952, pp. 129–30) to consider the following piece of reasoning:[6]

1 If it is not the case that Franz is in Berlin, he is in Rome.
2 It is not the case that Franz is in Berlin.
3 So Franz is in Rome.

When, says Frege, I think that if it is not the case that Franz is in Berlin he is in Rome, I am not thinking it not the case that Franz is in Berlin, so my first thought is of the form:

If not-P then Q.

Since, however, in 2 I do think it not the case that Franz is in Berlin, if this is taking a negative view of the thought that he is in Berlin, the content of my thought will be that he is in Berlin, and I shall merely be adopting a negative attitude to it. So my second thought will be of the form:

P

And in that case the reasoning will be invalid.

This argument has been thought a clincher by some, and the first point is unimpeachable: in premise 1 my thought has the logical form *If not-P then Q*. But the second point, that if in 2 I am thinking negatively of Franz's being in Berlin, then the premise must have the form *P*, simply begs the question. The rival view is that one way of thinking to be true is thinking that one thing is located in another, and another is thinking it not to be the case that the one is located in the other; these are two ways of thinking of the same things. Frege does not *argue* that differences in the form of what we think cannot be explained by differences in the form of our thinking (differences, his opponent might say, corresponding to different grammatical operations); he assumes that this is impossible.

He feels able to do this, I suggest, for two reasons. In the first place, the only alternative he can imagine to his own view is that thinking something not to be the case is some kind of division or separation. His source for this is probably Aristotle. Aristotle does not have a theory of absolute denial; he concentrates on thinking one thing true or false of another; but he describes thinking one thing true of another as thinking of them as put together, and thinking one thing false of another as thinking of it as divided from the second. He says thinking truly is thinking to be together things that are together and thinking to be apart things that are apart (*Metaphysics* Θ 1051b1–5). Both thinking to be together and thinking to be apart, however, he correctly calls 'weavings together', *sumplokai*, of thoughts (*De Anima* 3 432a11).[7] Secondly Frege was chiefly interested in mathematical thought, and mathematics deals with things untouched by time or causation: things like numbers, numerical functions and geometrical figures. Dwelling among such entities he found it easy to add to them a further set of things (misleadingly called 'thoughts') which are true or false independently of our speaking or thinking. If there are such entities, they would be complete with logical forms before we accept them or put them forward, and not owe their logical forms to how we think or say them.

Had Frege's interests lain more in grammar than mathematics, he might have noticed that when we report a thought that something is not the case we usually do so by negating, not the verb in the object-clause, but the verb of thinking.

We say 'The police don't think Franz was in Berlin,' meaning, not that it is false that they think he was, but simply that they think that he wasn't. This suggests that thinking that something is not the case is rather thinking negatively about something positive than thinking positively about something negative. Similarly with some verbs of saying. In Greek when you want to say that someone absolutely denies something you negate the verb of saying *phanai*, not the verb in the object clause. *Ou phêmi* means 'I deny' or 'Say "no"'.

6

Existence and Quantification

Existence is a philosophical topic if anything is. McTaggart entitled his two-volume *magnum opus* 'The Nature of Existence'. It is also a topic which touches everyone, however unphilosophical. We find existence pleasant or burdensome, and it is sobering to think that we might never have existed.

In Chapter 3 I distinguished simple sentences like 'Mars is red' in which we predicate one thing of another from simple existential sentences like 'Mars has two moons' or 'There are planets beyond Saturn' in which we *quantify* things. The word 'quantify' means 'say how many or how much'. In this chapter I shall argue that existence is not something we predicate, not something a thing can have or do, but something expressed by our form of speech when we quantify or refer. I first consider quantifying things signified by common nouns like 'wasp' and 'wine'. 'Wasp' is a word for things we count – we say 'two wasps', 'many wasps' – and 'wine' is a word for something we measure – we say 'two litres of wine', 'much wine' – but counting and measuring are both ways of reckoning quantity. Having discussed quantifying such things and referring to them I indicate briefly how the account of truth I offered in Chapter 5 for predications can be applied to statements of existence. Finally I consider apparently predicative uses of words like 'wasp' and 'wine', and quantification of properties and events. Quantification also applies to change, but I defer considering how we quantify change to Chapter 9.

Sentences in which we express existence are grammatically of subject–predicate form. In 'The Man in the Iron Mask existed', 'existed' is the grammatical predicate. Locke said that 'exist' signifies something simple, distinct from anything we may believe to exist, knowledge of which comes to us 'by all the ways of sensation and reflection' (*Essay* 2.7.1), and would probably have said that in our sentence we attribute this thing to the Man in the Iron Mask, as in 'Snow is white' we attribute the colour white to snow (*Essay* 4.5.2; 4.9.1–3). Hume, in contrast, said 'the idea of existence is the very same with the idea of what we conceive to be existent' (*Treatise* 1.2.7, p. 66), and would have said that thinking that the Man in the Iron Mask is having your idea of that man brighten up with increased 'force and vivacity' (*Treatise* 1.3.7, p. 96). Likewise Kant: 'To be [*sein*] is clearly not a real predicate, that is, a concept of anything that can be joined to the concept of thing' (*Kritik der reinen Vernunft* A598/B626). These thinkers do not associate existence with quantification. Plato associates it with number and quantity (for instance at *Republic* 7 524d–e; *Theaetetus* 185c–d), and perhaps construed saying things exist as a form of speech like saying things are the same or different (*Sophist* 250–4; Ryle 1971a, p. 67), but to analyse existence in terms of quantification I must distinguish predication and quantification more sharply than he does.

When the verb 'to be' is used to express existence or non-existence, it is used with adjectives of quantity like 'some', 'no', 'much', 'little', 'many', 'few', 'one', 'two'. 'There is', we say, 'much cocoa but little wine; there are many guests but no glasses.' In saying such things we are counting or measuring more or less precisely. Saying that scorpions exist is saying that there is at least one of them – and if we say 'There is a scorpion here' we say there is indeed one of them. Instead of 'There are many mosquitoes' or 'There is little wine left' we may say 'Mosquitoes are many', 'The wine left is little'. It is not English to say 'Centaurs are none' or 'The wine left is none', but in 'There are no centaurs' we deny that there is any number of centaurs, and in 'No wine is left' we deny that wine is left in any amount.

Adjectives like 'few' and 'many' do not signify predicates or things true or false of anything. As I said in Chapter 2, if Tom's enemies are mean-spirited, each of his enemies is mean-spirited, but we cannot say, if his enemies are few, that each of them is few. To say 'That enemy is few' is to speak not falsely but ungrammatically. Whereas adjectives like 'honest' and 'green' signify properties that can be had or lacked, 'few' and 'many' do not. Nor, therefore, do verbs of being used absolutely. In what way, then, do they have meaning? They give a speech the form of a quantification. There is no such thing as existing, but there are such forms of speech as saying that things exist or do not exist. There are no such properties as being many or being few, but saying that things are many and saying that things are few are ways of quantifying.

Aristotle says that existing is different for different things: for a house, being constructed in a certain way, for breakfast, being at a certain time, and for animals, living (*Metaphysics* H 1042b25–31), and this might suggest that it is something predicated 'by analogy' (*Nicomachean Ethics* 1 1096b25–9). But in fact when we say 'a house was constructed' we are not predicating being constructed of a house – we do not mean that there was a house and someone came along and constructed it – and in 'Dinosaurs once lived in Yorkshire' 'lived' is used not to predicate anything of dinosaurs at a time in the past but to quantify them. Aristotle's point could be that quantifying houses is saying how many *were built*, whereas quantifying dinosaurs is saying how many *lived*.

No philosopher today thinks that words like 'few' and 'much' signify predicates of things like poets or butter; but it is sometimes said that they signify 'second order' predicates, predicates of things predicated of such things. 'Great poets are few' is taken as equivalent to 'The property of being a great poet is had by few,' or 'That he is a great poet is true of few men' or 'Greatness in composing poetry has few instances.' Frege argued that 'There are four moons to Jupiter' is equivalent to 'the concept of a moon of Jupiter has four things falling under it' (1953, pp. 68–9). On this view, there is only one basic form of indicative speech, predication, and existential statements like 'There are several chairs' differ from predicative statements like 'Theaetetus is seated' only in the nature of the predicates and subjects. In 'There are several chairs', *belonging* to several things is predicated of the *property* of being a chair.

I prefer to take quantification as a form of speech different from but coordinate with predication. On both views, words like 'few', 'many' and 'four' belong to a second-order vocabulary, but on the Fregean view they enable us to specify properties of properties while on mine they enable us to specify forms of speech, saying things are few or many or four in number. Mine does not require us to recognize as many forms of speech as there are numbers. There is saying how many, and saying how much and we can do these things either in general terms or precisely. 'Much' and 'many' are general terms and relative: many cats are more cats than is usual or desirable. 'Two' and 'twenty' are precise terms, with can be combined with words for units of measure like 'gallon' and 'acre', and there are rules for constructing number-expressions out of a few primary number-words.

I have several reasons for preferring this approach. The Fregean requires a multiplication, not of forms of speech, but of increasingly abstract objects. Second-order predicates are entities known only to philosophers. And number words like 'four', the rules for constructing indefinitely many number-expressions out of them, and even quantitative expressions like 'all' and 'some' are all normally included in the grammar of a language and not just in the vocabulary. These number-rules are 'recursive'. Hauser, Chomsky and Tecumseh Fitch (2002, pp. 1577–8) suggest that they are *similar* to grammatical rules, and that since 'rats and pigeons' can 'represent number' the ability to use them might have evolved before the ability to construct sentences and be the origin of the ability to speak. In fact, however, they seem to be already *part* of grammar, and there is no evidence that any rat's or chimpanzee's ability 'to represent number' involves a grasp of them.

The words 'all', 'no' and 'some' are quantitative in a different way from 'many' and 'three'. Modern logicians like to interpret sentences like 'All men are mortal' as negative existential statements. To say that all men are mortal, on this view, is to deny that there is anything which both is a human being and isn't mortal (or, perhaps, to deny that there is any *human being* of whom being mortal is not true[1]). Similarly with sentences like 'No pigs have wings': to say this is to deny that there is anything which both is a pig and has wings (or any *pig* which is so equipped). And they interpret sentences where the grammatical subject is formed with 'some' as positive existential statements. 'Some pigs are black' is taken as equivalent to 'There are pigs that are black.'

Earlier logicians favoured a different interpretation. They took 'All men are mortal' as a simple assertion about all men. To say that all men are mortal is to say it is true of all human beings that they are liable to death. To say than no pigs can fly is to say it is false of every pig that it can fly. In 'Some birds do not have wings' 'have' is existential rather than predicative, but the sentence may be taken as equivalent to 'It is true of some birds that there are no wings attached to them.'[2] On this earlier view, just as saying that the Moon *is* spherical and saying it *is not* are two alternative ways of predicating a shape, so saying that *all* moons are spherical and saying that *some* are not, are further forms of predication. Besides asserting and denying something of a particular individual we can assert or deny it of all or some individuals of a specified kind. 'All' and 'some' combine with the nouns to which they attached and, as Ockham says (see above, p. 38), make them refer to or stand for things in a certain way.

Both these ways of understanding 'all', 'no' and 'some' are defensible. The first works better, perhaps, in mathematics, when we are talking about numbers or geometrical figures – and modern logic was founded by Frege and Russell who had a special interest in mathematics. The second is more natural when we are talking about physical objects, and brings our use of 'all', 'no' and 'some' into line with our use of proper names, demonstratives and definite descriptions to refer to particular individuals.

* * *

By a 'definite description' I mean a phrase like 'the author of *Waverley*' or 'your aunts' as contrasted with one like 'an author', 'some aunts'. This is the second way in which we express existence: using such a word or phrase to refer to something is speaking of that thing as actually existent. That is why, if you say 'Sherlock Holmes was at Oxford,' someone may retort 'That's not true, because there is no such person as Sherlock Holmes.' Early logicians thought that when I say 'all men' or 'no men' I say that there are several human beings and assert or deny something of all of them.

I do not mean that in using a definite referring construction we predicate actual existence of anything or anyone; I mean that our speech has the form of a singular existential statement. That holds whether or not the referring expression is the grammatical subject of the sentence. In 'The thieves overlooked that picture' I speak of a particular picture as existent. 'That picture' is the grammatical direct object, not the subject, of my sentence, though the picture to which it refers and the thieves are all equally subjects of my statement or speech. The same holds when the referring expression is used in a question or order. If I ask 'Is that man asleep?' I say that there is a man in the direction I indicate, and ask (or ask you to say) whether he is asleep.

That existence is expressed by adjectives of quantity like 'some' and 'many', by demonstrative adjectives like 'this' and by the definite article are grammatical rules. They would not be formulated in this way in ordinary grammar books, because while grammarians have to tell us how to perform acts like referring to definite individuals, they do not have to analyse these acts. They assume that anyone doing grammar already knows what they are, and that is reasonable. To grasp the meaning of a word which signifies a property we must know the difference between saying that something has a property and saying that something lacks it. To grasp the meaning of 'elephant' we must know the difference between saying that there is an elephant (in your garden, for example) and saying that there isn't, but we soon learn to use this knowledge in referring to particular elephants.

Do we then use different notions of existence when we quantify, saying that there are planets beyond Saturn, and when we refer to individuals, saying that the next planet beyond Saturn has rings? We certainly use different constructions, but I do not think the constructions express different concepts of existence, since the things we quantify, as distinct from the things we predicate, are precisely things to which we can refer.

Truth comes into simple existential statements much as it does into simple predicative statements. If I say 'There are crocodiles', I speak truly if there are *some* animals of the sort signified by 'crocodile', and falsely if there are *none*. If I say 'There is no wine' I speak truly if there is none of the liquid signified by 'wine', and falsely if there is some. Plato might have said 'Referring to things that are a certain quantity *as* that quantity is speaking truly, and referring to them as a quantity *other* than that quantity is speaking falsely.'

Up to now I have been considering speech; what about thought? There are grammatical rules for saying that there are or are not things of various kinds and referring to particular individuals. To these forms of speech there correspond forms of thought. I can *think* that there are giant sloths or that there aren't, that all tarantulas are venomous or that *not* all are, that *a* tarantula bit me or that *your pet tarantula* did. The conditions for thinking truly are the same as those for speaking truly. Knowing what it is for there to be no giant sloths is part of knowing what a giant sloth is, and knowing what it is for there not to be any wine is part of knowing what wine is.

Using relative terms like 'many', 'few', 'much' and 'little', and having the thoughts they express, depends on the ability to count, measure and make comparisons of number and amount. This is not part of knowing what a quantifiable thing is, though for human beings it is an elementary extension of that knowledge. We are inclined to attribute concepts of various sorts of thing to animals without also thinking they can count or measure. Similarly while it is part of knowing, say, what a lion is, to know the difference between the presence and the absence of a lion, this knowledge does not involve having a general idea of presence or existence. But we have a general idea of existence if we know the constructions for quantifying and for referring to things as existent.

*　*　*

Common nouns like 'elephant' and 'wine' are words for things we quantify; but grammar permits us to use them as predicate-terms, complementing verbs like 'is', and also allows us to quantify things expressed by abstract nouns like properties and events. What are we to make of these usages?

We count both natural organisms like crocodiles and products of human skill like clocks. Suppose I say 'That's a crocodile.' Philosophers usually take this predicative use as primary, and Rundle (1979, Chapter 4) suggests that the existential 'are' in 'There are crocodiles' is like 'are' in 'Those things are crocodiles.' What do I predicate in 'That's a crocodile'? Presumably a set of specifiable intrinsic properties: either properties which we believe necessary and sufficient for being a crocodile or properties which really are necessary and sufficient.

Now although crocodiles have a distinctive shape and size, we think it most important that they are living things with abilities to perceive, pursue and avoid. No doubt they could not do these things without intrinsic physical properties, but using 'crocodile' as a complement is hardly just predicating those properties. As to the properties which really are essential to being a crocodile, these cannot be known before scientists have studied crocodiles, though a word for crocodiles will already be in use. Moreover Hilary Putnam argued (with the aid of his 1973 'Twin Earth' thought-experiment) that no definition in terms of specifiable properties can determine what a word like 'water' applies to; that is fixed by the real nature of the stuff to which the first users of the word applied it (or, if they introduced it to translate a word used by speakers of another tongue, the stuff to which that translated word was first applied). A similar argument holds for words like 'crocodile'. No set of intrinsic specifiable properties is necessary or sufficient for being a thing to which the word applies; it applies to animals of the same species as the animal to which it was first applied.

Clocks and tables are not products of nature, but there is a similar difficulty in supposing that words like 'clock' and 'table' signify properties. It is hard to specify the properties an object must have to be a table or a clock. Such artefacts come in various shapes and sizes, and what is common to them is rather a range of uses than a range of intrinsic properties. Tables are things on which we write and off which we eat; clocks tell the time.

One objection to taking the predicative use of words like 'crocodile' and 'clock' as primary is the difficulty of specifying what is predicated. There is a second. Predicating one thing of another presupposes identifying the subject of which we predicate it. When I say 'That's an elephant' you may ask me 'That what?' I cannot just answer 'That entity' or 'That thing'. I might say 'That grey shape in the trees' or 'The thing that's making that noise.' But the referring expressions 'that grey shape' and 'the maker of that noise' are not typical. The subject of our predication is being indicated as the source of a particular auditory experience or visual appearance, but sounds and appearances are usually identified by the objects that give them off rather than the other way round. We normally indentify what we are talking about as a particular object of some kind. 'That marmoset', we say, or 'that little animal'; 'that theodolite', or 'that peculiar instrument'. Elephants and tractors may be identified by sight or hearing, but it is they, not sounds or appearances, that are the primary things we identify.

Things we measure, like things we count, are some of them natural like water and some artificial like bronze. There are similar objections to taking words for them as signifying predicates. Such words, like words for countable things, are used to identify subjects. We say 'This air is tainted' 'That clay is not suitable for china.' There is also a further difficulty: when we use them with 'is' and say 'That table is wood' or 'The liquid in that bottle is wine,' we are saying not what the subject *is* but what it contains or is composed of. The table is composed of wood; the bottle contains wine. Ancient Greek called for an adjective here: 'That table is wooden [*xulinos*]' (Aristotle *Metaphysics* Z 1033a18).

In Chapter 3 I said that words for things we quantify have reference, not sense; I might summarize the preceding argument by saying that they signify not properties but things that are popularly believed, or have been discovered, to have distinctive properties.

Yet sentences like 'That's an elephant' are grammatically correct. If they are not predicative, how should we understand them? As equivalent, I suggest, to sentences like 'There's an elephant there, in that direction.' When a small child is learning to speak, it often just points and says 'Elephant' or 'Tractor', without using a verb of being. If we have a choice between taking it to say that some identified object is an elephant or tractor, and saying that there is an elephant or tractor in the direction in which it is pointing, the second interpretation is the easier. The objects and materials which we notice and of which we form concepts are those of practical significance to us. A lion is something the presence of which is a reason to timid city-dwellers for evasive action. The presence of wine in a glass is to self-indulgent adults a reason for raising it to their lips. To little children mastering their mother-tongue, the presence of an animal for which they have learnt a word is a reason for uttering the word. Having a good time, avoiding trouble and indeed staying alive depend upon recognizing the presence in our vicinity of various sorts of object and material. I might say 'That monkey is a marmoset' meaning that the species to which it belongs is the species marmoset, but in general using 'to be' with a word for a sort of object or material as complement is rather expressing existence than predicating. Even if someone says 'I thought "That's an adder"', or 'I said to myself "That's petrol"', we can take the speaker to be reporting an existential thought.

It is different if someone says 'Arthur thought' (or 'saw', or 'knew') 'that the snake was an adder' or 'Arthur thought that the liquid was petrol'. A statement like this can be true even if the person referred to does not say to himself anything like 'There's an adder there' or 'There's petrol in that tin'. We learn to recognize objects and materials under various conditions and by various perceptible signs, sounds, colours, shapes, movements, odours. And the presence of an adder or of petrol is a reason for behaving in a certain way – if only for pausing, or refraining from striking a match. If Arthur perceives an indication of some kind, the odour of petrol or the diamond pattern indicative of an adder, and behaves accordingly, it may be true to say 'He thought the snake was an adder' or 'He could tell the stuff was petrol'. These remarks are abridged explanations of his behaviour.

'Elephant', 'chair' and 'hand' belong to a different class of words from 'red' and 'spherical'. The difference is not simply that they signify things we quantify. They answer a different question, 'What is it?' as distinct from 'What colour is it?' or 'What is it like?' and seem to signify things of a radically different kind. But whereas 'red' and 'green' signify colours and 'honest' and 'arrogant' signify traits of character, it is not so clear what sort of thing 'elephant' and 'chair' signify. Aristotle, who noticed that they answer the 'what is it?' question, seems to have thought that they signify precisely things that exist, the things of which the world primarily or basically consists. I have just argued that their primary use is in existential statements. This is a grammatical point, but it can be presented so as to sound metaphysical. We can say 'Elephants and chairs exist of themselves. Colours and traits of character exist too, but existing for them is being qualities of things like elephants and chairs, being had by such things, whereas existence for elephants and chairs is not being had by anything further.'

Countable objects take precedence in language not only over predicates such as qualities and modes of action, but also over materials that are measurable like flesh and clay. For materials can be quantified, and said to exist, only in so far as they form countable objects like elephants and teapots. At first that sounds false. Can't you have clay which has not yet been worked up into anything? Cannot air just blow about loose without being contained in anything? I reply that any actual quantity of material must form something, even if what it forms is not very interesting. Clay before it is dug out forms a layer in the ground; the air we breathe in the country is part of the earth's atmosphere. If we dislike the idea that the existence of a quantity of material depends on the existence of an object it constitutes, we can say it depends on the existence of the particles of which it is composed, since we conceive these as countable; we then, of course, conceive a pound of clay, for example, not as a quantity of material but as an aggregate of countable objects.

So much on using these common nouns as complements of 'to be'. My second residual topic was our quantifying things signified by abstract nouns, things other than objects and materials. We certainly say 'There are many shades of red,' 'There are several forms of animal locomotion,' 'There are four prime numbers between 10 and 20.' This is not multiplying realities beyond necessity.

I said that properties are not separate in reality from things that have them. For a shade of red to exist is for it to be a possible colour for something or the actual colour of something; there is such a mode of locomotion as flying if it is a possible way of moving for something or the actual way of moving of something – flying exists if things are flying or can fly. We may say that a number exists if there are or could be that number of things of some kind. It may not be possible for there to be a transfinite number of actual stars or atoms, but with some ingenuity we can stretch the notion of number to cover the more exotic objects of arithmetic like negative numbers and numbers of possible series.

As we can quantify objects and refer to particular objects, so we can quantify events and refer to particular events. I can say 'There were several shootings' or 'I witnessed *the* shooting'. Events that go on for a time, such as battles and Atlantic crossings, can, in fact, be quantified in two ways; they can be counted and also, as I shall argue in Chapter 9, measured. Events are said rather to occur or to take place than to exist. In 'I witnessed the shooting' I refer, strictly speaking, to a particular occurrence of the event signified by 'shooting'. If occurrence is really analogous to existence, it should follow that in 'Curtis shot the elephant' I refer to a particular existence of the animal signified by 'elephant'. In English, however, instead of 'existence' here we use 'instance' or, sometimes, 'specimen' or 'example'. The elephant shot by Curtis was a particular specimen of the species.

Discussing our predicative use of common nouns and our quantifying of properties and events has taken me some way from our central notion of existence, the notion that applies to ourselves and our possessions. To revert to that, we speak of things as existent in two ways. First, we quantify. For human beings or books to exist is simply for them to be one or more in number; for wine or water to exist is for it to be more or less abundant. There are grammatical rules for quantifying, and they tell us how to express existence in one way. Secondly we refer to things, we say things about them. The rules for referring to things are rules for speaking of them as actually there.

In this chapter I have concentrated on statements, but, as will appear in Chapter 7, existence is also expressed in imperative sentences. 'Bring out *more* wine', we cry, 'and open *that* window!' And we speak of things as actually existing not just in simple sentences but when we speak of them as interacting causally or as beneficiaries of any kind of action: as Plato observes (*Sophist* 247 d–e): 'Anything that has any power, however small, to act upon anything else or be acted upon by anything else, really exists.'

7

Goodness, Counsels and Commands

We say that some things are good and that some are bad; that some actions are right and that some are wrong. Simple people take these utterances in their stride, but our sophisticated societies sniff at them suspiciously. We do not argue only about *what* is right or wrong. That has always been controversial. We also ask *what it is* for something to be good or bad, right or wrong. Utterances to the effect that something is good or bad, right or wrong, are labelled 'ethical' or 'moral'. Perhaps the task philosophers are most often called upon today to perform is to settle the character of these utterances. Are they just expressions of feeling? Or can they be true or false in the same way as statements of historical or scientific fact? In classical antiquity and in the medieval West philosophers were not asked these questions, but in spite of that they handled the notions of goodness and its kin with kid gloves. Since the seventeenth century philosophers have supposed that either they are notions of relational properties, or notions of intrinsic properties, or the words that purport to signify them must be meaningless. I shall run through some accounts this supposition has inspired before defending my own position, which is that 'good' and 'bad' relate to counsels and commands as 'true' and 'false' relate to statements, that the basic notion of goodness is that of an objective, and that thinking something good is desiring it.

* * *

> Things [says Locke] are good or evil only in relation to pleasure and pain. That we call good which is apt to cause or increase pleasure, or diminish pain in us ... and on the contrary we name that evil which is apt to produce or increase any pain, or diminish any pleasure in us. (*Essay* 2.20.2)

Locke's theory of goodness and badness was followed, on the whole, by Shaftesbury (1699) and the Scottish philosophers Hutcheson (1725), Adam

Smith (1759) and Hume. 'An action or sentiment or character', Hume says, 'is virtuous or vicious; why? because its view causes a pleasure or uneasiness of a particular kind ... To have the sense of virtue is nothing but to *feel* a sensation of a particular kind from the contemplation of a character' (*Treatise* 3.1.2, p. 471). That is, for an action or a feeling or a trait of character to be good or bad is for it to cause a particular kind of pleasure or 'uneasiness' in people when they think of it; Hume refines on Locke's view only by insisting that the people should be good judges and contemplate the action, feeling or trait in a detached way (*Essays*, 1.23). His version of this theory is accepted by philosophers today like Mary Warnock (1998).

Locke has a second theory, a development of the first. 'Morally good and evil', he continues, 'is only the conformity or disagreement of our voluntary actions to some law whereby good or evil is drawn on us from the will and power of the law-maker', and he distinguishes three such laws, the law of God, set out, supposedly, in the Old Testament, state law, enacted by human legislators, and 'the law of opinion or reputation', the rules accepted by people generally, breaches of which are punished by disrepute (*Essay*, 2.28 5–10). By 'moral' goodness and evil here Locke means what are usually meant by 'rightness' and 'wrongness'; for an act to be right, he is saying, is for it to be ordained by some kind of law, and to be wrong is to be against some kind of law.

This thinking is not peculiar to Locke but seventeenth-century orthodoxy, shared to a greater or less extent by Grotius, Hobbes, Puffendorf, Suarez and Vazquez. In the eighteenth century it is taken over by Kant: actions are right or good, he says, in so far as they conform to a special kind of law, a principle somehow dictated by pure reason.

A completely different theory was put forward by G. E. Moore in *Principia Ethica* (1903). '"Good"', he says, 'if we mean by it that quality which we assert to belong to a thing when we say that the thing is good, is incapable of any definition' because '"good" is a simple notion just as "yellow" is a simple notion.' Like 'yellow', 'good' is a predicate-expression signifying a quality which is 'simple and has no parts' (pp. 7–9), though the quality it signifies, unlike the colour yellow, is not 'natural'. What stops it from being natural is the impossibility of imagining it 'existing *by itself* in time, and not merely as the property of a natural object' (p. 41).

If, as Hume thought, the words 'good' and 'bad' signify the powers to cause certain feelings of pleasure or 'unease', approbation or distaste, then using them, saying 'Truthfulness is good', or 'Incest is bad', is making a kind of causal statement which is true or false, like 'Petrol is explosive'. Twentieth-century philosophers denied this. They maintained that using them is not saying anything true or false, but merely expressing feelings of pleasure or distaste. They are like the exclamations 'Hurrah!' and 'Boo!' In the words of A. J. Ayer:

> If I say to someone, 'You acted wrongly in stealing the money,' I am not stating anything more than if I had simply said 'You stole that money.' In adding that this action is wrong I am not making any further statement about it. I am simply evincing my moral disapproval of it. It is as if I had said, 'You stole that money,' in a peculiar tone of horror, or written it with the addition of some special exclamation marks. (1936, p. 107)

A similar theory was developed by C. L. Stevenson (1944).

The divergences between these theories should make us suspicious of the assumption from which they spring: that either words like 'good' and 'right' mean nothing at all, or they have meaning in the same way as words like 'yellow' and 'intoxicating'. R. M. Hare put forward a theory which at the time was thought similar to Ayer's. Like Ayer he denied that saying something is good or bad is making a factual statement which is true of false. Whereas Ayer, however, said it was expressing or 'evincing' a feeling, Hare said it was counselling or commanding. Hare's basic idea, I think, was correct, but since he did not satisfactorily distinguish counselling and commanding, which are acts *of* speaking, from things we do *in* speaking like evincing or betraying feelings, I shall develop it in my own way with only minimal reference to him.

English-speaking philosophers usually assume that 'good', 'bad', 'right' and 'wrong' are primarily used by themselves in predicative sentences like 'This wine is good' and 'That action was right.' Those sentences have the same surface grammar as 'This wine is yellow,' 'That action was hesitant,' and that naturally suggests that the words signify qualities which an object or an action or a state of affairs can have or lack. Wittgenstein does not mention this as a case where a grammatical similarity has led to a metaphysical misapprehension, but it is a fine example of one. As J. L. Mackie complained (1977, p. 38), the qualities they signify would have to be very strange. In point of fact, the meaning of these adjectives is similar to that of 'true' and 'false', and to grasp it we should look first at their use in constructions like those in which 'true' and 'false' are used, not by themselves, but with 'of'.

* * *

As we say that one thing is true or false *of* another, so we can say that one thing is good or bad *for* another. We say 'It is true of Theaetetus that he is seated' or

'It is false of him that he is seated', and we can also say 'It is good for Theaetetus to be seated' or 'It is bad for Theaetetus to be seated.' In the one case we say that the seated posture is had or lacked by Theaetetus; in the other, that it is a good or bad one for him. And just as the posture is sometimes had and sometimes lacked, so it is sometimes good and sometimes bad.

'True' and 'false' are used not only with 'of' but also 'absolutely' or by themselves. We can say 'It is true *tout court* that Theaetetus is seated.' There is also a quasi-absolute use of 'good' and 'bad': we can say 'It is good that Theaetetus is' (or 'should be' – I shall come to this use of 'should' presently) seated. There is, however, a difference. Even when we say 'It is good' (or 'a good thing') 'that Theaetetus is seated', we still conceive goodness as relative.

We must distinguish two ways in which one thing may be said to be good for another. When the advertisements said 'Bovril is good for you' they meant that it is *beneficial* to people. When I say 'Green is a good colour for that wall' I do not mean it is beneficial to the wall. Only living things can be benefited. Rather I mean that it is a good thing that the wall is green, or perhaps that it would be a good thing if it were. What is a good thing in this way must be a good thing for some beneficiary. But when it is a good thing that some object should have a certain property, the beneficiary need not be that object. Whereas truth and falsehood, then, are relative only in one way, goodness and badness are relative in two. Properties are good or bad relatively to objects that can have them. What is a good colour, shape or size for one object may be a bad one for another. A good size for a bed-sheet might be a bad size for a pocket-handkerchief. But a property can be good or bad for an object only relatively to a beneficiary. And a property which, from the point of view of one beneficiary, is a good one for an object, may, from another's point of view, be a bad one for the same object. Consider the auditorium of a theatre. If you have a seat in front of me, the sitting position is a good one for your body so far as I am concerned, in that if you are seated I have an unimpeded view of the stage. But it might be a bad one for your body so far as you are concerned if you have cramp. A good size for a bed-sheet for a human being would be a good size for a pocket-handkerchief for a giant.

Besides being had or lacked, properties can be acquired and lost. An object can not only *be* or *not be* red; it can *become* or *cease to be* red, and it can not only stand or not stand in a definite relationship to another object but come to stand or cease to stand in that relationship. To say that a property is a good one for an object to have – that white, say, is a good colour for the woodwork to have – is to say that it is a good one for the object to acquire and a bad one for it to lose, that the object's acquiring it, if it doesn't already have it, would be a good thing, and its losing it, if it does already have it, would be a bad thing. A property which is a bad one for an object to have is the contrary: it's a bad thing for the object to acquire it and a good thing for the object to lose it.

The words 'right' and 'wrong' can be used of properties – we say 'the right size', 'the wrong colour' – but they are appropriate also to actions. We say that doing something or not doing something is right or wrong. If it would be a good thing for your woodwork to acquire the colour white, then it would be right to do what will cause it to become white, for instance to paint it white; and it would be wrong to do something that would prevent it from becoming white, for instance to stop you from painting it white. And if it would be wrong to stop you, it would be right to refrain from stopping you. Similarly if it would be a bad thing for the woodwork to cease to be white, it would be wrong to bring that change about, say by scribbling on the paintwork or chipping it, right to refrain from such action, and right to prevent the bad change coming about, say by stopping a child who is idly kicking it. (Right, that is, at first sight or *pro tanto*; for in general it is wrong, unfriendly, to stop people from doing what they want to do.)

I offered a simple theory of truth for predicative statements: in saying that an object has a property you speak truly if the property is had by the object, if what you assert of it is true of it. In saying 'Theaetetus is *not* seated' you speak truly if what you deny of Theaetetus is false of him. Can a similar theory be found to cover saying that something is good or bad, right or wrong?

Saying that white is a good colour for the woodwork is a way of predicating it of the woodwork. In 'Let the woodwork be white' or 'If only the woodwork were white' 'white' is the grammatical predicate. But it is not speaking truly or falsely. Rather it is recommending white as a colour for the woodwork. Recommendations cannot be true or false but they can be right or wrong. You recommend white rightly, and therefore speak rightly, if white *is a good* colour for the woodwork, and wrongly if it *is a bad*.[1] It is a good colour, as we have just seen, if either it would be a good thing for the woodwork to acquire it, or it would be a bad thing for the woodwork to lose it. What if you say that purple would be a bad colour for the woodwork? We have no single English word for your form of speech comparable to 'recommend', but since recommending a colour is advising in favour of it we can say that you advise *against* the colour; your advice is right if it is a bad colour for the woodwork, if it would be a bad thing for the woodwork to acquire it or a good thing for it to lose it.

If you say that some action would be right, 'It would be right', for instance, 'to paint the woodwork white', you are counselling or commanding the action;

and while counsels and commands cannot be true or false they can (a point to which Hare gave insufficient attention) be right or wrong. You counsel rightly if it would be right to paint the woodwork white, and the action would be right if the change to white would be good for the woodwork. Your counsel is wrong if the change would be bad. Saying 'It would be wrong to paint the woodwork purple' is forbidding the action or counselling against it, and you speak rightly if the change the action would produce would be bad, and wrongly if it would be good.

So far goodness and badness are analogous to truth and falsehood. It seems, however, that there is a difference. It is either true or false of your paintwork that it is white, and it cannot be neither true nor false; a property is either had or lacked, and there is no third possibility. Couldn't the colour white, however, be neither good nor bad for your woodwork? Mightn't it be neither right nor wrong, say, to make a trip to Margate? It has been argued, indeed, that no action is morally indifferent; so, recently, John Haldane (2011). But it seems implausible to hold that if advising in favour of Margate is wrong, advising against it is right and vice versa.

It is disputable whether a property must be either had or lacked. Colours shade into one another, and while one emulsion may be definitely white and another definitely 'magnolia' someone might say that an intervening shade neither is white nor isn't. And that apart, absolute denial can be used when something is predicated of something non-existent. If there is no such person as Mrs Harris, then saying that she admires Mrs Gamp is asserting wrongly, and so is saying that she doesn't. If we recognize a form of imperative speech analogous to absolute denial, we can say that advising in favour of a colour or journey can be counselling wrongly, and so can counselling against it.

Besides saying that the sitting position would be good for Theaetetus, or that it would be right for him to adopt it, we can say that it was yesterday good for him and that he was right to adopt it. We are not here counselling but rather praising. Praising and censuring are not the same as ordering and forbidding, and nor is expressing a wish that something should have happened in the past, or shouldn't in the future. These forms of speech, however, can be correct or incorrect in the same way as counsels and commands. We censure Theaetetus rightly for not having risen when Xanthippe came along, if the standing position was then a good one for him to assume. They are grammatically closer to counsels and commands than to statements, even if they have different constructions. Greek, for instance, has an optative mood for wishes, different from the imperative; in English we have forms like 'O, to be in Paris!' and 'If only the rain would stop!' They are more expressive of goodness and badness than of truth and falsehood.

I have been speaking of counsels and commands corresponding to indicative predicative statements; but there are also imperatives and optatives corresponding to indicative quantifications. 'Let there be lights in the firmament,' the Creator is reported to have said; 'Would that there were no mosquitoes' rises sometimes to the lips of his creatures. Nothing is so bad that its presence is always bad, but if the presence of mosquitoes in your area is bad, action to reduce their numbers like spraying the pools where they breed would be right, if more light in the room would be good, action to prevent it like drawing the curtains or disconnecting the electricity would be wrong. Counselling rightly in connection with numbers of objects and quantities of materials presents no special problems.

* * *

It may be thought, however, that there is one major problem I have not addressed. A property is a good or bad one for something to have only if the thing's acquiring or losing it benefits or would benefit some beneficiary. What are we saying when we say something would be beneficial? The core notion of goodness, goodness for someone that can be benefited or harmed, has yet to be analysed.

Aristotle says: 'Let good be defined as that which is an object of choice for its own sake, and that for which we choose something else, and that at which all things aim, or all sentient or intelligent things' (*Rhetoric* 1 1362a21–4). This quotation will perhaps show what I mean when I say that, in comparison with modern philosophers, ancient philosophers handled the notion of goodness with kid gloves. Aristotle seems to take the basic notion of goodness to be that of an objective, of a thing, as he puts it 'for the sake of which', *hou heneka* (a phrase, he notes (*De Anima* 2 415b20–1) that may be used either for a benefit or for a beneficiary: 'I planted the tree …' you can say, 'for the sake of shade', or 'for the sake of my children'). Listing the things we offer as explanations he says: 'And there are the things which stand to the rest as their end and good; for what the other things are *for* is by way of being (*ethelei einai*) best and their end. It may be taken as making no difference here whether we say "good" or "apparent good"' (*Physics* 2 195a23–6). Similarly medieval philosophers. Aquinas says it is part of what goodness is, that it is an object of appetition and a final cause (*Summa Theologiae* 1a, question 5, articles 1 and 4).

That the basic notion of goodness is that of an objective seems to me a sensible line to take, whether or not these thinkers really took it. Someone might object that it rules out saying that anything is good or bad in itself. For an objective must be an objective *to* someone; nothing is an objective in itself. So if to be good is to be an objective, nothing can be good absolutely; things can be good only to this or that person. Aristotle did not overlook this possible objection, and I paraphrase his answer:

> If what I say doesn't please you, we may distinguish between what is good without qualification and in truth from what is good to a particular person. We say that what gives pleasure to someone in good bodily health and what preserves and increases that sort of person's health is naturally or truly healthy and pleasant; and other things are healthy or pleasant only to people who have some kind of physical disability. In the same way we can say that what is truly and naturally good is what is aimed at by people who are in a good condition psychologically, whose intellectual and emotional functioning is good, who have had experience of critical situations and so forth. (*Nicomachean Ethics* 3 1113a15–b2)

People may be unable to accept this reply because we seem to evaluate objectives. We ask not only whether people do aim at this or that, but whether they *should*; and when an objective is proposed to us we can ask 'Why should I aim at that? What's good about it?' To defend the thesis that to be good is to be an objective we must recognize that human beings have objectives of at least three kinds.

First, we are sentient organisms and we experience pleasant and painful bodily sensations. Anything that preserves our health and keeps our organs functioning is good for us, and also anything which causes or prolongs pleasure is an objective to us, as individual organisms. So far the Scottish philosophers were right. We are also social beings, living in societies with regard to the laws and customs of those societies. Anything which is required by our laws and customs is an objective to us as social beings and anything forbidden by our laws or customs is an object of aversion. To that extent the emphasis placed on law by Locke and Kant was not misplaced. And we have concern for other people and also for other living organisms, whether or not they belong to the same society as ourselves; we care for them independently of any benefit to ourselves as individuals or to our society. Anything, then, which is an objective to others, either as individuals or as members of some society, is an objective to us in so far as we have this disinterested concern for them, and anything that is bad for them is, as such, an object of aversion to us. Every sane adult has these three types of objective I have specified; they correspond partly, but not completely, to the 'parts' Plato distinguishes in the human psyche (*Republic* 4 435–42); and to be a good person psychologically in the sense required is to have them well balanced and working in harmony.

If a sceptic asks 'What is good about health?' or 'Why should we conform to custom or have concern for others?' we may reply that any such question presupposes some standard of practical rationality. To ask it is to assume that there are or can be reasons for acting. What I have just said is that reasons may be of three kinds: it is reasonable to aim at health and pleasure, to conform to the customs of your society, and to make the aims of others your own. These are principles of practical reasoning in the way that *modus ponens* is a principle of theoretical reasoning. *Modus ponens* explains why the premises 'If these lines are equal to the same thing they are equal to each other,' and 'These lines are equal to the same thing,' make rational the conclusion: 'These lines are equal to each other.' But as Lewis Carroll's Tortoise showed Achilles, it is not itself a premise, and does not require justification (Carroll 1939, p. 1105). Similarly 'Health is good' explains why 'Outdoor exercise is necessary for health if you work in an office,' and 'You work in an office,' make reasonable the advice: 'You should take some outdoor exercise.' Health is much the same for every human being, whereas different societies have different customs. That is how custom differs from nature. But 'It is good to conform to the customs of your society' explains why the premises 'In Thebes (there being no welfare provision by the state) it is obligatory for children to help parents in need,' and 'Oedipus (being blind) needs someone to lead him about, and I am his daughter,' make it reasonable for Antigone to think 'I should lead him about.' This is a reasonable conclusion for her not just as a social being, a being to whom life in some society or other is an objective, but as a Theban.

To take in the notion of badness or evil we need to recognize that we have negative as well as positive objectives. I may act or refrain from acting either in order that something *should* come about, or in order that something *should not* come about. In the first case I have a positive objective, something's coming about or occurring, in the second a negative, something's not coming about or occurring. To be good is to be a positive objective, and to be bad is to be a negative objective. A change that is good is a change *in order to cause which* we act, and *lest we should prevent which* we stay inactive, and a property that is good for a thing is one a change *to* which is good and a change *from* which is bad.

Objectives come into speech in two ways. I can explain an action in terms of purpose; I can say 'The hunter stifled his sneeze lest he should startle the stag'; here I give the stag's becoming aware of him as the (negative) objective of the hunter's stifling. But I can also simply express something *as* a positive or negative purpose. I can whisper 'Don't startle the stag' or 'It would be bad to sneeze aloud.' Simply expressing something as a positive objective is saying it would good or right; expressing it as a negative objective is saying it would be bad or wrong. In these cases, of course, it is expressed as an objective to the person to whom we are speaking.

Ordering something is expressing it as a positive objective, forbidding something is expressing it as a negative objective. Wittgenstein overlooked this when he imagined rudimentary languages consisting of orders. He imagined a master-builder uttering the sounds 'pillar', 'slab', 'tile', and workmen bringing pillars, slabs and tiles. When you learn to sail a yacht you learn to react to changes in the wind or current in such a way as not to have the yacht upset, and Wittgenstein gives us no reason to think that his workmen have done more than learn how to react to these sounds issuing from the master-builder's mouth in such a way as not to be injured by him. Yachtsmen do not think the wind is giving them orders, and if the workmen are merely reacting in the same way, they are not taking the master-builder's utterances as orders. To take them as orders they must take him as saying that it would be *right* to bring a pillar or slab, that the position indicated would be a *good* one for the pillar or slab.

To return to the analogy between goodness and truth. There is no such relation as *being true of*, but there are linguistic acts of saying that something is true of something and saying that something is false of something. Similarly there is no such relation as being good for something, or being right for someone, or being an objective to someone, but there are such linguistic acts as advising for and against properties and ordering and forbidding actions. As 'true' and 'false' have a use in explaining indicative constructions, so 'good' and 'bad', 'right' and 'wrong' have a use in explaining imperative. I said that anyone who knows what a property is, knows the difference between having and lacking that property, but to know what in general it is to be something or have something we must know a construction for affirmative predication. Equally anyone who knows what a property is can have that property as a positive or negative objective, but to know what in general it is for something to be good or bad you must know a construction for advising for or against it. Different languages have different imperative constructions. Latin and Greek verbs have a range of moods and gerunds, and these are used to express goodness. Badness is expressed by means of particles like the Latin *ne* and the Greek *mê*. In Polynesian languages verbs are not inflected, and an imperative particle takes the place of an imperative inflection. English verbs are not much inflected, but 'should' 'would' and 'were' are used where in Latin or French the subjunctive might be used. We say 'It would be good if Theaetetus were to sit,' 'It is good that he should be seated.' We also use the modal auxiliaries 'may', 'must', 'have to' and, of course, 'ought'. In the way in which 'not' is expressive of not being or of being false, these words are expressive of goodness or being right.

Under the general heading of counsels and commands there are a number of varieties of linguistic act. Frege drew a sharp distinction between asking what he called a 'sentence question' (*satzfrage*) like 'Is the Earth spherical?' and giving an order. Orders do not express anything true or false; in a sentence question, he says, we express something true or false, but do not assert it (1967, p. 21). In fact, however, to say 'Is the Earth spherical?' is to ask your hearer to *say* whether it is spherical; it is to ask for a certain type of statement. In general constructions for asking questions are constructions for requesting linguistic acts. If I say 'Where is my umbrella?' I ask to be *told* where it is, though if you just point I may be satisfied. It is reasonable to distinguish questions from other requests, because linguistic acts, as I shall argue in Chapter 13, are different from more purely causal acts like pushing, cutting and washing. But requesting a linguistic act is like requesting such a causal act; it is saying it would be good if it were performed.

Hare (1970) proposed a theory of counselling and commanding similar to the theory of asserting which Plato tries in the *Cratylus*. Plato's suggestion is that saying 'Theaetetus is seated' is like producing a picture of Theaetetus seated and saying 'That shows how things are.' Hare's theory is that saying 'Theaetetus, sit down!' is like showing the same picture and saying 'Make that how things are!' It suffers from the same circularity as Plato's *Cratylus* theory. How a sentence can order something is explained by a sentence that itself orders something; all the explanatory work is done by the imperative construction of 'Make that how things are!'

When Hare said that using words like 'good' and 'right' is counselling or commanding, it was objected that we can use them without doing this; for instance in sentences like 'If it is good to forgive enemies it must be good to forgive friends' or 'It is not wrong to refuse unwelcome invitations.' Obviously as using 'not' is denying one thing of another only in certain simple sentences, so using 'good' is recommending one thing for another only in certain simple sentences. But only if we can give conditions for speaking truly or counselling correctly in uttering simple, elementary sentences, are we in a position to give conditions for truth or correctness in uttering sentences constructed out of these. Suppose I say: 'If it is right to paint the wall green it is right to paint the ceiling green.' No doubt I counsel wrongly if green is a good colour for the wall but a bad one for the ceiling.

In Chapter 5 I said that truth *sans phrase* is expressed by the indicative, and that this explains why 'T sentences' look self-evident and why philosophers are tempted by 'redundancy' or 'deflationary' theories of truth. I am now saying that goodness or rightness *sans phrase* is expressed by imperative constructions, and an analogous point can be made about them: as the statement that Theaetetus is seated is true if and only if Theaetetus *is* seated, so the counsel or command that Theaetetus should sit down is right if and only if Theaetetus *should* sit down – if the seated position would be a good one for him.

Simon Blackburn has seen the parallelism, but I do not think he has worked it out, and, perhaps because counsels and commands can have the surface grammar of statements, he calls them 'assertions' and speaks of 'assenting' to them. 'You assent', he says, 'to the assertion [sc. that an action is good] if and only if you are disposed to endorse, choose or otherwise practically orientate yourself in favour of the action' (2010, p. 12). The word 'assent' suggests saying that something is true rather than saying it is right, and Theaetetus 'orientates himself practically in favour' of the action counselled in 'Sit down' not by smiling and saying 'Yes' but by doing as counselled.

We can strengthen Blackburn's parallelism (I don't know whether he would welcome the amendment) if we say that assenting to an indicative sentence too is orientating yourself practically. You assent sincerely to 'Theaetetus is seated' only if you believe that Theaetetus is seated, and in Chapter 12 I shall argue that believing he is seated is simply being disposed to act for the reason that he is. So we can say: 'Assenting to "That Theaetetus is seated is true" is being disposed to act for the reason that he is seated' and 'Assenting to "That Theaetetus should sit down is right" is being disposed to act for the purpose of his becoming seated.'

* * *

I have been considering what it is to *say* something is good or bad. What is it to *think* something is good or bad? Since the basic notions of good and evil are notions of a positive and a negative objective, I think something is good in having it as a positive objective, and I think of it as evil in having it as a negative. And what is it to have something as a positive or negative objective? An easy question: it is to desire it or be averse to it. To think a property good for something is to want it for that thing, and to want a property for something is to desire that it should acquire it or be averse to its losing it. It is significant that in some languages there are single words, like the ancient Greek *axioun* and *dokein*, corresponding to our phrases 'think good', 'think right', 'think fit'. When I say that to think something good is to desire it, I do not mean it is to have an overmastering desire. We think things good in various ways, have different kinds of desire, and we often have desires that cannot all be fulfilled or cannot all be right; but we cannot think something good without desiring it in some way; if we appear to, our thought is probably that other people think it good.

Two objections might be made to the claim that thinking something good is having it as an objective or to desire it. The first fastens on the notion of an objective. This is something we can bring about or prevent, but we can think things good or bad over which we have no control, such as past events. I can think that green was a good colour for you to wear yesterday, or that Brutus was wrong to kill Caesar. Similarly I can wish it will be fine tomorrow for my picnic, though there is nothing I can do to bring about this desirable weather. And when I read a novel I hope that the hero will prosper and regret that he is deceived and betrayed; but he is a fictitious being and his world is totally closed to me.

Our feelings about past and fictional situations are strange, and being able to analyse them is not a precondition of offering an account of our feelings about situations we can influence; I have argued elsewhere (1984), however, that it is not impossible to analyse them in terms of objectives. Perhaps we can have conditional objectives. If I am glad you wore green yesterday, perhaps besides desiring to remember how you looked, I desire that if a similar situation arose I should make your wearing green an objective. If I think Brutus did wrong to kill Caesar, besides contradicting those who make him out a hero, I should wish to prevent similar assassinations. If I hope it won't rain at the picnic, besides being averse to waterproofs and sodden sandwiches I wish I *could* make it fine.

The second objection concerns desire rather than objectives. It is obvious, surely, that we desire many things we don't think good, and think good many things we don't desire. At best thinking something good *makes* us desire it; at worst, desiring something *makes* us think it good. Hobbes may have thought the latter when he wrote:

> Whatsoever is the object of any man's appetite or desire, that it is which he for his part calleth *good*: and the object of his hate and aversion, *evil*; and of his contempt, *vile* and *inconsiderable*. ... *Good*, and *evil*, are names that signify our appetites, and aversions. (*Leviathan* 1.6; 1.15)

Hobbes says that desire and aversion are physical movements in our bodies, the beginnings of our so-called voluntary movements towards and away from things (*Leviathan* 1.6). Russell, in contrast, says that desire is 'some sensation of the sort we call disagreeable', and that a desire is *of* or *for* whatever causes that sensation to stop, so that it is not part of experiencing a desire to know for sure what it is desire for (1921, pp. 65–7). Although Hobbes and Russell stand at opposite ends of the philosophical spectrum that runs from saying that there is nothing but matter to saying that there is nothing but mental states, they both hold that desire is not, properly speaking, a kind of thinking, and philosophers who come between them in time draw a broad distinction between thought and feeling or 'passion'. By a 'passion' they mean a passive state of mind that does not involve any awareness or consciousness of anything except itself. They class emotions like anger, fear, pity and sexual desire as passions; and include desire and aversion among passions in this sense. Ancient and medieval philosophers, in contrast, think that having certain beliefs is part of feeling an emotion like anger or fear, and that desire and aversion are forms of awareness or consciousness of things other than themselves.

This earlier view has been defended in recent times by Anthony Kenny (1963), Martha Nussbaum (in many places, including her 1996) and others, and I here take it as broadly right. Desiring something is being aware of it as a positive objective, and being averse to it is being aware of it as a negative objective. There are different types of desire and aversion, corresponding to the different ways in which something can be an objective. One way of desiring something is simply being aware of some state of your body as pleasant, since this is being aware of it as something the continuance of which would be good and the interruption or cessation of which would be bad. Another is awareness of something as useful or necessary to you as an individual organism, necessary to prevent injury, useful in contributing to health or the enjoyment of your activities or the satisfaction of future desires. You also desire something in thinking it obligatory upon you, or necessary or useful for fulfilling an obligation. And we desire what we think good for other individual people and animals we care for. Corresponding to these modes of desire are modes of aversion. You can be aware of a state of your body as painful and good to get rid of, of objects as dangerous to you and actions as debilitating; you can be aware of an action as forbidden by your society; and you can be aware of things as bad in one way or another for your friends.

If desire and aversion are ways of thinking in this way, we may draw two conclusions. First, the notions of rightness and wrongness apply to them. We desire rightly if we desire what is good or right, and our aversion is wrong if we are averse to what is good or right. And since a desire can be right or wrong it can be reasonable or unreasonable. Hume denied emphatically that a 'passion' can be 'opposed by, or be contradictory to truth and reason' (*Treatise* 2.3.3, p. 415), but that was because he supposed the passions are passive states involving no thought.

A second conclusion is that thinking that something is pleasant, or useful, or contrary to custom, or beneficial or harmful to someone else, is not just thinking something true or false. Hume thought that 'pleasure' is a word for a genus of sensations united by similarity: 'Under the term *pleasure* we comprehend sensations, which are very different from each other, and which have only such a distant resemblance, as is requisite to make them be expressed by the same abstract term' (*Treatise* 3.1.2, p. 472). On that view, effectively criticized by Kenny (1963) and others, thinking a sensation pleasant would be spotting the resemblance, and thinking anything else pleasant would be thinking it a cause of such sensations. Instead, for a sensation or an activity to be pleasant is for it to be an object of desire for its own sake. Being objectives is what unites the things we call 'pleasant'. To think a sensation or an activity pleasant is to want it to continue, or be averse to its stopping, or, in the case of pleasant momentary sensations, perhaps to be averse to any immediate activity. Thinking that doing something would give you pleasant sensations is making a causal judgement, but this judgement is not purely theoretical: it involves a certain desire, eagerness or willingness to do it. This eagerness is rather right or wrong than true or false. It is wrong if the action would be wrong in some other way, for instance causative of some grievous harm to yourself or to someone else, or if it would violate the rules of your society.

Similarly thinking that something is forbidden in the society to which you belong is not just making a true or false anthropological judgement, or believing it to be forbidden in some official document or inscription. If you know that the society which forbids it is yours, your thought that it is forbidden involves having a particular kind of aversion to it that may amount to horror. Oedipus's thought 'Sleeping with one's mother is illicit' involved his viewing it as damaging to his society's life and cutting him off from other members of that society.

And it is the same with thinking that something would benefit or harm some other individual. This will involve a judgement that is true or false. But to think that doing something would give another individual pleasure is to think of that individual as sentient, and this, I shall argue in Chapter 12, involves either wishing to benefit or wishing to harm the individual, and hence having either a desire or an unwillingness to do the deed in question – for in general, I take it, the good of others is an objective for its own sake to intelligent agents; altruism is both possible and a form of rationality. The thought 'This would give pleasure', is not just true or false but right or wrong. It is right if giving your friend pleasure in this way is really beneficial to your friend in these circumstances and you have no overriding reason to act otherwise. But inasmuch as it is a desire to do the deed, the thought 'it would give pleasure' is wrong, and you should not entertain it, if it would be wrong on balance for your friend to obtain pleasure in this way in these circumstances. Conversely the thought that doing something will cause acute pain to your friend involves an aversion to doing it, and that feeling of aversion is wrong if the action – removing a large splinter, say, or amputating a gangrenous limb – is necessary for your friend's wellbeing.

* * *

That completes the first part of my case. Truth, I say, and goodness, existence and being, are not realities that we predicate, but they are expressed by the grammar of simple sentences. I have argued that our grasp of what they are is not just manifested in constructing and understanding simple sentences but also dependent upon it. We can attribute to animals without language some ideas of things for which we have words, warmth and coolness, kinds of food, prey and predators; and with these ideas goes the ability to distinguish between presence and absence of specific quantifiable things, and between a thing's having and lacking specific properties. A cow can distinguish between a shady spot and a place that isn't shady. With these ideas, also, goes the ability to have particular positive and negative objectives, particular desires and aversions. But it is language that separates things from what is true or false of them, from what is good or bad for them, and from the numbers and measures in which they are quantified. It is hard, therefore, to see how any animal without language could have any idea of truth, existence or goodness themselves. Acquisition of these metaphysical concepts must go in step with mastery of elementary grammar.

Truth, existence and goodness are the most general of metaphysical topics. I pass next to change, time and causation. These things make up our idea of the physical. The world of physical science, unlike that of mathematics, is temporal, things change in it, and changes are brought about by causal action. In Chapters 8–11 I argue that change, time and causation are not, like magnetism or the seasons, themselves physical phenomena, and cannot be explained or even defined by physical scientists. Nor are they, as some philosophers have argued, illusions. I show how grammar differentiates changes from states of affairs; also how it distinguishes processes that begin, go on and end from their going on, and how this distinction provides us with general notions of time and causation.

8

Change and Tense

'What is change?' is a fine specimen of a metaphysical question. It differs in that respect from 'What has changed?' or 'What change has taken place?' Locke held that change is indefinable, and made fun of a definition proposed by Aristotle (*Physics* 3 201a10–11), which he translates: 'The act of a being in power, as far forth as in power'. 'What more exquisite jargon', he asks, 'could the wit of man invent? ... [It] would puzzle any rational man, to whom it was not already known by its famous absurdity, to guess what word it could ever be supposed to be the explication of' (*Essay* 3.4.8). Locke thought Aristotle stood for everything he disliked; he would not have thought that of Russell, yet his words could as fairly be applied to Russell's definition:

> Change is the difference, in respect of truth or falsehood, between a proposition concerning an entity and a time T and a proposition concerning the same entity and another time T', provided that the two propositions differ only by the fact that T occurs in the one where T' occurs in the other. (1903/1964, p. 469)

Locke himself deals as lightly with our idea of change or motion as with our concept of existence: it is a 'simple' idea we get from both sight and touch (*Essay* 2.5).

In this chapter I consider two features of simple indicative sentences: that they may express either change or a state of affairs, and that they have tenses. I suggest that using a verb of coming or ceasing to be is expressing something as a thing that can be caused or prevented, but I postpone developing this suggestion to later chapters, and proceed to discuss doubts about the reality of change and time inspired by the phenomenon of tense.

We say not only that objects have and lack properties but that they acquire and lose them. 'Maple leaves in autumn', we say, 'cease to be green and become red.' We also say not only that things exist, but that they come into being and cease to exist: 'Pots come into being out of clay; wood passes away into smoke and ashes.' To put it succinctly, we express changes as well as states of affairs.

I here use 'change' and 'state of affairs' as technical terms. They have untechnical uses in ordinary speech. 'Here's a state of things, here's a pretty mess' sing characters in *The Mikado*. Politicians seeking office sometimes promise 'We will bring you change.' But 'An object's acquiring a property is a change' is something nobody would say who wasn't doing philosophy. A philosophical account of change must tell us how changes differ from states of affairs.

If we are asked 'Is there a difference between being red and becoming red?' it is hard to know what to answer. One suggestion might be that being red and becoming red are different properties we can predicate of things. If, as Alvin Goldman (1971) said, phrases like 'broke a chair' signify properties attributed to the object designated by the subject-expression, the same should presumably hold for phrases like 'turned crimson'. Being red, we might say, is a static property and becoming red a fluid property. If, however, any property can be acquired and lost, that will lead to a regress. Besides the property of becoming red we shall have the property of acquiring that property, the property of *becoming* becoming red.

Davidson (1982b), instead of postulating such properties, proposed that we quantify events in the same way as objects. We should analyse 'The cherry became red' as equivalent to 'There was an event *e* such that *e* was the cherry's becoming red.' He did not, however, offer an analogous analysis of 'The cherry was red.' He did not say it was equivalent to 'There was a state of affairs *s* such that *s* was the cherry's being red'. Rather he understood 'The cherry *was* red' as equivalent to 'There was a cherry *c* such that *c was* red'. Why not say, then, 'The cherry *became* red' is equivalent to 'There was a cherry, *c*, such that *c became* red'?

The words 'change' and 'state of affairs' correspond to the Greek words *kinesis* and *stasis*. In the *Sophist* (252d–254d) Plato groups *kinesis* and *stasis* (which may be translated 'change' and 'staying unchanged') with being, sameness and otherness, and calls these things specially 'large' or 'pervasive' forms. What are they forms of? Ryle suggested that they are forms of speech. *Kinesis* is:

> the generic verbal noun for all live verbs [by 'live verbs' he means what grammarians call 'finite' parts of the verb, as distinct from infinitives and participles] and verbal inflections of happening, doing, beginning, stopping and the like. *Stasis* is the verbal noun for all verbs and verb inflections of continuing and remaining. (1960/1971a, p. 67)

Interpreted along these lines, Plato takes expressing a change and expressing a state of affairs as two forms of speech comparable with three others:

quantifying, or saying that something is or exists; identifying, or saying that something is the same as something; and differentiating, or saying that something is other than something. On this view, 'The world contains changes and states of affairs' does not announce the existence of entities overlooked by natural scientists; it specifies two ways of speaking, and to say what change is is to say how they differ.

The verbs 'to be' and 'to become' are grouped together by grammarians and should have meaning in the same way. Both are copulas; using them is predicating. 'Red' signifies a property that can be had, lacked, lost or acquired. The difference between saying that something was red and saying that it became red is like the difference between saying that something *was* red and saying it *was not* red. Those, I argued in Chapter 5, are different ways of predicating, and so are saying that something *had* a property and saying it *acquired* or *lost* it. The same goes, I shall argue in a moment, for differences of tense – 'The leaves *were* red' and 'The leaves *will be* red'.

What, then, *are* the ways in which we predicate when we use verbs of being and becoming? Precisely *how* does saying the leaves became red differ from saying they were red? Russell's answer is that it is saying they were red *after* not being red. In Chapter 7, however, I said we use a verb of becoming rather than a verb of being when we speak of a property as good or bad, when we speak of it as a positive or negative objective, an object of aversion or desire. A good property for a thing is one it would be good for it to acquire or bad for it to lose. And we advise for or against causing or preventing changes. So predicating something with a verb of becoming is predicating it not only as something good or bad but as something causable or preventable; it is expressing it, we might say, as a causal *explanandum*. Conversely predicating something with a verb of being is predicating it not only as true or false of something, but as an object of belief; and this, I argue in Chapter 12, is predicating it as a reason, a kind of *explanans*. The distinction between being and becoming is connected with the distinctions between belief and desire, and between rational and causal explanation. That probably sounds surprising, and the argument for it will take up much of the following chapters. Meanwhile I may say that the basic theory of truth I provided in Chapter 5 can easily be applied to statements in which we report change. It is true absolutely that the leaves are becoming red if it is *becoming* true of them that they *are* red.

* * *

Although Aristotle and Russell offer definitions of change, the question about change which, on the whole, has most occupied philosophers is not 'What is it?' but 'Is it real?' Non-philosophers might think it incredible that anyone should ask if change is real. Surely nothing could be plainer than that things come into being, acquire and lose properties, and cease to exist. What is this if not change? In fact, however, the reality of change has been called into question not only by philosophers but by mystics in India, China and medieval Europe. So has the reality of time, which everyone agrees to be closely related to change, though there is less agreement about what, exactly, the relation is.

Some people have compared the world of change and time to its disadvantage with a transcendent world that is unchanging and timeless. In the *Bhagavad Gita* (2.16–17, 20–2) we read: 'What is not does not become, and that which is can never cease ... Eternal and indestructible, this is unborn and unchangeable,'[1] and a similar line is taken by some Western thinkers influenced by Plato. Plato, speaking in *Timaeus* 37e–38a of what he calls 'eternal' (*aidios*) being, says: 'We say that it was, is and will be. But in truth only "is" belongs to it.' Plato himself may have had in mind only the atemporal present we use in mathematics ('9 is the square of 3'), but Boethius, acquainted with Christ's words in *John* 8.58, 'Before Abraham came to be, I am', says: 'Eternity is the complete, simultaneous and perfect possession of everlasting life' (*Consolations of Philosophy* 5.6), and Meister Eckhart says: 'Once beyond time and temporalities, we are free and joyous all the time. ... The now wherein God created the first man and the now wherein the last man disappears and the now I speak in are all the same in God, where there is but the now' (1988, pp. 68, 69). This conception of eternity, however, is rather ethical or theological rather than purely metaphysical, and I shall not discuss it here.

Philosophers who have denied or questioned the reality of change have mostly been led to do so by reflecting on pastness, presentness and futurity. That is not true of Russell, whose definition of change reduces it to a succession of states of affairs. But Aristotle (*Physics* 4 217b32–218a30) and Augustine (*Confessions* 11.15) air the problem that the past no longer exists, the future does not yet exist, and the present shrinks under scrutiny to an instant with no duration. This is not in fact a ground for scepticism. It is sufficient for the reality of time that past events should really *have* occurred, and future events should really be *future*. The past would be unreal only if there were no past, that is, only if nothing had ever happened, and the future would be unreal only if there were no future, that is, only if nothing were ever going to happen. And the present need not shrink. We can speak of the present day, year or millennium, and we can use the adverb 'now' to refer to any period during which we are using it.

Neither Aristotle nor Augustine accepted any sceptical conclusion, but J. E. McTaggart argued at considerable length that holding time to be real is incoherent or self-contradictory. He took 'past', 'present' and 'future' to signify properties that events or states of affairs can acquire or lose, and he thought that change and time are possible only if an event can cease to be future and become present, and then cease to be present and become past, rather as a fruit can cease to be green and become red, and then cease to be red and become black. The argument goes like this. Past, present and future, he said, are 'incompatible determinations. Every event must be one or the other, but no event can be more than one.' Nevertheless, 'every event has them all. If M [any arbitrarily chosen event] is past, it has been present and future.' So the supposition that change and time are real involves a contradiction (1927, sections 325–9).[2]

Some philosophers writing after McTaggart have claimed not that time is unreal, but that tense is. By 'tense' they do not mean what grammarians mean, something I shall discuss in a moment; they don't say that there are no tenses of verbs, that the future indicative or the pluperfect subjunctive is unreal. They talk of 'tensed facts', where a tensed fact is whatever makes true an utterance containing an expression like 'past', 'present', 'future', 'now', 'then', 'yesterday', 'next year', 'a long time ago'.[3] Hugh Mellor says '*Last century and last week* are tenses, and so are *this month, tomorrow and next year*.' He also says that the word is to cover 'the temporal positions in McTaggart's A series',[4] and 'thus include not only the rather extended positions PAST and FUTURE but also more restricted PAST and FUTURE positions like YESTERDAY and NEXT YEAR, and PRESENT ones like TODAY and THIS YEAR' (1981, p. 16; 1968, p. 171).

I think he means that 'tense' in his special sense is to be a word for the entities designated by the linguistic items he has had printed in italics or capitals. In fact these linguistic items are a mixed bag. 'Past' and 'present' are primarily grammatical terms; 'yesterday' and 'next year' are expressions referring in a special way to movements or changes, a rotation of the earth on its axis and a revolution of the earth round the sun. When I use such an expression I refer to a particular movement by relating it temporally to my utterance, and the movement I refer to is not unreal. The movement I refer to if I use 'yesterday' will really have occurred, and we hope or fear that the movement I refer to as 'next year' will really occur.

Mellor probably imagines, like McTaggart, that 'past' and 'future' are words for properties like 'red' or 'pale', since he says 'Past and future admit of degrees:

future events are not all equally future, nor are all past events equally past' (1981, p. 14)[5] If to be past is to have happened and to be future is to be going to happen, past and future do not admit of degrees. This is a grammatical point. We can say that one thing is more red or more pale than another, but the 'more' goes with the adjective, not with the verb of being. We cannot (except by way of a joke) say that one object exists more than another or that one event took place more than another. The American Civil War occurred before the First World War, but it did not occur *more*.

If pastness, presence and futurity are not properties, what are they? 'The past', we are told, 'is a foreign country: they do things differently there'. Not, however, in the University of Cambridge. 'If it were now the eighteenth century', asks Mellor, 'how different would the world be?' and he answers that there would be no real differences at all (1981, p. 29). In fact, however, the past is not a temporal theatre of action, and to analyse our concept of it we must consider how we express temporal relations.

By 'temporal relations' I mean those of being earlier than something, later than something and contemporaneous with something. Temporal relations are not mutable like spatial relations or relations of comparative magnitude. Those are relations in which a thing can stand at one time and not at another. I am lighter than you now, but was heavier than you when you were a child. Temporal relations are not like that, a fact that bears on the question whether time travel is possible and on other philosophical questions about time. But we can relate one event or one state of affairs temporally to another in speech. One way of doing this is by conjunctions: 'Telemachus', we say, 'was born *before* Odysseus went to Troy'; 'Helen patched up her marriage with Menelaus *after* he brought her home from Troy'; and 'Clytemnestra lived with Aegisthus *while* Agamemnon was besieging Troy.' Another way is expressed by parataxis: 'I came', says Caesar, 'I saw, I conquered.' 'Before' is no more an expression *for* temporal priority than is an order of words; but using either is speaking of one thing as earlier than another. And temporal relations to a speaker's utterance are expressed by what grammarians call 'tense'. That word is taken from *tempus*, the Latin word for time, and although it does not mean the same as 'time', people are liable to feel about tense what Augustine felt about time, that if you do not ask them what it is, they know, but if you do ask them, they don't. It is easy to give examples – 'The future and the pluperfect are tenses' – but hard to give a general account. Let me, however, try.

We say 'That pear is ripe' or 'was ripe' or 'will be ripe'. In the first case we express the pear's ripeness as contemporaneous to our utterance, in the second as prior, in the third as posterior. The forms of a verb by which we say something is contemporaneous with our utterance are called the 'present' tenses of the verb, those by which we say it was prior are called 'past' tenses and those by which we say it will be posterior are called 'future' tenses. 'Is' and 'are' belong to the present tense of 'to be', 'was' and 'were' to the simple past, and the phrase 'will be' forms a future tense. Verb-inflections expressing such relations are called 'tense-inflections' and the auxiliary verbs and particles (used, for instance, in uninflected Polynesian languages) which do the same work are called 'tense-auxiliaries' and 'tense-indicators'. When Aristotle observed that verbs, unlike nouns, signify time [*khronos*] in addition to whatever else they signify (*De Interpretatione* 16b6), he probably meant that they express temporal relations to the utterance. The grammatical notion of a tense is that of a group of words or phrases formed from a single verb and united by the way in which they are expressive of temporal relations. If I say that the tense of 'are' or *sumus* is present, I mean that the word is one of the forms of the verb ('to be' or *esse*), using which is speaking of something as contemporaneous with the utterance; it is a form expressive of that contemporaneity.

Besides speaking of things as temporally related directly to our utterance, we can speak of them as temporally related to events that are themselves earlier or later than our utterance. We say 'When he had conquered Persia Alexander invaded India' speaking of the conquest as prior to the invasion. R. I. Dordillon, writing for nineteenth-century missionaries, gives the Marquesan for 'When you get there we shall have been eaten' (*'ia tihe mai 'oe, 'ua pao matou 'i 'e kai*) (1931, p. 40). Survivors may have said: 'When you got here they were about to eat us,' in Latin, *manducaturi erant*. All these are tense forms.

Not all languages have the same range of forms. English differs from French in not having future inflections – it uses 'will' instead – and Latin does not differentiate the perfect from the simple past in the way English does. When children are first learning to speak they do not use past or future tenses, and I can imagine a human society in which people never express anything as prior to or posterior to their utterance, though I have not myself heard of any human beings so primitive or so parsimonious of the truth. Whorf's claim that the Hopi Indians lack our concepts of past, present and future (1991, pp. 47–64) was based on conversations with a single Hopi Indian in New York, and is questioned by E. Malotki (1983); but even if it were accurate I do not think it would follow that Hopi speakers are unable to say that anything is past or future. According to Rundle (1979, p. 41, on the authority of Boas 1911), in Eskimo languages temporal relation to the utterance is expressed rather through nouns than through verbs. Perhaps what passes for speech among animals is tenseless. Tense, aspect and voice have no meaning in mathematics. A mathematician might say '6 can be divided by 2 and 3' but the passive is not used here as it is in 'The cake was divided into six slices': nothing acts upon the number six. But they are essential for speaking of the physical world; I consider tense here and aspect and voice in Chapters 9 and 10.

Grammarians apply the words 'past', 'present' and 'future' to verbs or tenses. We can also speak of past and future politicians, or say that summer is past, and using a past, present or future tense is speaking of things as being or not being past, present or future. I say 'being or not being' to avoid recognizing negative entities. Saying 'Achilles will not overtake the tortoise' is not saying that a negative event, his not overtaking the tortoise, is future, but rather that a positive event, his overtaking it, is *not* future: no such overtaking will occur. Similarly saying 'There were no mosquitoes yesterday' is not saying that the non-existence of mosquitoes was a state of affairs yesterday, but rather that the existence of mosquitoes was *not*, yesterday, a state of affairs.

The word 'future' comes from the Latin *futurus*, which is the future participle of *esse*, 'to be'. What is future is what *will be*. Similarly what is past is what *has been*, and what is present is what *is*. Since being is not an activity or state, nor is having been or being about to be; so saying that something is past, present or future is not predicating anything of it, but merely relating it temporally to your utterance. If I say: 'You said something was past' or 'You denied something was future' I describe the construction of your speech, the way in which you predicated or quantified, I do not specify something which you predicated, namely pastness or futurity. This holds even if you use the word 'past' or 'future'. In saying 'Summer is past, over' you say no more than if you had said 'We have had summer' or 'The Sun has left this hemisphere.' E. J. Lowe (1998, p. 47) correctly says 'presentness' is not 'some sort of *property* of events', and he is expressing my positive view when he says that tenses are 'predicate modifiers' (p. 50) if by that he means that they modify, not what we predicate, but the way in which we predicate it

Since confusion about the grammar of tensed sentences leads to scepticism about time and change, it may be well to add a few more words on the subject.

I said that tense has no meaning in mathematics. In mathematics we use the present tense – we ask '*Is* 83 a prime number?' but not to relate its being prime temporally to our utterance. This usage should be distinguished from the use of the present to say what is natural noted by Michael Thompson (2012). In 'Swallows arrive in May' we do relate the natural time of their arrival to our utterance; migratory habits can change. Numbers have their properties timelessly. Philosophers sometimes ask us to choose between 'tensed' and 'tenseless' (or 'tensed' and 'detensed') theories of time; so R. Le Poidevin and Jeremy Butterfield in Le Poivedin, 1998. Time itself is not tensed or tenseless, but a tenseless theory of time is one according to which we can give a full description of the physical world using only the present tense as it is used in mathematics. Philosophers may be motivated to do this by a Fregean desire to make all speech like that of mathematicians. There are at least three strategies they can adopt. They can postulate moments of time and say, for instance, that if a cherry is red there is a moment at which it is red, and the two-place predicate 'is red at' is timelessly predicated of the cherry and a moment of time. That, in effect, was Russell's strategy. (Properties can then be predicated of numbers at *all* moments.) Or they can introduce dated properties. In McTaggart's day academics had open fires in their rooms, and could put a poker into such a fire, with the result that it became red hot. McTaggart thought that if his poker was black on Sunday but, having been put in the fire, it was red on Monday, it did not really change because 'from eternity to eternity' the poker had the property of being red on that Monday (1927, section 315). He took 'on Monday' with the adjective 'red', understanding it to signify a special kind of redness, not dark redness or bright redness but Monday redness. A third strategy (David Lewis, 1986, pp. 203–4) is to treat objects extending in three dimensions as faces, so to speak, revealed by slicing through objects that extend in a fourth temporal dimension, analogous to the two-dimensional faces revealed when you slice through a loaf. A cut through the middle of a French baguette will show a larger face than one near the end. These four-dimensional objects have temporal parts, and the Monday part of the poker is timelessly red.

I take up Russell's view below and the other two strategies are ruled out by grammar. 'On Monday' and 'yesterday' are adverbial expressions. Some adverbs modify adjectives and other adverbs – 'For someone so clever', we hiss, 'she solves sujikos surprisingly slowly'. But adverbial expressions of time go with verbs, and in 'The poker was red on Monday' 'on Monday' must be construed neither with 'the poker' nor with 'red' but with 'was'.

Aristotle asked whether, if we say 'Tomorrow the navies will engage in battle', we are speaking either truly or falsely (*De Interpretatione* 18a33–19a6). The question has been debated since the earliest times; for recent surveys see the 'Introduction' to Ammonius (1998) and Crivelli (2004) Chapter 7. We fear that if we are speaking truly, the navies cannot help engaging, and if we are speaking falsely they cannot possibly engage. This appearance arises, if we suppose that if we are *now* speaking truly, it must *now* be true of the navies that they will tomorrow engage, and if falsely, it must *now* be false of them that they will tomorrow engage. But grammar does not oblige us to suppose that. Suppose a gardener says 'Next week the tomatoes will be red': he *then* speaks truly if it *will next week* be true of the tomatoes that they *are* red. The adverbial phrase 'next week' and the tense auxiliary 'will' can be taken with 'be true of'. To understand the gardener's prediction as equivalent to 'It is now true of them that they will next week be red' is to understand it as 'it is now true of them that it will next week be true of them that they are red'. That not only sounds complicated and regressive but suggests, what I have argued is a mistake, that 'true of' signifies a relationship in which one thing can stand to another. Similarly with Aristotle's prediction, though there we have the verb 'engage' in place of 'be'. 'Engage' is a verb of action, expressive of becoming. 'The navies will engage tomorrow' is equivalent to 'It will tomorrow *become* true of the navies that they are engaged', and we prophesy truly if this will tomorrow become true of them.

9

Time and Aspect

'Time', says Aristotle, 'is either change or some aspect of change; and since it is not change, it must be some aspect of change' (*Physics* 4, 219a8–10[1]). His arguments for the premises of this disjunctive syllogism leave something to be desired, but his conclusion is correct: time, I shall argue, is the taking place or going on of processes of change. That being so, time stands to change as existence stands to things like horses and water. As existing is not something we do, so the going on of a process of change is not a further process that goes on; but as there are ways of speaking of things as existent, so there are ways of speaking of changes as temporal. We have constructions for speaking of a change as a period of time, a period of so many hours or minutes, and also constructions for speaking of a change as something instantaneous, something without duration. In order to establish this I shall have to distinguish between processes that begin, go on and end, and the beginnings, ends and goings on of these processes. The task is delicate because constructions for expressing change vary from language to language, but I shall start with the choices European grammars allow us.

First, we may use either a verb of becoming (or ceasing to be) with a complement ('The trees *are turning* yellow'), or a verb of making or doing like 'build' or 'sail'. I say more about verbs of making and doing below, but it is obvious that sentences like 'Palladio built a villa' or 'Columbus sailed across the Atlantic' report changes.

Next, we have a choice of moods. We can express changes in statements, or in commands, counsels and wishes. In Chapter 7 I considered utterances like 'Sit down', 'Stop fidgeting', 'It would be no bad idea to adopt a less supine position,' 'O that this too, too solid flesh would melt.' In this present chapter I concentrate on indicative constructions.

Thirdly, our verbs have tense and aspect. In European languages there are *simple* tense-forms, like 'builds', 'built', 'will build', *continuous* or *imperfect* forms, like 'will be building', *construisait, aedificabat* and *perfect* forms like 'has built', *a construit, aedificavit*. Perfect forms express states of affairs subsequent to changes. The distinction marked in English by simple and continuous forms is the most important for understanding time, but it appears differently in different languages. In general continuous forms express changes as going on and incomplete. We do not normally, in expressing change in English, use a simple form of the present indicative. We say 'I am turning grey' rather than 'I turn grey'. We use the simple form to express frequency – 'You go to Paris (sc. quite often)' – or to give a stage direction – 'He goes to the door' – or to make a story more vivid (the so-called 'historic' present). It is different when we are expressing a state of affairs: then we use the simple forms, not the continuous. We say 'The grapes are ripe,' 'There was no whisky' and 'Caesar will be in Egypt,' rather than 'The grapes are being ripe.' 'There was not being any whisky,' and 'Caesar will be being in Egypt'.

Bernard Comrie (1976) gives a valuable description of aspectual forms in English and many other languages, but writes rather as a linguist than as a philosopher. Antony Galton (1987, pp. 169–96), whose interests are at least partly philosophical, sketches a logic of aspect comparable with A. N. Prior's logic of tense, but does not suggest, as I do, that time is what is expressed by certain aspectual forms. Michael Thompson (2012) uses distinctions of aspect to analyse the notions of life and action: see below p. 187. Thompson's notion of an 'event- or process-form' (2012, p. 125) corresponds fairly closely to my notion of what I call a 'process'. Lakoff and Johnson speak of aspect (1999, pp. 39, 41, 93 and elsewhere) but fail, I shall suggest, to grasp its significance.

Besides different forms of verb we have adverbial constructions that quantify time like 'in an hour', 'for many years', 'after 20 minutes'. (English uses different prepositions here; Latin uses different case-inflections.)

Finally we may express the termini of a change in positive or negative terms. We may say 'Autumn leaves change from being green to not being green,' 'They change from not being yellow to being yellow' or 'They change from being green to being yellow' (or, more concisely, 'from green to yellow').

I shall use the word 'process' in a restricted sense for changes like the change from green to yellow; I call expressing a change in positive terms as a change from one thing to another expressing it as a 'process'. Processes other than changes of colour are a change of temperature, say from blood heat to boiling point, a change of shape from spherical to pear-shaped, growing from three feet high to four, a change of posture from sitting to standing, a rotation from facing north to facing east, a translation from London to New York.

Processes (we say) take place or go on; they also begin and end. For example I walk from my house to the pub, a distance of a mile. That is a process. It takes place and is completed *in* a time, say in 20 minutes. It goes on *for* a time, for 20 minutes. It starts at my house and ends at the pub, and it ends *after* a time, after 20 minutes. The distinctions between a process, its beginning or ending, and its going on are not like those between flying, running and swimming. 'Start' (I mean as in 'start moving', not as in 'start the engine'), 'finish' and 'go on' are not expressions for modes of action we can investigate empirically. Starting, finishing and going on are expressed by constructions we use in speaking. My walking from my house to the pub is not separable from my leaving my house, my reaching the pub and my walking for 20 minutes between the two. But

'I walked from my house to the pub'
'I walked a mile'
'I was walking between my house and the pub'
'I left my house,' and
'I arrived at the pub'

are different sentences and illustrate different ways of speaking of a movement. In the first two I speak of my movement as a process, in the third I speak of it as a going on of a process, in the fourth as a beginning of a process, and in the fifth as an end of a process. Distinctions similar to mine were made by Aristotle (*Metaphysics* Θ 1048b18–35; *Nicomachean Ethics* 10 1174a13–b10) between what he calls 'changes' and 'activities' (*kineseis* and *energeiai*), and by Zeno Vendler (1957) between what he calls 'activities', 'accomplishments' and 'achievements'.

Lakoff and Johnson (1999, pp. 39–42) report that in every society people, when they act on purpose, distinguish starting, going on and stopping (and also other phases) and that the physiological processes that take place when they act are found to have corresponding parts with distinct neurological structures. Might our ideas of starting, going on and stopping derive from these bodily processes? Are they picturings or projections of them? Lakoff and Johnson say that the 'single general structure governing all neural control systems ... provides a literal skeleton for our conception of event structure' (1999, pp. 175–6). (By 'our conception of event structure' they mean our idea that processes start, go on and end.) But there are two difficulties. First, animals without language act in much the same way as human beings. Birds build nests; carnivores go hunting. But it is doubtful if they have concepts of starting, continuing and stopping. Secondly the physiological processes scientists observe in starting, continuing and stopping do not have the features by which I have just distinguished startings, goings on and stoppings. They are all simply processes in a broad sense, within which my distinctions can be drawn. No doubt if they didn't occur we shouldn't act as we do, and if we didn't act as we do we shouldn't speak as we do. But starting, going on and stopping as I have defined them are differentiated only in speech and our notions of them are taken from speech.

* * *

Equipped with the notions of a process, the beginning or end of a process and the going on of a process we can say what time is. I shall first argue that the notion of an instant is the notion of a beginning or end of a process; then that the notion of a stretch of time is the notion of a going on of a process.

Instead of saying I arrive *after* a time, I may say that I arrive *at* a time; and if I leave my house *after* a period of repose and *before* a period of gentle activity, my departure may also be said to be *at* a time. By a 'time' here, however, is not meant a period, but rather an instant, something without duration or temporal extent. A line, which extends in one dimension, terminates at points which have no spatial extension at all, so a stretch of time, which seems similarly to extend in one dimension, should begin and end at entities which have no temporal extension at all.

Temporal extension and spatial extension are indeed analogous, and we do say things like 'The train started at five minutes to two' or 'I reached the pub at five to two precisely.' 'Five minutes to two', however, is an expression for a position of clock-hands. To say 'The train will start at five minutes to two' is to say that its starting will be simultaneous with the passage of clock-hands through the five-to-two position. If clock-hands move continuously and not (as they often do) in jerks with intervals between each jerk and the next, then the end of the movement *to* each position is identical with the start of the movement *from* it. The hands pass through a position after a period of moving towards it and before a period of moving from it, but the passage itself has no duration. Nor has a switch (the word used by Colin Strang, 1974) from motion to rest or vice versa. If an instant, however, is analogous to the terminal point of a line, these events rather *are* instants than occur at instants. The period of moving towards the five-to-two position ends with the passage through that position, the period of my movement between my house and the pub ends with my reaching the pub. These startings and stoppings occur at spatial locations or whatever may be analogous in alterations and changes of size. If we postulate further unextended temporal items for them to occur at, they will have to occur simultaneously with these items, and if one thing cannot be simultaneous with another unless there is a third thing with which both are simultaneous, we shall have a Third Clock regress to add to the Third Man.[2]

What then is it for two events to be simultaneous? There are several possibilities. They might be identical. As Aristotle (*Physics* 6, 231a21–4) recognizes, if I pass through a point without stopping, my reaching that point and my leaving it are the same event. Or they might be parts of the same event. If wax is heated, its starting to rise in temperature is part of the same event as its starting to become liquid. Or if two events are separate, we can draw upon the Special Theory of Relativity: we can say they are simultaneous if equal stretches of time separate them from a single event that is earlier or later than both, for instance if rays of light emitted from both meet half way between them. If no such processes can occur to relate them they are not temporally related.[3]

In colloquial speech we sometimes use expressions which in themselves signify starting or stopping to signify extended processes. We say 'It took us a long time get started' or 'Thanks to our new brakes, the car came to rest in four seconds.' Here the words 'took a long time' or 'in four seconds' make our report one of a process. Similarly with coming into being. Coming into being is not a change undergone by the thing that comes into being; it is not like coming into a room. What comes into being does so out of something else; this may either remain like the bricks out of which a house is built, or pass away like the snow that turns to water. In 'Ice came into being in my freezer *after* a few minutes', we express a coming into being as the end of a process (a change of temperature undergone by water); in 'Ice came into being *in* a few minutes' we express it as that process.

So much, for the moment, on beginnings and ends of processes; now for their going on. A process and a going on of that process are the same thing spoken of (or thought of) in different ways. When we speak of it in one way, as a change from one thing to another, we quantify or measure it in units of one kind, and when we speak of it as a going on of such a process we use units of another. My walk, spoken of as a movement from one place to another, is quantified in units of distance; it is a mile-long walk, a walk of 1,760 yards. The growth of a tree, spoken of as a change from one height to another, is measured in units of extension in one dimension, it is a one-foot growth. The temperature change of the water in a kettle, spoken of as a change from one temperature to another, is a change of so many degrees, whereas a movement spoken of as a change from facing in one direction to facing in another, or a change of shape such as a straight piece of piping undergoes when a plumber bends it, is reckoned in degrees of arc.

All these units of measurement quantify changes considered as possibilities. What do I mean by 'possibility'? They are changes from one possible thing to another: from one possible place to a second, or one possible height, or degree of heat, or shape or direction. And they are themselves possible changes; they are changes that can go on or take place many times, as contrasted with actual goings on or occurrences of changes. We have no accepted unit for quantifying a change from one colour to another, though a scientist might use wave-length (or what is called 'reflectance') for this purpose, but green and yellow are possible colours for things, and spoken of as a change from green to yellow an alteration in colour is spoken of as a possibility.

Spoken of, on the other hand, as goings on of change, all changes are quantified in the same way. We measure them and give their extension in units of time like hours and years. Since these are units in which we measure the going on of a change of any kind, and they are units of time, it seems that the time or temporal extent of a change is its going on. A 20-minute translation is a 20-minute making of a movement from one place to another; a one-year change of size or colour is a year-long taking place of a possible change from one size or colour to another.

This is not unambiguously clear from ordinary English. There are locutions which could suggest that speaking of a movement as extending for a time is still speaking of it as a possibility, as a movement that might be made many times. I might say 'In my new car, I can make a 20-minute journey in ten minutes.' This, however, is a way of saying 'I can make a movement which usually takes 20 minutes in ten.' It is correct to speak of a ten-minute making of a ten-mile journey, but not of a ten-mile making of a ten-minute journey. We cannot say 'It took me ten miles to travel ten minutes'. It is grammatically permissible to say 'To keep fit, I run for 20 minutes every day.' This, however, is equivalent to 'Every day I engage for 20 minutes in the activity of running'. It is not permissible to say 'To keep fit I run two miles for 20 minutes every day.'

We use time units to quantify not only modes of locomotion like running but other things we do like fighting, laughing and thinking. These may be quantified in two ways. 'There was a lot of fighting' may mean 'A lot of people fought' in which case we really quantify the fighters. Or it may mean 'People fought for a long time' and then what is quantified is the going on of combative activity.

It might be objected that even if time-units measure the going on of processes rather than the processes which go on, still it does not follow that a going on of a process *is* a time; all that follows, surely, is that it is *for* a time, that it *lasts* for a time. But to say that the going on of a process lasted for a time could only be to say that it *went on* for a time or *was taking place* for a time. Processes go on and take place, but the going on of a process does not go on or take place.

Another possible objection concerns contemporaneity. Two processes which are contemporaneous go on for the same time, but the going on of one is not the same as the going on of the other. Suppose I walk three miles in an hour, and you walk the same three miles simultaneously; we walk together. Then the hour for which I am walking is the same as the hour for which you are walking, but my walking is not the same as yours. So the hour for which we are both in motion must be something over and above my making of the three-mile journey and yours.

I might reply as I did to the similar objection about instantaneous events. What good is this extra hour supposed to do? To say it is an hour for which we are both in motion is surely to say that it is an hour contemporaneous both with your making of your movement and with my making of mine. But if your making of your movement and my making of mine can be contemporaneous with this hour, why can they not be contemporaneous directly with one another? They will be contemporaneous if their beginnings and ends are simultaneous.

But the objector may complain that this does not meet the difficulty, which was that the hour for which I move is the same as the hour for which you move, but my making of the journey is different from yours. If your making of the journey actually were identical with an hour, and so were mine, that would make two hours and not one.

My answer is that there are indeed two hours, an hour of motion by you and an hour of motion by me. These hours are contemporaneous in the way I have indicated: they start and stop simultaneously. That sounds strange, but if two people cleaned my house for an hour contemporaneously, I should have to pay for two hours of cleaning. We are sometimes told that time began a finite number of years ago, and that suggests that that number of years is the total amount of time there has been. In this way of speaking, however, what is quantified is not time in general but a particular process, the expansion of the universe after the Big Bang.

The real question is whether there can be an hour which is not an hour of any kind of motion or change. S. Shoemaker (1969), followed by W. H. Newton-Smith (1980, chapter 2) argues that we could have empirical grounds for thinking there are periods of universal rest. Such periods, however, could not begin or end without violating conservation laws, and would destroy the analogy between temporal and spatial extension. Length, area and volume are called 'extensive magnitudes', magnitudes in which things extend, and time is similar. As we say that water or sand extends for miles or acres or cubic feet, so we say that travelling from England to Australia or changing from green to yellow goes on for days or hours or minutes. But there are no lengths, areas or volumes which are not lengths areas or volumes of some material. A cubic metre is a cubic metre of wood or wine, not of nothing at all. Similarly an hour is an hour of motion or growth or rise in temperature.

People may imagine that there can be empty times, times in which no change occurs, because there can be empty spaces, gaps between things in which nothing material extends. But this is to confuse extension with distance. The confusion occurs because we use the same words to signify units of length – units, that is, of spatial extension in one dimension – and units of distance, in which we reckon translations. We say 'That rod is a yard long' and 'The distance between the windows is a yard.' That is not surprising, since we might measure the distance between the windows *with* the rod. But this possibility may make us think that the distance between two objects is a length of some tenuous material which is like wood or steel except that it is not only invisible but offers no resistance and is incapable either of acting upon anything else or of being acted upon. If what I say below about matter and causal powers is correct, the notion of a material that has no causal powers at all, or confers none on objects containing it, is incoherent. A unit of distance is a unit in which we measure, not the *extension* of anything, but a possible *movement* from one place to another. To say that the distance between the windows is one yard is to say that the movement from one to the other is a one-yard movement. To say 'There is space beyond the furthest star' is to say that it is possible to get further from the Earth than the furthest star. The units in which we reckon distance are analogous to the units in which we reckon changes of size or temperature. If the tree grows in height from three feet to four feet, that is a change in height by a foot, but the foot between its height at the beginning of the change and its height at the end is not a foot of any material. Nor is it a foot of distance; it is a foot of change in height. The fifty-foot distance, likewise, between two possible places for an object is 50-feet of change of place.

Whereas an hour is analogous to a piece of string a yard long, it is not analogous to a movement a yard long. The going on of a movement is not analogous to a movement that might go on; and therefore while time is analogous to extension in spatial dimensions, it is not analogous to space itself.

Changes can be counted as well as measured, and that also in two ways. They can be counted as processes which go on, and then they are distinguished by their termini. The movement from London to Paris and the movement from Rome to Athens are two different possible movements. Alternatively they can be counted as goings on of processes. My making of the journey from London to Paris and yours are two different actual movements, two different goings on of the same process, and hence two different stretches of time. But the position is the same with lengths, breadths and volumes. A volume may be measured in cubic inches, litres or some such units, but volumes can also be counted. Each bottle in a case of Bollinger contains a different expanse, a different 750 ml, of the same wine, each human being is a different expanse of flesh and bone.

If there are no empty times, that enables me to meet a further objection that might be made to my identification of time with the going on of change. States of affairs go on as well as changes. London has been the capital of England for centuries. Things exist for periods of time. So isn't time just as much the going on of states of affairs as it is of change? I reply that a state of affairs exists for a time only if its coming into existence is simultaneous with the beginning, and its ceasing to exist with the end, of a process that goes on for a time. 'How long, porter,' a traveller asks in a perhaps legendary phrase book, 'will the train be at this platform?' 'From two-to-two to two-two,' replies the porter. 'Good God, man!' exclaims the traveller. 'Do you think you're a trumpet?' The train's coming to rest is simultaneous with the passage of clock-hands through the two-to-two position, and its starting again with their passage through the two-minutes-past-two position. What is not the case is that a state of affairs could exist for a period during which no change whatever in anything goes on. That would really be like a yard for which no material whatever extends.

Someone might say that physicists in the last 100 years have given us new knowledge about time, knowledge that Augustine was not just unable to put into words, but didn't possess. In fact their speculations and experiments have been directed towards the measurement of time, not towards what it is that we want to measure. Whereas the question 'What is gold?' is a question about the material structure, or the utility in society, of an identifiable substance, the question 'What is time?' is equivalent to 'What are questions concerning time questions about?' and that is for philosophers, not physicists, to say. Time is of practical importance to us; it is bound up with causation and our desires and fears.

To sum up what I have been saying, an instant of time, if we wish to have durationless temporal items,[4] is the beginning or end of a process, and a stretch of time is the going on of a process. I have described the grammatical constructions by which periods of time and instants are expressed in English; and I have argued that as expressing existence is quantifying things like elephants and water, so expressing time is quantifying changes. Small children have difficulty with the idea of time. Phrases like 'in two days', 'after a month', 'for three years' and even words for time units like 'day', 'hour' and 'minute' seem to mean little to them. A day, a month and a year are defined by the relative movements through 360 degrees of the Earth and the Sun, the Moon and the stars, and an hour by the movement of clock-hands. To grasp the idea of time a child must not only grasp the notion of turning through an angle but distinguish a rotation or revolution from its going on. That is no small intellectual feat. The two are not distinct in reality; they are distinguished by language; so knowing what time is is a matter of knowing constructions that make the distinction.

* * *

Having offered what I believe to be a correct account of time, I shall now consider some mistakes I think philosophers have made.

The principal trap into which we fall when we consider time has already been mentioned. Topics of metaphysics have the property that staring at them induces a kind of double vision. We shall find this in connection both with matter and with mind, but it happens also with time. The end of a process, which is itself something with no duration, projects an image of itself that we construe as a durationless instant at which it occurs, and the going on of a process projects an image of itself as a further process which goes on and which we construe as a stretch of time.

A classic case of this double vision is to be found in Newton's Note to the Definitions in his *Principia*:

> Absolute, true and mathematical time of itself and from its own nature flows equably without relation to anything external. … Absolute space, in its own nature, without relation to anything external, remains always similar and immovable.

Newton pictures time as a process which itself goes on, like the pouring of treacle from a jug, and space as a kind of substance which itself extends. These mistakes are like thinking that existence is a process or state; you might say it is a translation of that mistake to physics. Newton probably imagined that space and time exist as well as extending, though what existence could be for them apart from extending he does not say;[5] he stops at double vision and doesn't attempt triple.

His Note continues:

> As the order of the parts of time is immutable, so also is the order of the parts of space. Suppose those parts to be moved out of their places, and they will be moved (if the expression may be allowed) out of themselves. For times and spaces are, as it were, *the places as well of themselves as of all other things*. All things are placed in time as to order of succession; and in space as to order of succession. (My emphasis)

He may have thought that materials cannot extend unless there already extends space in which they extend, and that processes cannot go on unless there already goes on time in which they go on. He imagines that there are locations in absolute time as there are locations in space, and that one location in time is a certain number of years from another (no doubt in the direction of earlier or later) as one place in space is a certain number of miles from another (as it might be in a northerly or southerly direction). If that were the case, temporal locations would be possible properties for objects or events, and it would in theory be possible for something to change its temporal location. Such a change would be a possible movement of so many years, as changing your spatial location from London to Paris is a possible movement of so many miles. Contrary to what I said just now, a 20-minute movement would be a movement someone could make, and a movement of 750 years is one the Battle of Waterloo would have to make in order to change from being later than the Battle of Hastings to being earlier than it. I say that if temporal locations could be acquired, lost and predicated of objects like spatial locations, these movements would be possible *in theory*, possible 'logically'. Whether they would be possible physically is another question; but then 'Is it physically possible to move from Waterloo to Hastings?' is a different question from 'Is it possible in theory?' It is possible in theory, if Waterloo and Hastings are spatially related; whether it is possible physically depends on what is being moved, what the motive power is, what obstacles there are and other such matters. Of course, if a 20-minute movement were a movement we could make, we should not make it *in* a time or be making it *for* a time. The going on of a movement from one part of Newton's absolute time to another would have to be reckoned in units as yet unimagined.

The notion of a location in time is coherent, but it is not that of something to or from which there can be change; rather it is a notion of change itself. If we think of a temporal location as a time *within* which something occurs, then to express a change as a going on of a process is to express it as a location in time. Odysseus's visit to Circe was located within his ten years of wanderings. If we think of temporal locations as analogous to *end-points* of spatial lengths, to express a movement or change as the beginning or end of a process is to express it as a temporal location. The end of Odysseus's wandering was his arrival in Ithaca.

Russell said:

> We must entirely reject the notion of a *state* of motion. Motion consists *merely* in the occupation of different places at different times, subject to continuity as explained in Part V. (1964, p. 473)

The continuity which he had explained in his Part V is the continuity which attaches to a certain series defined by Cantor (1955, pp. 133–6) (roughly speaking, the continuity of the series of so-called 'real' numbers), and by different 'times' here he means different durationless instants – not, however, beginnings and ends of processes, but purely temporal items without temporal extent. Russell urges us, then, to reject the notion of being in motion for a time-stretch, and with it any notion of the going on of a process. As a line can be viewed, thanks to Cantor, as a continuous series of points, so time is to be viewed as a continuous series of instantaneous events, events similar, in the way in which they are spoken of, to startings and stoppings, but not, like startings and stoppings, entities known to non-philosophers. Russell would have us think of time as made up of the existences of objects at places at instants, and his definition I quoted at the beginning of Chapter 8 reduces change generally to having different properties at different instants. The idea behind this definition is that if, for example, 'The poker was red on Sunday' and 'The poker was red on Monday' are one of them true and the other false, then there has been a change.

That is undeniable; but it does not follow that time or change simply consists in existences of objects (or instantiations of properties) at instants. To accept Russell's definition it is not enough to say that if a body moves, say, from one place to another, it must pass through an infinity of intervening points; we must also say that its existence at each of those infinitely many points is logically independent of its existence at every other point. Only then will its motion consist '*merely* in the occupation of different places at different times'. For certain purposes we might want to divide a movement or change into instantaneous existences at points, and say 'At this instant the projectile will be here' or 'At that moment the pumpkin weighed exactly one kilogramme.' But it is hard to believe that these are logically independent momentary events, as we should have to if we want them to be the materials out of which time is constructed. The so-called 'event' of the projectile's being at a point is its passing through that point,[6] and its passing through the point is not so much an event as a non-event, its *not* coming to rest at that point. We can construct a story out of events, but out of non-events nothing can be constructed. Russell's vision of a continuous series of logically independent durationless states of affairs is a picture not of a physical but of a mathematical world. Whatever else they may be, the things that enter into these states of affairs are not physical objects.

Far from rejecting the notion of a state of motion we should recognize it as a notion of a stretch of time, and whereas Russell says 'The concept of motion is logically subsequent to that of occupying a place at a time' (1964, p. 469), the notion of time seems logically subsequent, if not to that of motion specifically, at least to that of change. The concept of an aspect of something is subsequent to that of the thing of which it is an aspect; the concept of a human body, for instance, is logically posterior to that of a human being.

I have been using 'a state of affairs' for what is expressed by a verb of being or having; but we might decide instead to use the phrase for anything that has temporal extension. In that case Russell's existences at instants would not be states of affairs, but a going on of a change would be, and expressing a change as a going on of a process would be expressing it as a state of affairs. 'Columbus was travelling between Europe and America for two months' and 'The water in the kettle was rising in temperature for three minutes' quantify dynamic states of affairs.

* * *

My concern in this chapter is with the relation of time to grammar. Time has been the subject of millions of words of philosophical discussion, and any reader even slightly acquainted with that literature will be aware of many topics I have not discussed and think of questions I have not answered. I cannot deal with these topics and questions here, but I will fill out a couple of grammatical observations I made at the start.

First, we often express change by using verbs of making and doing. In English building and sailing are things we are said to do, and so are pushing, singing, resting and sleeping, though various distinctions are drawn between them. Building is a kind of making, sailing a way of moving, pushing a mode of action, singing an activity, resting a kind of inactivity and so on. Some of these distinctions are unimportant for understanding how time is expressed, but it is useful to recognize that the English word 'action' is used in two related but distinct ways.[7] We call bringing about a change – building a house, for instance, or stabbing an enemy, or taking a friend to the theatre – 'an action'. Using 'action' in this way, we can use it in the plural and speak of performing several actions. But we bring about change by acting, and we use 'action' for such acting. The word used in this way is not used in the plural; we say, not that pushing and swimming are two actions, but that they are two kinds of action. But a phrase like 'Othello's action' is ambiguous. It might refer either to *an* action by Othello, killing Desdemona, or to *the action by which* he killed her, pressing on the pillow.

We build a house or swim a mile *in* a time, and actions like these are processes that are completed in times. On the other hand we act upon things for times; we swim and sing for hours, we are active or inactive for days. Verbs which are used to report actions can also be used to express ways of being active. Building and walking are ways of being active – both, in fact, are exercises of acquired skill – and we are said to build or walk or exercise any skill *for* a time. 'Watch' and 'listen' are not used to report actions – we do not watch *in* a time – but they are used as if they signified ways of acting or being active; we watch or listen for a time. Resting and sleeping are ways of being inactive, and we rest or sleep rather for than in a time.

Secondly I said that perfect tense-forms like 'has built', 'has been building', 'had built', and 'will have been building' express states subsequent to changes. (I ignore here what Comrie (1976, p. 58) calls the 'experiential perfect'.) It is not correct, I think, to say that in 'Palladio has built a villa' we predicate of Palladio a state of having done something. As there is no such property as being red on Monday, so there is no such property as having been red, and no such state as having done something; there are only states that follow upon doing things. If we say 'Palladio has been building a villa for three months,' we say that he is now in a state subsequent upon three months of building. In 'When it's finished he'll have been in Vicenza for three months', we say that he will then be in a state subsequent to being for three months in Vicenza.

10

Causation

From the twelfth century to the fourteenth philosophers in western Europe were obsessed with universals and the meaning of words for things. When grammar gave place to physical science they turned to causation, and agonizing over that culminated with Hume. Hume argues that the things we take to be causes and effects regularly attend each other, but that is all. We see that one object[1] is followed by another, and that objects similar to the first seem always to be followed by objects similar to the second, but we never 'perceive the tie, by which they are united'; ''tis not, then, from any one instance that we arrive at the idea of cause and effect, of a necessary connection, of power, of force, of energy and of efficacy' (*Treatise* 1.3.14, p. 162). Experience 'never gives us any insight into the internal structure or operating principle of objects, but only accustoms the mind to pass from one to another' (p. 169). When we see a new object of the first sort we expect an object of the second, and we project our feeling of expectation onto the objects, and imagine that the first is making the second necessary. He concludes (in opposition to ancient Greek philosophers) 'that all causes are of the same kind' and 'that there is but one kind of necessity' (p. 171).

Hume was pleased with his treatment of causation. He sets it out in the *Treatise*; he presents it as a sort of flagship for his philosophy in the *Abstract*, his anonymous favourable review of that work; and there is a polished restatement of it in the *Enquiry Concerning Human Understanding*. The wit and force with which he writes entitle him to the credit he has received for exorcising the ghost of causation from the universe, but he stands in a long tradition. Berkeley had said in 1710: 'Whoever shall attend to his ideas, whether of sense or reflexion, will not perceive in them any power or activity; there is therefore no such thing contained in them' (1964b, p. 51). Hume's principal source was probably Malebranche (1638–1715), whose works will have been readily available to him during the three years he spent in France in his 20s composing the *Treatise*, and whom he several times cites by name. It is not hard to find the bases of his argument in Locke and Descartes. Etienne Gilson shows how it was anticipated by Franciscan theologians in the thirteenth and fourteenth centuries, and by Muslim theologians in the tenth and eleventh (1937, chapter 3).[2] Hume will not have been acquainted with Muslim philosophers like Al Ashari (873–935) and still less with the extensive writings on causation by early Hindu and Buddhist thinkers. But he does claim acquaintance with the Pyrrhonians (*Enquiries* p. 158) and their spokesman Sextus Empiricus preserves plenty of sceptical arguments (*Outlines of Pyrrhonism* 3, 13–29; *Against the Physicists* 1, 207–79).

In this chapter I first describe the place causation actually has in our thinking, and distinguish three uses we make of the English word 'cause'. We use it for causal agents, for the action by which they bring about or prevent change, and for the conditions under which this action is effective. Aristotle is sometimes said to distinguish four sorts of cause; but the words he uses, *aition* and *aitia*, are better translated 'explanation' or 'responsible factor' than 'cause', and his distinction is rather between ways of being responsible or senses of 'explain' than between kinds of thing that explain in a single sense. What we call '*causal responsibility*' he classes as one way of being responsible as a *source of change*. Collingwood (1939, chapter 29) undertook to distinguish three senses of the English word 'cause', but they are different from mine. A cause in his first sense is a deliberate act affording someone 'a motive for doing something'; a cause in his second is intentional action in order to cause or prevent; and a cause in his third is an event that renders something physically necessary. I would call the first 'providing a reason' rather than 'causing', and I would class both the second and third under causal action.

Next I look at the constructions by which we attribute a change to something as the agent responsible, and explain a change by the action responsible. In neither case, I argue, do we make use of a special concept of causing; rather we make special uses of ordinary concepts of modes of action and properties things acquire and lose. I complete this positive account with some remarks on preventing as distinct from causing.

Finally I try to explain how philosophers became perplexed by causation, and how they replaced the notion of causing by the notion of continuation.

* * *

In Chapter 9 I considered how change is expressed in the indicative, but perhaps it is primarily expressed in the imperative moods, since it comes into our thought when we think properties good or bad. To think of a property as good for something, as I said in Chapter 7, is to think it would be good for the thing to acquire it or bad for it to lose it. We *believe* properties to be had or lacked, we *want* them to be acquired or lost. And if we think it would be good for some object to acquire a property, or bad for it to lose it, we think it would be right to cause that object to acquire it, and wrong to cause it to lose it; also that it would be wrong to prevent the object from acquiring it, and right to prevent it from losing it. The notions of causing and preventing are therefore built into human desire and aversion.

They are also built into counsels and commands. Although we tell children to be quiet, and advise our friends not to be silly or naive, it is really a waste of breath to order a person to *be* something. We can sensibly order or forbid people only to *do* things, and *being* something is not a thing we *do*. Children can be told to become quiet, or to stop making a noise, and friends can be advised to refrain from foolish acts, or exhorted to acquire experience and prudence. It is a presupposition of giving any counsel or command that the person addressed is capable of causing or preventing change.

The most primitive human beings of whom we have any trace had skills of the sophisticated type we call 'arts' or 'crafts'. The term 'skill' may be applied to any ability to bring about a desired result on purpose. Controlling our hands and feet are skills in this sense; so are the abilities to recognize objects of different kinds by sight and hearing. Skills are acquired, not inherited, but they may be acquired unconsciously. We learn to move our hands and feet in the womb; we learn to identify human beings by sight and hearing at a very early age; our genetic inheritance makes it easy and natural to acquire basic skills, and if animals teach their offspring skills by instinct, so, presumably, do we. More or less consciously we learn to achieve desired effects by using parts of our body: to move swiftly over the ground by using our legs, to make a variety of significant noises by using our vocal organs. More consciously still we learn to bring about changes in objects by acting upon them in various ways, either with our hands and feet or with sticks, stones and manufactured tools. Learning how to do this is acquiring an art, and arts are usually imparted to us deliberately by other people, with the aid of speech and example. Pottery, tool-making, shelter-building and medicine are arts of this kind; so are hunting and agriculture.

Anyone who acquires or imparts an art must think that we can bring about a change we desire, or prevent one to which we are averse, by a period of action. It must also be understood that the efficacy of our action is conditional, that there are conditions under which it will or won't be effective. In every society, then, in which arts are acquired and transmitted there are three causal notions. We have the notion of a causal agent, a person or thing that can bring about or prevent change; we have the notion of causal action, action by which an agent brings about or prevents a specified change; and we have the notion of a causal condition, a condition under which the action will be effective or preventive of the change. Lakoff and Johnson are right in saying: 'It is conscious volitional human agency acting via direct physical force that is at the center of our concept of causation' (1999, p. 177). Unfortunately they fail (see pp. 377–9) to distinguish between analysing our modern concept of causation and the ancient Greek project of distinguishing different concepts we have of explanation.

An artist is an intelligent agent, and the action of an artist is intentional, but it is not part of the notion of causal action which we need for acquiring or practising an art, that it should be intentional, or that causal agents should do things on purpose. The causal notions which prevail wherever arts exist are notions that can be applied quite generally: to inanimate objects and to their action as well as to human beings and animals.

Natural science as we understand it today started with applying them to natural phenomena. The ancient Greeks applied them first to arresting phenomena like eclipses, earthquakes and rainbows. They asked what agents cause them, and by what action upon what. Scientists go on to ask this about more ordinary occurrences like the changes undergone by leaves in autumn. And they also ask a question which artists do not ask: they ask why causal action is effective. It is enough for a potter to know that he can cause his pot to become hard by putting it in an oven. If this action is not effective, he will enquire why; perhaps some condition that is usually satisfied is not satisfied on this occasion, for instance the supply of electricity to his oven is not connected. But it is no business of the potter to know why it is that hardening of clay results from heating, whereas softening of wax results from the same action; that is a question for the scientist.

We say that a dropped cigarette or a careless smoker was the cause of the forest fire, meaning it was responsible as a causal agent. We say the smoker's dropping of his cigarette, or the cigarette's heating some grass, caused the fire, meaning it was the causal action responsible. And we say that the dryness of the grass was the cause, meaning it was a condition without which the action would have been ineffective or insufficient.

* * *

The notions of a causal agent, causal action and a causal condition are found in every society and appear perfectly clear.

Causal conditions are very straightforward. They are states of affairs like grass's being dry or the presence of air in a container or the falling of rain. In English we can give something as a causal condition by using a conjunction like 'because' or a conditional construction. 'Striking the match', we might say, 'caused it to light *because* there was air', or 'If the grass hadn't been dry your dropping your cigarette wouldn't have caused the forest fire.' A state of affairs causes something as a condition simply by existing. Philosophers find nothing puzzling in this, and in fact show little interest in causal conditions, either because they do not feel they are genuine causes, or because they do not distinguish them from causal agents. The absence of a steersman might be a causal condition of the wind's driving a boat onto the rocks, but as Aristotle observes, we should say that the steersman is responsible for this disaster as a causal agent, either by not preventing it or by leaving his post (*Physics* 2 195a11–14). I mention causal conditions only for the sake of completeness.

A causal agent is a material object like a human being or the Sun, and it causes a change by acting, by doing something. There are various ways of saying that something caused a change as a causal agent. We can use a verb that signifies causing a specific change, as in 'Odysseus blinded Polyphemus', 'The Sun melted the butter', 'The stone broke the glass', 'The ceiling was blackened by smoke'. The verb 'to blind' means 'make unable to see'; 'melt', 'break' and 'blacken', used transitively, mean 'cause to become liquid', 'cause to become fragmented', 'cause to become black'. In the first three examples the change in the object (the thing designated by the object-expression) is attributed to the subject by the active voice, and in the fourth a change in the ceiling is attributed to the smoke by the passive voice. In French, instead of verbs like 'blind' and 'blacken' we can use 'faire' with a predicate-term like *aveugle* or *noir*. In Marquesan, which has no verb like 'make' or 'faire', we prefix *haka* or *ha'a* to a predicate-term.

Alternatively we may use a verb like 'push' or 'pull' which simply specifies a mode of acting, and add a phrase to specify the change effected, for instance 'He pushed the barrow *half a mile*', 'She pulled me *out of the river*'. Here a change in the barrow or in me is attributed to the subject, and 'half a mile' and 'out of the river' specify the change. Pulling me out of the river is causing me to leave the river.

Or again, we may use a verb for causing something to come into being, as in 'Mrs Beeton baked a cake'. Here what is attributed to Mrs Beeton as causal agent responsible is not a change in the object. Coming into being is not a change in what comes into being and, in our sentence, though the words 'a cake' form the grammatical object of 'built', they are not a referring expression as they are in 'Mrs Beeton iced a cake'. The coming into being of a cake is a change in the ingredients. In 'Mrs Beeton baked a cake' we do not refer to those ingredients, but the coming of something into being is a kind of occurrence, and we attribute to Mrs Beeton the coming into being of a thing of the sort signified by 'cake'.

Attributing to something a mode of action like running or pushing is a very simple kind of linguistic act, bare predication. Ascribing a change or an occurrence to something as the agent responsible is a more sophisticated act, and my examples show, I hope, that it requires more complicated procedures such as using a verb transitively or adding *haka*. Causal agency is what is expressed by these procedures. To understand them is to know, not *how* to cause change, but *what it is to do so as an agent*.

I said that the question 'Is there a difference between being red and becoming red?' is hard to answer. 'Is there a difference between becoming red and being made red?' has, I think, a negative answer. On Russell's atomistic view of change, for a thing to become red is simply for it to be red after not being red, so the notion of becoming is untainted by any notion of causation. But I criticized the atomistic view as such, and even if it were unobjectionable, becoming would still require identity. It must be the *same* thing that earlier isn't red and later is. If what is later red has not been *made* red, how can it be identical with what was earlier not red?

When we say that a change is going on we use a continuous present: 'The plums are becoming ripe.' Vendler (1957, p. 145) says that such statements are covertly predictive: we say the plums will go on changing in flavour till they reach ripeness. Thompson (2012, p. 126) disputes this, and it is better to view them as covertly causal: we say that a change to that flavour is being caused in them. It is significant that the English suffix 'en' may be expressive either of becoming, 'They are ripening', or of causing, 'The sun is ripening them.'

But though there is no difference between becoming ripe and being made ripe, there is a difference between saying that something is ripening, using the verb intransitively, and saying it is being ripened, using the passive. The constructions for attributing a change in something to that thing as something it undergoes are different from those for attributing a change in one thing to a second as something caused in it by that second thing. Learning how to say that one thing made another ripe is not learning a word for a new thing, *making*, but learning a new construction in which to use a vocabulary item you already know, 'ripe'. To put this in terms of thought rather than speech, if I know what ripeness is, thinking that the Sun is making a plum ripe is not using a new concept of causal agency, but using my concept of the ripeness in a new way, as the concept of an effect.

* * *

Agents bring about changes by periods of causal action. Michelangelo causes a likeness of David to come into being by chipping marble for many days. The Sun makes the butter melt by bombarding it for an hour with its rays. Causal action does not cause change in the way an agent does; instead it *is* the causing of the change by the agent. What is it for a period of action to be that? What is it for it to be efficacious? This is the question 'concerning the efficacy of causes' which Hume called 'one of the most sublime questions in philosophy' (*Treatise* 1.3.14, p. 156). The change that is caused, the thing we want to explain, will be either a process or the beginning or end of a process. Whatever action is the causing of a process of change from one state or place to another is the causing also of the beginning and completing of that process. Every process takes time, and a period of action is the causing of the process when it *is* that time, when it is *the going on* of that process.

Put in these abstract terms, that sounds complicated and paradoxical. But a sculptor causes a statue to come into being out of a block of marble by chipping away at the block for a month if it was *that month of chipping* which was the going on of the change in the block. In this case it is hard to think what else could be the going on of the change. In general, that action is the cause of a change which is the going on or taking place of that change; and since the going on of a change is its temporal extension or time, for action to be the cause of a change is for it to be the time of that change.

Time is of practical significance in that it is a cause, that it brings things to birth and destroys things. It does so not as a causal agent but as the action of agents. The time that blunts the lion's paws is the time for which stones and other material objects are acting upon them. Any time stretch is the going on of some process, and any going on of a process is the causing of some change. A period of time may be expressed either in the active voice or in the passive. We may speak of an hour of pushing or an hour of being pushed, an hour of heating or an hour of being heated, but in either case it is spoken of as a period of causal action.

I am saying that every piece of causal action is a time-stretch, and every time-stretch is a piece of causal action. The first claim may seem uncontroversial. Odysseus caused Polyphemus to become blind by thrusting a heated stake into his eye and twirling it, we are told, as a carpenter twirls a drill: obviously a prolonged piece of acting. Enlightenment philosophers, however, were fascinated by the less gruesome example of causal action provided by billiard balls. Malebranche (*Éclaircissements*, 15) says: 'When I see a boule qui en choque une autre, my eyes tell me, or seem to tell me, that it is truly cause of the movement it impresses', but reason says otherwise. So too Locke (*Essay* 2.21.4), Hume (*Treatise* 1.3.14, p. 164; *Abstract*, 1951, pp. 252–3; *Enquiries*, pp. 28, 63), and Berkeley notes: 'Doctrines of liberty, prescience etc explain'd by Billiard balls' (1964a, p. 21). One billiard ball rolls up to a second, hits it, and the second moves off. The philosophical onlooker sees the first ball set the second in motion, but does not see by what action it makes it move. I am told by scientists that the first ball pushes on the second and deforms it, presses it out of shape; and the second ball starts to move as it resumes its shape. This takes place so quickly that the player doesn't see it; nevertheless there is this short period of action by which the first ball makes the second ball start to move.

Against the claim that every time-stretch is a piece of causal action, it might be argued that states of affairs can go on for a time. If an unopened letter lies on my desk for a week, must its week on my desk be the causing of anything? It is a week of pressing gently on the desk and, as I said in Chapter 9, it is a state of affairs measurable in time-units only in so far as the letter's ceasing to change and its starting to change once more are events simultaneous with the beginning and end of some process that is caused, like the movement of clock-hands.

Uniform motion in empty space is in itself a state of affairs: it is not a change in the moving body but a staying unchanged in velocity. The motion, however, must be relative to something and, if not to Newton's Absolute Space, to some material body. Say a spaceship is moving away from Saturn at 100 miles an hour. Then an hour of its uniform motion may be given as the cause of a 100 mile increase in the distance between it and Saturn (and perhaps a proportional weakening of the force of gravity between the two).

In Chapter 9 I said that a process that begins, ends and goes on is not a different thing from its going on; rather the same thing, the same change, may be expressed either as a process or as a going on. Expressed as a process, it is expressed as something that can be given a causal explanation. Expressed as a going on of a process it is expressed as something that can be given *as* a causal explanation, but not as something that can itself be explained causally. I can ask 'What caused the wagon to start moving?' 'What made it stop?' 'By what action was it moved a distance of 50 yards?' It is not English to ask 'What made it *be moving for 30 seconds*?' or 'What caused it to *be moving 50 yards*?'

It is the same with other changes. We can ask 'What caused that tomato to become red?', that is, 'What was the cause of its becoming red?', but not 'What caused it to be becoming red?', which would be 'What was the cause of its *being becoming* red?'

This is a grammatical point, and a similar point may be made about desire and about imperative moods. I said that a change is an object of desire or aversion: we desire or are averse to changes. A change, however, is an object of desire thought of as a process, or as the beginning or end of a process, not as a going on of a process. You can say: 'I want those tomatoes to become red' or 'to start becoming red' or 'I don't want them to stop becoming red' but it is odd English to say 'I want them to be becoming red'. You can say 'I *hope* they're becoming red', but hoping and wishing are different from desiring. Oedipus first hoped and then wished he hadn't killed his father, but grammar forbids his saying 'I desire not to have killed Laius'. Desire and aversion are expressed in ordering or forbidding, and in ordering or forbidding changes we express them as processes, not as goings on of processes. 'Drink me', says Alice's bottle, not 'Be drinking me'; 'Don't steal', Moses tells us, not (unless he is attempting Irish) 'Don't be stealing'.

It might be thought that these are peculiarities of English, with no general significance. But languages which have very different grammars have comparable constructions expressing the same distinctions. Marquesan, for example, which has no verbs of being and becoming, has a word, *'i'o* for passing to a state and a prefix, *ha'a*, for making. Where we say 'The fruit is becoming ripe' Marquesans would say *E 'i'o ana pa'a te puku*, 'Passing now to ripe, the fruit', and where we should say 'I want the fruit to become ripe' they would not use *'i'o* but say *O tu'u hia e ha'apa'a tia te puku*, 'My desire, to be made ripe, the fruit'.[3] As for importance, the distinction between the two ways of expressing a change is, I believe, the key to the notions of cause and effect. Our notion of a piece of causal action is the notion of something expressed as a going on of a process, and our notion of an effect is that of something expressed as a process that begins, ends and goes on. These two modes of expression are not, in themselves, causal. The first occurs in true or false statements, the second in counsels and commands; and making statements and giving orders are linguistic acts different from explaining causally. We explain a change causally in giving a period of action as the going on of that change, and we do that by using an explanatory construction: perhaps a conjunction like 'because' ('The wheelbarrow moved 50 yards *because* I pushed it for a time') or an adverbial phrase ('I moved it 50 yards *by* pushing'). But using an explanatory construction is not applying a concept of a special, elusive thing, causing. It is using concepts of ordinary things, open to investigation by non-philosophers, in a way philosophers find elusive.

Action can cause change but it can also prevent it. Let me supplement my account of what it is for action to cause with a word about prevention.

Is preventing a genuine alternative to causing, or is it the causing of something negative, causing something *not* to occur? Is it a kind of causal action which differs from other kinds in what it is a causing of? There are several reasons for recognizing bringing about and preventing as distinct causal concepts.

First, if preventing a change is causing its non-occurrence, causing it should be causing its occurrence. Now McTaggart thought that occurrence, or becoming actual, is a kind of superchange that befalls changes. Though he does not use the comparison, it is rather like *entering*, which is a superchange that befalls characters in tragedies, as contrasted with being murdered, which is an ordinary change befalling them enacted by actors. If occurring is indeed a kind of change, it will make sense to talk of causing an occurrence. But construing occurrence as a change changes undergo is multiplying entities as prodigally as making existence a property acquired or possessed by objects. It is thriftier to say that causing is from the start causing-to-occur. We can still say, if we like, that preventing is causing not to occur. But if causing as such is causing-to-occur, *causing not to occur* is not causing-to-occur something called 'non-occurrence', an even more problematic event in the lives of changes than occurrence; causing not to occur must from the start be causing-not-to-occur. That is, causing-to-occur and causing-not-to-occur are different ways in which we think agents and modes of action are related to changes;[4] we do not think that there is single way, causing, in which action can be related to two things, changes and non-changes or occurrences and non-occurrences.

Moreover the concept of bringing about differs formally from the concept of preventing. That emerges when we consider time. Causal action is temporally extended. We push or heat for a time. Changes are brought about *in* a time. A ten-degree rise in the soup's temperature is caused-to-occur *in* 30 seconds *by* 30 seconds of heating over a fire. But changes are prevented *for* a time. A ten-degree fall in the room's temperature is caused-not-to-occur for an hour by an hour of central heating. To take another example, a 200-mile movement of my car from London to York is caused in four hours *by* four hours of action on the controls. Perhaps having reached York my car rests there for a week. But in acting on the controls for four hours between London and York I do not cause it to stay in York for a week. I merely cause it to move to York *in* four hours and arrive *after* four hours. On the other hand suppose I have cancer and my doctor treats me for a month. If he hadn't treated me, the cancer would have killed me in a month. So he prevents the cancer from, in a month, causing my death. But he does not, *in* a month, prevent my dying; he, *for* a month, prevents it.

But given that the concept of preventing is irreducible to that of causing, is there any serious purpose for which we need it, or is it just a fussy luxury like the battlements on a Victorian house? There are at least two purposes for which we need it. First, the notions of causing and preventing are bound up, as I said, with those of desire and aversion, and we need them to understand purposive behaviour. For purposive action not only causes some changes and prevents others: it is *for the purpose of* causing some of the changes it causes and preventing some of those it prevents. Secondly, we need the notion of prevention to analyse the concept of a fundamental physical force. Although we talk of gravitational pull, there is no action of pulling by which the earth causes a stone to fall; nor is there any action of pushing by which two magnets get further apart. Rather something must act on the stone to prevent its falling, act on the magnets to keep them together. Fundamental forces are measured by the force needed to prevent objects from moving towards or away from each other. If we think that physical action can only be causing we shall find ourselves foxed by the fundamental forces. We could say that force is needed to cause the non-occurrence of certain movements, but that dark utterance leaves us wondering what causes their occurrence if the inhibitory force is removed.

* * *

That completes my positive account; how did philosophers come to find causation perplexing?

In the first place, they did not distinguish between causal agents, causal action and causal conditions. That was partly because they thought that we never perceive, or have any direct access to, physical objects, physical action or physical states of affairs. The only things with which, as Russell puts it, we are actually *acquainted*, are Humean 'objects', sensations and mental representations; all else is shaky inference and conjecture; and Humean objects are neither agents nor action nor conditions. But philosophers also assumed that if 'cause' means anything it must mean the same thing for agents and for their action. Agents obviously cause things by acting. Odysseus caused Polyphemus to become blind by thrusting in the glowing stake and twirling it. So if the thrusting and twirling are to cause Polyphemus to become blind, they must do something in their turn. It was this further exertion of force that eluded the philosophers, and no wonder. An agent's action is what connects the agent with changes the agent brings about. Despite what Bradley (1902, chapter 2) thought, nothing has to connect a connection with the things it connects. A rope connects a boat to a bollard; at most a knot connects the rope to the boat and the bollard, and a knot is not a further rope.

The search for something causal action does to produce effects comes to a dead end. To find a positive account of the relationship between causal action and its effects philosophers looked to continuity. Newton's first law of motion is that a body in motion keeps moving uniformly unless something acts upon it: causal action is needed to prevent its continuing to move, but no causal explanation is needed for its continuing. It seems that if we can show that one process is just a continuation of another, in the way the movement of a projectile beyond a point on its path is a continuation of its movement up to that point, then although we haven't given a causal explanation of this further movement, we have shown it does not need a causal explanation; and that is as good as explaining it causally. Enlightenment philosophers believed that the only genuine properties of material objects were extension in three dimensions, shape and motion or velocity. This doctrine, which makes a debut in Plato's *Timaeus*, was forgotten in the later middle ages when Aristotelian science held the field, but it was rediscovered, so to speak, by Galileo, Descartes (*Principles of Philosophy*, Oeuvres 8-1, pp. 42, 52–4) and Boyle, and reflected the actual practice of the best physical scientists in the seventeenth century. The philosophers of the time consequently thought that all change is mere redistribution of motion, a matter of the passing of motion from one body to another.

The billiard table is a more or less closed mechanical system in which, once a player has set a ball in motion, all the subsequent states of the system can be predicted with great accuracy.[5] The movements of the balls after each impact can be explained as a mere continuation of their movements before. This came to be seen as a paradigm of scientific explanation. Later states of the system, later locations and states of motion of the balls, are a logical deduction from earlier states together with laws framed in terms well defined in physical science. In explanations of this sort, no appeal is made to causal action or causal powers. Their explanatory work is done by general descriptive laws, by statements, that is, of what always happens. So long as we are content with explanations like this, a Humean conception of causation is all we need. Intelligent behaviour is explained scientifically if it can be shown that the movements we make in speaking, writing and doing anything on purpose are in fact continuations of processes which start outside our bodies and are themselves continuations of processes going back to the Big Bang (or going back for ever, if time has no beginning).

J. L. Mackie (1974, p. 221) argued for 'extensions of the concept of causing to include both the persistence of objects, and the persistence of self-maintaining processes' (processes like the spinning of a top), saying that 'in both of them we could regard an earlier phase as a cause and a later phase as an effect'. That is, the existence of Mars, for instance, between the Battle of Hastings and the Battle of Waterloo, could be regarded as the cause of its existence between the Battle of Waterloo and the detonation of the Hiroshima bomb; and the uniform movement of a spaceship from one point far distant from the Earth to a second further point could be given as the cause of its movement from the second to a third further still.

Mackie's extensions of the notion of causation are very hard to take: how can an earlier period possibly be the cause of a later? The supposition that a cause must be earlier than its effect was challenged in antiquity, by Aristotle (*Posterior Analytics* 2 95a22–b1) and authors summarized by Sextus Empiricus (e.g. *Outlines* 3 16; 3 25), who thought that any effective causal action must be contemporaneous with its effect. It is more tolerable to say that the end of a process is the cause of the beginning of any process which is continuous with it. These events are not successive but simultaneous and, indeed, identical. To take the billiard balls, the first ball's coming into contact with the second, which is the end of its movement up to the second, is the beginning of the second ball's being dented or deformed. There is no time interval between these events; and we might say 'The first ball made the second move by coming into contact with it at ten feet per second.' But there remains a major difficulty. According to Enlightenment philosophy of physics, physical objects have only geometrical properties and motion. Geometry tells us nothing about what will happen if one sphere comes into contact with another of the same size. Why should the second be deformed? Why shouldn't the first pass straight through it? The communication of motion, therefore, remains, in Locke's words, 'obscure and unconceivable' (*Essay* 2.23.28).

The belief that we are 'acquainted' only with sensations and mental images is supported by bad arguments like those in the first chapters of Russell (1912) and Ayer (1964), but really arises, I think, from the irrational thinking identified by Wittgenstein (*BB*, pp. 160, 174). The idea that if causal action is to cause anything it must do so by further acting is an instance of philosophical double vision, but also an instance of confusing a grammatical concept with a physical. There are real modes of action by which an agent brings about an effect, and these may be said to constitute a real physical relationship between the agent and the effect. There is no such relation between causal action and an effect. The feeling of philosophers that there ought to be one is betrayed by the incautious way in which they speak of causation as a relation. 'Of cause and effect and other relations', Locke entitles chapter 26 of his *Essay*, Book 2. At the beginning of his *Treatise* (1.1.5, p. 15) Hume says: 'which relation of cause and effect is a seventh philosophical relation, as well as a natural one'. And in his *Enquiries* (p. 26) he says: 'All reasonings concerning matter of fact seem to be founded on the relation of *Cause and Effect*.'

I argued that the causal action by which a change is caused is the going on of that change. In many causal explanations what we give as the agent's action is not in fact the going on of the change caused but something earlier like a murderer's putting poison in a bottle or pulling a trigger. Davidson (1982c, pp. 149–62) gives as an example of a 'causal statement': 'The short circuit caused the fire.' Here the coming into contact of the wires was probably the beginning of the fire. Nevertheless in cases where the agent's acting is the rendering necessary of the effect (and philosophers want genuine causing to be making necessary) it is the going on of the change caused. The going on of any process is, as such, the rendering of it logically necessary. It is not logically necessary that any bit of acting is the going on of any particular process; that is something to be established empirically. We sometimes bring about a change we desire without knowing exactly which of the things we did was the causing of it. But the particular bit of acting which is the going on of a particular process is, we may say, the rendering of that process *physically* necessary.

It is not wrong to speak of a 'relationship' between a going on of a particular process and the process of which it is a going on. But this is not a physical relationship. It is like the relationship between an object and its shape or movement, or between a specimen and that of which it is a specimen. *Being* is not a relationship between a thing and what it *is*, and *being a going on of* is not a relationship of a time-stretch to a process of which it is a going on. To be a going on of a process is, in fact, to be an instance or specimen of that process. Objects and the things they are or do are distinguished by language, and the relation between them is expressed by predicative constructions. Processes and goings on of processes are likewise distinguished by language. In saying 'I moved the wheelbarrow by pushing it' or 'The wheelbarrow moved because I pushed it' I use separate words for the wheelbarrow's change of place and for my action of pushing. And I say that my pushing was an instance in the wheelbarrow (or an example by the wheelbarrow) of the change of place. I do this not by a predicative but by an explanatory construction. We say that it was *by certain action* that an agent brought about some event, that it was *because of some period* of acting that the event took place. Whereas a causal agent acquires, through acting, a real relation to the effect of that acting, causal action is related to what it effects only in language, by the grammar of explanatory utterances. The search for a real relationship between the two is bound to fail.

There is no need here to spell out different forms of negation in causal explanation, but it may be worthwhile to emphasize that grammar supplies a variety of causal constructions: bare parataxis, parataxis with a connective like 'and' or 'so', the use of a conjunction like 'because' or *cum* with the subjunctive, a preposition like 'by' with a verbal noun, an adverbial phrase like the ablative absolute, and so on. Languages generally have a good deal of ambiguity, and grammarians have to flag different meanings of the same inflections of case or mood, and say when certain connectives express causation and when they express other things like temporal relations or purpose.

Scepticism about causation is similar to scepticism about goodness. Philosophers think that if anything is to be objectively good or bad, goodness must be a real property or predicate; since there is no such real property, they conclude that it is an illusion that anything is really good or bad. They think that if any action is really to be the cause of anything, there must be a real relation between the action and what it allegedly causes; since there is no such real relation, they conclude that it is an illusion that anything really causes anything. In actual fact agents really bring about change by acting, and their action really is the going on of the changes they bring about. But the word 'cause' itself does not signify any real action. We use it to explain the meaning of the constructions by which we attribute changes to the agents causally responsible – transitive use of verbs, of verbs of making, and so on – and to the action that is the causing of them.

11

Materiality

Natural science differs from art in two ways. First, scientists apply the causal concepts we use in the arts and crafts to natural phenomena. That gives rise to no philosophical problems. Secondly they ask why causal action which is agreed to be effective does in fact do the trick. Why, for example, is clay made harder by heating, and wax softer? Philosophers found these questions puzzling because they thought the scientists must be asking by what action the *act* produces the effect, a question we have seen to be unanswerable. But why did they think the scientists must be asking this question? Partly from a defective concept of materiality. For the answer to questions of this sort lies in the material of which the agent and the thing affected are composed. The action of the first of the billiard balls is the cause of the second's starting to move, not because it, the first ball's action, does something, but because the balls are composed of ivory, an elastic material. Holding the poker in the fire is causing it to become red because it is composed of iron.

Although Berkeley was the first Enlightenment thinker to deny explicitly that there is such a thing as matter, Descartes denied this implicitly in saying:

> The substance which is the immediate subject of extension in space (*extensionis localis*) and of the properties (*accidentium*) that presuppose extension, such as shape, situation, movement etc., is called body. (*Replies to the second set of objections, Oeuvres* 7, pp. 161–2)

> The nature of matter, or body viewed in general, consists not in being something hard or heavy or coloured or in any other way affecting the senses, but solely in being something extended in length, breadth and depth. (*Principles of Philosophy* 2.4, *Oeuvres* 8-1, p. 42)

Descartes identifies being a material thing with being a body, and then identifies being a body with being extended, tacitly dropping its corporeality. Plato in the *Timaeus* had run the speculation that bodies consist of regular three-dimensional figures such as cubes and tetrahedra projected in space rather like modern holograms; they are composed, if they can be said to be composed of anything, of space, *khôra* (literally 'room' as in 'please leave room for me'). Descartes's view is exactly the same, except that his basic particles are not all constructed out of right-angled triangles as Plato's were. Both see bodies as objects not of physics but of solid geometry. Locke tried to retain for bodies what he called 'solidity', a power of a body to exclude other bodies from the place it occupies. In this he was well inspired; he was groping for the idea of a fundamental repulsive force. But it slipped through his fingers – Rom Harré (1970, pp. 285–9) gives the credit for discerning the need for it to R. J. Boscovich (1711–87)[1] – and solidity faded from the philosophical picture when philosophers abandoned hope of finding any clear notion of causal power.

'Matter' is our translation of the Greek word *hulê*, which originally signified wood (wood in its unworked state, as distinct from beams or planks), but which Aristotle appropriated as a technical term. He started from the idea (already stated pretty clearly by Plato, *Phaedo* 70e) that anything that comes into being does so *out of* something. Bedsteads come into being out of wood, pots out of clay, cakes out of eggs, butter and flour; and these things may be called the matter, or materials, respectively of the bedsteads, pots and cakes. Oaks and human beings come into being out of seeds, gametes and other inconspicuous materials, and substances like water and air have materials of their own out of which they arise. In bedsteads and houses the material out of which the thing arises is clearly still present in it throughout its existence; in cakes and human beings it is not. Nevertheless in such cases there is something of which the thing is composed or by which it is constituted. The Aristotelian notion of matter extends to these components or constituents; it can even be extended to what a container like a bottle contains.

Have these materials anything in common besides being things 'out of which' other things arise? Aristotle assigns to them an explanatory role. They are that in virtue of which a thing causes changes in other things and has changes caused in itself by certain action. The wax of which a candle is composed is that in the candle by virtue of which we can make it liquid by heating it. It is what accounts for the fact that heating, or being heated, is the going on in it of a change from solid to liquid. The wood in a war club is that in the club which accounts for the fact that bringing it down on your enemy's head is causing his skull to become cracked; if it arose simply out of wool your blow would be ineffective.

When the material out of which something arises is not plainly present in the thing, when, in fact, it has passed away, as the gametes of the human embryo pass away when fertilization takes place, it may be thought that they cannot play this explanatory role. In that case the material of which the object *is* composed plays this role. In us, for instance, our flesh and bones account for the fact that if you prick us we bleed. But flesh and bone are able to play this role because of the materials out of which they arise – the food consumed, and ultimately the gametes, which, scientists tell us, contain our parents' DNA, without which flesh and bones would not develop in the embryo. For a cake to come into being out of eggs, butter, sugar and flour, is not for the eggs and the rest to pass away into nothing and for a cake to come into being out of nothing in the same place without a time-interval. To say the cake comes into being out of the ingredients is to say that it has roughly the same mass as the ingredients, the same liability to be affected by action upon it and the same ability to nourish. The development of a human embryo is more complicated than the baking of a cake, but it results in human limbs because the material of the embryo arises from human parents. Something which has passed away can still account for the efficacy of causal action, if it is action upon, or by, *that into which* it has passed away; since it is has not passed away into nothing but into that thing.

Discussing words like 'gold', 'wine' and 'air' in Chapter 6, I said that though they may be used as complements of 'is', they do not signify properties that may be had or lacked. They are used primarily in existential statements, and when they are used predicatively, the statement is still often existential in meaning; 'That's wine' often means the same as 'There's wine there'. I also said that the presence of a material like wine is of practical significance, and that when you say of me 'He thought it was wine' you are not so much attributing a definite thought to me as giving an abridged explanation of my behaviour, perhaps my drinking the stuff. When we act intentionally we not only have a purpose; we are exercising causal knowledge or skill and we think our action will be effective. If you say of me 'He thinks the object is composed of wood,' you explain my behaviour in so far as that behaviour is an application of causal knowledge or skill. You say why, for instance, I think that if the object is placed on a fire it will go up in flames and turn to ashes. If you say 'He thinks that the bottle contains wine' you explain why I think that drinking it will cheer me up or make me dozy. To be composed of ivory, or to contain petrol, is to be liable to being changed by certain action, and capable of changing other things in certain ways if they in their turn are composed of certain material. What is composed of ivory has a certain elasticity, and is therefore set in motion by certain action. To contain petrol is to be liable to explode.

From the earliest times natural scientists have thought of themselves as investigating causal powers. Although in the *Timaeus* Plato tries to mathematicize physics, elsewhere he endorses a view reflected in the Hippocratic treatise known as *Ancient Medicine*:

> See what Hippocrates and the truth say about nature. Is not this the way in which we should think about any nature? First, we see if that about which we wish to make ourselves skilful (*tekhnikoi*) or teach someone else to be capable, is some one thing or several in kind (*polueides*), and then, if it is one, to look at its power, and see what it is naturally such as to do to what, and to undergo by the action of what. (*Phaedrus* 270c-d)

Locke observes:

> Powers make up a great part of our complex ideas of substances. He that will examine his complex idea of gold will find several of its ideas that make it up to be only powers, as the power of being melted, but of not spending itself in the fire; of being dissolved in Aqua Regia; are ideas as necessary to make up our complex idea of gold as its colour and weight. (*Essay* 2.23.10)

But unfortunately it turned out that we have no idea of power. Locke concedes at the start that 'we have but a very obscure idea of an active power of moving in bodies' (*Essay* 2.21.4), and he soon admits that 'the communication of motion by impulse … is as obscure and unconceivable as how our minds move or stop our bodies by thought' (*Essay* 2.23.28).[2] And Hume, of course, declares 'There is no part of matter that does ever, by its sensible qualities, discover any power or energy; … external objects as they appear to the senses give us no idea of power' (*Enquiries* pp. 63–4).

How did philosophers convince themselves of this? In the first place, they thought that causal powers, if they exist, must be qualities. This idea goes back at least to Aristotle's great commentator, Alexander of Aphrodisias. Unlike us, but like early Greek thinkers, he took fire to be a kind of natural substance like water and air, and he says:

> Fire is a natural simple body, and its form is heat and dryness and the lightness that arises from them and supervenes on them; its matter is what underlies these things which, being in its own nature none of these things is receptive alike of them and their contraries [sc. coldness and wetness]; and it is because it has this nature that the simple bodies [sc. fire, air, water and earth] change into one another. Neither of them [neither the matter of fire nor its form] is a body, but what is composed of them is already a body, having for nature and form lightness, the source of its upward movement. For how could lightness move all by itself, being a property of something else and not a thing existing on its own? Lightness is a power of the body that has it. (*De Anima*, p. 5, lines 4–14)

Similarly Locke says that the qualities which are found that are in bodies are of three sorts, of which powers are the third (*Essay* 2.8.23). 'Hardness, friability and the power to draw iron, we say, are qualities to be found in a loadstone' (*Essay* 2.23.3).

'Friable' and 'soluble' are adjectives with a grammar superficially, at least, similar to that of 'yellow', 'round' and 'angular', and in Wittgenstein's words (*BB* 7), 'When words in our ordinary language have prima facie analogous grammars we are inclined to interpret them analogously; i.e. we try to make the analogy hold throughout.' Locke and his successors, then, thought that causal powers, if they exist, must be properties we can predicate of things; and they took shapes and colours as paradigms of properties. That already ensured that they would fail to find ideas of power. For properties like shape can only modify the effect of causal action that is already efficacious; the shapes of billiard balls and billiard tables explain why balls when struck move in straight lines; they do not explain why they move at all.

Next, philosophers thought that if an object has a causal power because of its matter, its matter must have that causal power. If a candle is made liquid by being heated because it is composed of wax, then it is melted by heating because the wax of which it is composed is melted by heating. This sounds plausible, but it leads to a regress. If the candle has a power to be melted because its material has, surely the material must have the power because its own more basic material has. Scientists will be constrained to seek ever more basic materials, but destined never to understand the causal powers of the most basic material they have discovered as yet. In point of fact, though it is correct English to say 'Wax is melted by heating' or 'Gold is dissolved by immersion in Aqua Regia', what is meant is that things composed of wax or gold are affected in this way. If we said this, the regress should never get under way.

Instead of saying that if causal powers exist they must be properties like colour or texture, and that if objects have causal powers it must be because their materials have, we can say that the causal powers of an object *are* its material. The idea of a material is from the start an idea of the causal power of the object it composes. Imagining that causal powers are powers *of* materials, that materials *have* causal powers, is an instance of philosophical double vision.

Perhaps it sounds shocking to say that materials are the causal powers of the objects they form or constitute. But a causal power of an object is that in virtue of which it affects other things and is affected by them, and that is simply its matter. The ability of objects to cause changes and to have changes caused in them is their materiality. To be a physical object, to be a thing the behaviour of which can be explained physically, is to be composed of matter; that, it might be said, is the formal cause of their physicality. In a way this is not disputed. Descartes held that what makes physical things physical is their extension, which he identified with their matter. He thought he had a clear idea of extension, and no clear idea of anything else of which bodies might be composed. But in fact our ideas of gold, clay, oxygen and the rest are ideas of that in virtue of which action on and by objects is effective, whereas the idea of extension in three dimensions is not.

The idea of a causal power is puzzling if we think of it as a property of matter; and the idea of matter is equally puzzling if we think of it as an owner of properties, 'the unknown support of those properties we find existing' (*Essay* 2.23.2) which embarrassed Locke and which Berkeley dismissed. A real man, says Proust in *À côté de chez Swann*, however well we may know him, has parts which retain a certain opacity, impervious to our understanding; 'the discovery of the novelist was to have the idea of replacing these parts which are impenetrable to the soul by an equal quantity of immaterial parts which our soul can assimilate to itself'. It is like that with matter: the happy discovery of the philosopher is to substitute for earthy materiality, impenetrable to the human intellect, pure extension which geometers at least can assimilate to themselves.

We might fear that even if our notions of materials are notions of the powers of objects to affect one another, recognizing this will not help us to understand fundamental forces like that of gravitation. Massive objects approach one another without being acted upon by anything else; why is that? Not, surely, because they are composed of gold or butter. Or *is* it because of that? The force with which they approach without being acted upon is proportional to their mass, and the gravitational mass of an object composed of gold is greater than that of an object composed of the same volume of butter. Our notion of the heaviness of a golden ingot is the notion of the gold of which it is composed. Philosophers have thought heaviness or gravity elusive, because they thought it must be a property of materials.

The puzzlement that comes from making causal powers qualities of matter is exacerbated by two changes that have occurred in the concept of matter. First, it acquired a new explanatory role. Being what, as Alexander says, 'receives' contrary qualities, it is what remains through change.[3] Instead of being what accounts for the efficacy of causal action (or the need for it), it becomes what accounts for the difference between one thing's becoming another and one thing's ceasing to exist, and another's coming into being in its place.

Secondly, in modern science bodies are composed of molecules, molecules of atoms, atoms of protons and electrons and so on. These are all, we think, present in the bodies they make up, and they make them up somewhat as individuals make up a crowd. We take material constituents generally to be components like these, and we think that if there are any ultimate or absolutely basic material constituents of the world, they will be components that are not composed of anything further. This conception is static as compared with that of Plato and Aristotle. For them composition was a process of putting together, and an absolutely basic material would be one that did not arise out of anything else.

Descartes not only stripped the physical world of all but geometrical properties; in his *Discourse on the Method for Conducting Reason Well, and Seeking Truth in the Sciences* he confesses that:

> The long chains of reasonings (*raisons*) all quite simple and easy, which geometers are accustomed to use to reach their most difficult demonstrations had given me occasion to imagine that all the things which can fall under the knowledge of human beings are connected in the same way. (*Oeuvres* 6, p. 19)

Later philosophers recognized that the whole of human knowledge cannot be obtained from a few definitions, axioms and postulates as the whole of Euclidean geometry could. They held, in contrast, that the direction of explanation should be from part to whole. At the end of his *System of Logic* Mill argues that we should apply 'the physical or concrete deductive method' to 'the moral sciences', that is, to the study of human beings, and especially to the study of human beings in society.

> Men [he says] in a state of society are still men; their actions and passions are obedient to the laws of individual human nature. ... Human beings in society have no properties but those which are derived from, and may be resolved into, the laws of the nature of individual man. In social phenomena the Composition of Causes is the universal law. (*System* 6.7.1)

> However complex the phenomena, all their sequences and coexistences result from the laws of the separate elements. The effect produced, in social phenomena, by any complex set of circumstances, amounts precisely to the sum of the effects of the circumstances taken singly; and the complexity does not arise from the number of the laws themselves, which is not remarkably great, but from the extraordinary number and variety of the data or elements – of the agents which, in obedience to that small number of laws, cooperate towards the effect. The Social Science, therefore, (which, by a convenient barbarism, has been termed Sociology[4]) is a deductive science; not indeed after the model of geometry, but after that of the more complex physical sciences. (*System* 6.9.1)

Philosophers could still call the method of science 'deductive' because from the laws scientists discover by observation and experiment, together with a statement of the conditions existing at a certain time, it should be possible to deduce what happened or will happen immediately after that time. If the inference is to be valid the laws must be general statements to the effect that whenever certain conditions are fulfilled, something specific ensues, statements like – I adapt examples from Alexander Bird 1992, p. 62 and Harré 1970, p. 20 – 'Whenever potassium is placed in water it dissolves', or 'When sodium salts are introduced into a flame, it turns yellow'.

Philosophers today, then, mostly view objects as aggregates of components and think that the explanation of an object's behaviour lies in its parts; they conceive its parts as objects in their turn; and they want scientists to divide things (in thought at least) into the smallest parts they can and discover general truths about these particles that will license factual deductions. Saying that we should explain the behaviour of a whole by whatever explains the behaviour of its parts taken separately may sound rational, but it is not very practical. Nobody can investigate separately the behaviour of each of the atoms, electrons or quarks of which a billiard ball is allegedly an aggregate, and although I have known natural scientists admit to conceiving these diminutive items on the model of ordinary material objects, it can hardly be supposed that one of them has any behaviour independently of everything else. Philosophers are at best offering scientists an ideal, imported from mathematics, or in Mill's case perhaps from political theory, towards which they are invited to look.

'What is science?' is not itself a scientific question. Scientists can tell us what particular problem is engaging them at the moment, but they are not qualified to say what makes an enquiry scientific or what, in general, is the scope of scientific enquiry. That is a task for philosophers. Probably philosophers and scientists would all agree that scientists investigate the material constitution of things, and that if their investigations are successful they can explain why causal action is effective, even why it is *necessary* that certain action should have a certain effect. But as we have seen, there are different ways of conceiving matter and different kinds of necessity. If the matter of a thing is its causal powers, then scientists are investigating causal powers, and their researches into the material constitution of things give them just what Hume thought they could never have, a knowledge of 'power and energy', an 'insight into the operating principle of objects'. Their examination of cells, molecules, atoms and the rest will reveal the *physical* necessity of what happens. If, on the other hand, causal powers elude us, and events at the level of the smallest material constituents of things merely take place, then scientists who investigate these constituents can at best uncover only a kind of *logical* necessity. Not the slightly exotic logical necessity I spoke of earlier when I said that the going on of a change renders that change logically necessary, but the humdrum necessity with which the conclusion follows from the premises of a valid piece of deductive reasoning: scientists see the logical necessity that this poker should become red if whenever an object composed of certain particles is placed in a fire it becomes red, and this poker is composed of the right particles and is placed in a fire.

Current orthodoxy is that scientists are uncovering or constructing a pattern of regularity: beneath the picturesque diversity of casual experience lie similar events that always follow or accompany one another in the same way. The cinematograph came into being only in the twentieth century, but now that we have it we can explain, perhaps more clearly than they could themselves, how earlier thinkers wanted to see the world. When we watch a film, black and white or coloured shapes resembling human beings and other objects seem to move across the screen and interact; but they don't. There is a rapid succession of still shots, like Russell's existences at points at instants except that they are not quite instantaneous. And when it seems that a swordsman transfixes an enemy and thereby causes him to fall dead, or that a potter is turning a wheel with his foot and causing clay to acquire the shape of a pot, in reality there is nothing but a sequence of stills none of which causes its successor or is caused by its predecessor. We believe that the film was produced by the causal action of a cameraman and light, and that it is projected by an unseen person at the back of the auditorium. Both the theologians mentioned by Gilson and modern philosophers think that all experience is watching such a vivid film in three dimensions. The theologians think it is made by God and projected by God; the philosophers for the most part think it was made by no one and is projected by no one; it just goes on.

* * *

Today the English word 'matter' is seldom on the lips either of scientists or of philosophers. Scientists speak more of mass and energy, and philosophers associate the word with ideas that are now exploded: with the prime matter of ancient syncretists and Western medieval philosophers, or with Locke's unknown subject in which solidity and extension 'inhere' (*Essay* 2.23.2). In fact, Locke's 'we know not what' substratum is a typical metaphysical illusion. Grammarians distinguish uses of words as subjects and predicates, and they might say that using a noun as a subject is referring to something without predicating of it what the noun signifies (though of course you cannot use a noun to refer to something unless you also use other words to predicate something of it). A philosopher may transfer this feature of a referential use of words to the things referred to; it will then seem that the things designated by subject-expressions are in themselves things of which nothing is true, things in which the properties signified by predicate expressions, properties like solidity and being a cubic foot in size, merely inhere like currants in a pudding. What Kant calls the 'categories of *Inhärenz und Subsistenz*' (*Kritik der reinen Vernunft* A80/B106) are the result of projecting grammatical concepts onto reality.[5]

But though philosophers have consigned prime matter and Locke's substratum to the metaphysical dustbin, they still contrast matter and mind, the physical and the psychological. These contrasts force some notion of materiality upon them. To be physical an object must be able to affect other things, and be affected by them, in certain ways by certain causal action. If, as I have argued, to be composed of any particular material is to have such abilities, then while there is no particular material (as it might be, hydrogen) of which philosophers need a notion for their contrasts, they need the notion of being composed of some material or other. And as the relation of an object to the material of which it is composed is expressed by grammar, by prepositions like 'of', case inflections, suffixes like 'en' and so forth, so *materiality*, being composed of some material or other, is expressed by the syntax of causal explanation. In 'The muffin turned black because it was heated', that the subject is a physical body is expressed by the causal construction.

'Matter' is not a word like 'truth', 'existence' and 'goodness'. I said that these are not words for anything real, not words for things the world contains. The world does contain matter, solid, liquid and gaseous, and the various kinds of matter are expressed by ordinary words like 'milk', 'hydrogen' and 'gold'. 'Matter' itself or 'material' is a generic term. Like 'object', 'quality' and 'action' it signifies a kind of thing that exists; and things are classified as materials partly by the way they are quantified and partly by the role they play in causal explanations.

Change, time and causation characterize the physical world. We are able to recognize these characteristics and to understand causally because we can distinguish processes which go on from goings on of processes. A process is not distinct in reality from its going on; the distinction is created by language and we grasp it when we understand constructions for expressing a change as something that happens and as a happening of something. We learn these constructions gradually as we learn how to cause changes we desire and prevent changes we fear. Human beings live in language-using societies, we are taught verbally how to cause and prevent change, and the constructions are used by our teachers. An animal without language might be shown how to cause desired changes, but it would have no idea of physicality.

12

Thinking

The physical gets contrasted with the mental: what does 'the mental' comprise? Plato called attention to reasoning, measuring, calculating, evaluating and comparing. Besides engaging in these intellectual activities we perceive things by sight, hearing and other senses and have feelings and desires. At least to heirs of Greco–Roman civilization, these seem very important facts about human nature. Plato (*Philebus* 38b–39c, *Sophist* 263d–264b) and Aristotle (*De Anima* 2–3) tried to say what perceiving, thinking and feeling are.[1] Their question was not how a species evolved that can do these things, but what it is to do them. They all fall under mind in a broad sense of the term; they are all mental states or activities, or, to speak more sonorously, they are all psychological phenomena. Many philosophers today write as if the one big task that remains for them is to show that these phenomena can all be completely accounted for in purely physical terms; when they've done that they can hand over to cognitive scientists and go home. Meanwhile, however, some concentrate on beliefs and desires, others on sentience. In this chapter I first argue that the concepts of belief and desire are explanatory, that we express them in explaining people's behaviour in a special, non-causal way; and I compare this account with alternatives. I then move on to sentience, and offer a similar treatment of that. Aristotle developed a notion of the psychological which was coextensive with that of life, and I discuss the distinction between the animate and the inanimate. Finally I indicate differences between thinking and saying.

English-speaking philosophers often use 'belief' and 'desire' as semi-technical terms, and I shall follow that practice. In ordinary speech believing that something is the case contrasts with seeing with your own eyes that it is the case and with knowing for sure that it is the case. We should not say 'Polonius believed Ophelia was present' if she was in plain view and he was speaking to her, or 'Cantor believes that 6 is an even number' if Cantor is a competent mathematician. But I shall use 'believe' to cover not only what would ordinarily be called 'believing' but also perceiving, remembering, imagining and surmising that something is the case. Similarly I want 'desire' to cover every kind of wishing and wanting, including negative kinds like aversion and regretting something happened.

That being understood, I say that the notion of a belief is the notion of a reason for or against a line of conduct, a reason for or against acting in some way or refraining. Reasons are of two kinds, which I call 'practical' and 'technical'. A practical reason is some real or supposed happening or state of affairs that makes some line of conduct good or bad. The presence of an injured man lying in the road would be a practical reason for stopping your car; that someone had recently been taken by a crocodile in a pool would be a practical reason against jumping in. A technical reason is something that renders a line of conduct effective or ineffective. That the road is rising steeply is a technical reason for changing to a lower gear. The distinction between practical and technical reasons corresponds to the distinction between character and skill. Being a good or bad sort of person is a matter of the weight you give to practical reasons; being skilful or unskilful is a matter of your disposition to act for technical reasons.

My claim, then, is that for you to believe that there is an injured man is for you to have this as a reason for stopping. You may not actually stop, but then you drive on despite the injured man's situation. For you to believe there are crocodiles in the pool is for you to have this as a reason for not jumping in. It may not be an overriding reason: the fact that your child has just fallen in might override it; but then you jump despite the crocodiles. To think of something as an object of belief to someone – as something, that is, of which the person is, or isn't, or should be aware – is to think of it as a reason to that person; and conversely to think of something as a reason to someone for behaving in some way, is to think of it as an object of belief. If the presence of crocodiles is a reason against swimming, then if you are contemplating a dip it would be well for you to know that crocodiles are present.

Two different objections are brought against this sort of account. The first is that we have many beliefs which not only are not actually reflected in our behaviour, but seem to have no tendency whatever to influence our behaviour. For instance I believe that there is no highest prime number, and that Mme de Maintenon was married to Louis XIV. Anyone who says we have beliefs that are not reflected in my behaviour probably conceives them as pictures in our minds. The examples I have just given are not readily associated with pictures – how does one depict the highest prime number? – and there is the obvious objection that the same picture would have to correspond to the belief that Louis and Mme de Maintenon were married and to the belief that they weren't. Beliefs are positive or negative; pictures are not.

But is it really true that beliefs about the distant past and the loftier regions of pure mathematics are not reflected in behaviour? These beliefs are verbal; they are expressed in words; and if I hold them I am disposed to utter them aloud when asked. If you ask 'Was Louis XV beheaded?' and I think he wasn't, I will say 'No' unless I have some special reason for speaking falsely. If I say 'Yes' it is perhaps for the reason that you are a bore, or are competing against my friend in some general knowledge test, and I say 'Yes' in spite of the fact that Louis XV was not, in fact, beheaded.

Besides beliefs we hold consciously we have unconscious beliefs we have never put into words. You probably think that there are blind women in China. This thought has never occurred to you, but if asked you would say 'Yes, I'm sure there are'. The belief follows logically from beliefs about China – that it has a large population – and about the incidence of blindness in human populations, which do influence your behaviour, for instance when you are making holiday plans or trying to decide which charities to support.

If, after these replies, the objector still claims to have beliefs that are not reflected in behaviour, we may ask 'What makes you think you believe these things?' We sometimes are in doubt whether we believe something of no immediate practical significance. Do I believe there is a life after death? Perhaps I do not know until my life is in danger; and then I can infer that I do really hold the belief or that I don't really hold it from how I behave. What are usually called 'moral' or 'political' beliefs, like the belief that abortion is wrong or the belief that referenda are democratic, should be classed rather as desires than as beliefs; but again we can be sure that we really have them, and are not just professing them, only when they are put to the test: perhaps when a close relative has an unwanted pregnancy or a referendum has an unwanted result. Or take suspicions. We want to trust our employees; you may discover that you no longer believe an employee honest if you find you are taking care not to leave open files lying about or small sums of money.

Anyone putting this objection probably thinks it is true by definition that we know what we think. Descartes defined thought (*cogitatio*) as 'everything that is in us in such a way that we are immediately conscious of it' (*Replies to Objections, Oeuvres 7*, p. 160). Locke attributed this 'immediate consciousness' to a faculty of 'reflection' which, 'though it be not sense, as having nothing to do with external objects, yet it is very like it' (*Essay* 2.1.4). G. E. Moore, in contrast, speaks of thought as 'diaphanous' (1922, p. 25), which would make it incapable of being an object of anything 'like sense'. I think (perhaps with Gareth Evans 1982, p. 225) that when we have no doubt we believe something it is because we have no doubt it is true. Do I think the window is open? I can see it is. Do I believe my sister is in Berlin? She said she was going, I know of nothing that might have prevented her, yes, I do believe she's in Berlin. Similarly with desires. Do I wish the President to be re-elected? My cousin is campaigning on his behalf, his opponent is advocating a hawkish foreign policy that is likely to cause more harm than good, so again, yes I do.

Alex Byrne (2011) puts forward the implausible suggestion that I *infer* (say) that I believe the Earth is spherical from the fact that it is. Matthew Boyle (2011) claims that if I believe something, it an *aspect* of my mental state that I 'tacitly know' I am in it, an aspect to which, as a 'reflective being' I can 'shift my attention'. He does not say how this shift of attention is possible without some introspective faculty, and his talk of a mental state of belief is consistent with conceiving belief on the model of a bodily state like being sunburnt. My view is that if I come to be sure that I believe something it is through shifting my attention not to my mental state, but to the grounds for believing it, and finding them adequate.

The second objection to my account is that even if beliefs are necessarily reflected in behaviour, even if they have to have some influence, however weak, that is because they are *causes* of behaviour. The Samaritan motorist braked because he could *see* that there was an injured man lying in the middle of the road, and that made him stop. In general, whenever it is true to say that you acted for the reason that something was the case, it is true to say that you did so because you thought or knew it was the case, and surely anything introduced by 'because' is introduced as a cause. Davidson (1982a) argued that reasons satisfy Hume's conception of a cause.

If we choose to use the word 'cause', rather as ancient philosophers used *aition*, for any kind of explanatory factor, no matter how it is explanatory, then we can say that beliefs are causes of action, but it remains an open question in what way they account for it. I think, however, that I follow ordinary present-day usage when I say that a cause must be one of three things: a causal agent or causal action or a causal condition. A belief is not a causal agent, nor is it any familiar kind of causal action. Nobody would say that Othello killed Desdemona by believing that she loved Cassio; he killed her by smothering her. A belief might be a causal condition. We might say 'The Turks captured Cyprus because Othello believed Desdemona loved Cassio; his jealous belief and his preoccupation with events within the castle made it possible for the Turkish surprise attack to be effective.' But those who say that beliefs are causes do not mean merely that they are causal conditions of the efficacy of action. They rarely distinguish between agents, actions and conditions; instead they follow Hume and take a cause to be an 'event' that is prior to what it causes, and is of a kind regularly followed by an event of the kind it is said to cause. That is a bad analysis of the notion of a cause, but when philosophers say that beliefs are causes they are trying to cast them in the role of bits of causal action.

The reply to that is that in 'Othello killed Desdemona because he believed she loved Cassio,' 'because' does not introduce a causal explanation. We can show that by a grammatical argument. In the sentence explaining Othello's action the verb of belief can be put in a parenthetical clause; we can say 'Othello killed Desdemona because, *as he believed*, she loved Cassio.' When 'because' introduces a genuine cause, that cannot be done. Consider the sentences 'Othello killed his wife because he took her with him to a town where there was cholera', and 'Othello killed his wife because Iago had mixed cyanide with the sugar he put in her morning tea.' Here, where 'because' introduces the causal action responsible for Desdemona's death, we cannot replace 'because he took' or 'because Iago had mixed' by 'because, as he took' or 'because, as Iago had mixed'. 'Because' in 'because he believed' is simply equivalent to 'for the reason'; it combines with 'he believed' to form a synonym for the conjunctival phrase.

The idea that beliefs are causes is central to functionalist theories, and I shall consider it further when I come to them. Meanwhile let me complete my own theory. In Chapter 7 I equated desire with having something as a positive objective; and aversion with having something as a negative objective. You have something as a positive objective if you act to bring it about or preserve it, and you refrain from acting lest you prevent it or bring it to an end. A negative objective is the opposite: you act to prevent it or bring it to an end, and refrain from acting lest you cause or perpetuate it.

This account of desire has to face objections just like those that are made to my account of belief. Surely we desire things we make no attempt to bring about, and even if we do act to bring something about, our desire is not identical with our acting but a cause of it.[2] These objections can be met by the same tactics as the objections to what I said about belief. Although we can say 'Macbeth killed Duncan because he wanted to become king', 'because' does not introduce a cause but combines with the verb of wanting to produce a phrase equivalent to 'in order that'; Macbeth acted in order that, as was his desire, be might become king. Similarly with 'because' in 'Othello killed Desdemona because he was averse to her betraying more men': he killed her *lest*, as he feared (Act 5, Scene 2), she betray more men.

We sometimes say that a person believes or desires something without mentioning any action. Most people know that wine intoxicates, and that the Earth is spherical. Most people want to have friends and are averse to mosquito bites. Since in saying these things we do not mention any behaviour, how can our statements be explanations? What are we explaining?

We must distinguish between having a belief over a stretch of time without, for most of the time, thinking about the matter, and believing or wanting something on a particular occasion. When I explain your doing something I attribute a belief or desire to you on the occasion when you act; the belief or desire is operative, so to speak, at the time of your action. When I say simply that you believe or know something, or desire or are averse to something, I attribute to you a long-term belief or desire which will (or may) become operative when appropriate situations arise. Philosophers speak here of dispositions. If you know that wine intoxicates the knowledge will become operative when wine is on offer, and you then refrain from drinking as much as might be pleasant when intoxication would be bad, though perhaps drink more than is pleasant in desperation. If you know that the earth is spherical the knowledge will become operative when you are planning a visit to the far side, or discussing latitude and longitude. Similarly with long-term desires. If you want to have friends, the desire becomes active when you meet strangers or when the friends you already have make requests of you. It is sometimes said that you know something over a stretch of time if you have acquired the knowledge and not lost it. That is reasonable, but what is it to lose it? To lose the disposition to act upon it. A disposition of this kind probably depends upon an acquired property of the brain, but it cannot be identified with such a property, unless teleological explanation generally can be reduced to causal.

I have been considering uses of 'believe' and 'desire' in statements, but my account can be extended to counsels and commands. 'Believe that you're going to get better' is not a command to engage in an activity signified by 'believe' but advice to do what you have to do, and refrain from what you mustn't do, if you are going to get better.

Explanations in terms of reasons and purposes I shall call 'teleological'. (The word ought to mean simply 'in terms of an end, *telos*', but I extend it to cover reasons and negative objectives.) I claim that verbs of thinking like 'believe' and 'desire' do not signify any sort of action or activity in which a person engages, nor any bodily or mental attitude a person can take up, nor, when they are supplemented by object-clauses like 'that the Earth is spherical' or 'to go to India', do they signify any sort of intrinsic state a person can be in; rather they signify what is expressed by the constructions of teleological explanation. There are many such constructions. In English we have, besides conjunctions like 'for the reason that', 'in order that' and their variants (and 'although', 'in spite of the fact that', though these words can also, of course, introduce ineffective *causal* factors), parataxis like 'He called me a liar. I hit him.' Anyone who has studied Latin knows how rich that language is in ways of expressing purpose. Besides *ut* and *ne* with the subjunctive you have the choice of such grammatical exotica as the gerund, the gerundive and the supine. A grammarian might say that in Latin belief and desire are often expressed by the subjunctive.

Nobody has ever thought that the inflections of the subjunctive mood signify some kind of non-physical act; has anyone really thought that 'believe' or 'desire' does? 'All the modes of thinking', says Descartes, 'which we experience in ourselves can be brought under two general heads: one of them is perception, or the operation of the intellect; the other is volition, or the operation of desire (*voluntas*)' (*Principles of Philosophy* 1.32, Oeuvres 8–1, p. 17). Likewise Locke: 'The two great and principal actions of the mind which are most frequently considered, and which are so frequent that everyone that pleases may take notice of them in himself, are these two: perception, or thinking, and *volition*, or *willing*' (*Essay* 2.6.2).

Introspection failed, in the end, to confirm the existence of anything active in the mind. Philosophers today, however, often call belief and desire 'propositional attitudes'. For some this is simply a way of labelling a class of psychological phenomena. The word 'attitude', however, suggests we should conceive belief and desire on the model of the attitudes we take up towards people who knock on the door. We can adopt a friendly, welcoming attitude or a hostile one, a credulous attitude or a sceptical. Conceiving belief and desire on this model is circular – the attitudes involve belief and desire – and they would have to be adopted towards entities which are true or false, Fregean thoughts or propositions. Trenton Merricks (2009, p. 210) undertakes to use 'propositional attitude' for 'a relation between an agent and a proposition'. Uriah Kriegel (2012), who counts 'entertaining' as a propositional attitude, says not that these attitudes are relations but that they are 'grasped by [what Russell calls] acquaintance' (p. 5), that is, by introspection. Whatever the attitudes may be, obviously if there are no Fregean propositions for them to be attitudes towards, this way of conceiving thought collapses.

Sentences like 'Columbus thinks the Earth is round' are of subject–predicate form, and Descartes supposed that predicate-expressions like 'thinks the Earth is round' signify properties thinkers can have or lack. He assumed the properties are non-physical and non-relational. In the last 80 years philosophers have rejected both assumptions. Beliefs and desires, they have argued, must be identical with physical properties of our nervous systems; and Putnam (1973) argues that they cannot be intrinsic: Columbus could have all his intrinsic properties identical with those of his double on Twin Earth, but his double would not share his belief that the stuff across which he is sailing is water.

* * *

Today many philosophers give accounts of belief and desire that at first look like mine. They accept that beliefs and desires must be reflected in behaviour. They also hold that material objects interact with our eyes, our ears and the other sensitive parts of our bodies, and that it is through their stimulation of these sensitive parts that we come to have the knowledge and beliefs we have. Our beliefs are thus causally dependent on the action of objects on our bodies; and our beliefs and desires must have at least the influence on our behaviour that I claimed just now. This approach is sometimes called 'functionalism'. The idea behind the word is that what gives a belief or desire its essential nature and identity is the part it plays in our life, not any intrinsic properties it may have as an activity or state, whether of mind or body.

On this showing, my account could be called 'functionalist'. It diverges in important ways, however, from current orthodoxy. The current theories of belief and desire are part of a programme to give an account of human life consistent with holding that all our movements are determined by earlier causal action upon our bodies. And instead of saying that we should not have beliefs and desires if parts of our bodies were not affected by physical stimulation, their exponents say, without qualification, that beliefs and desires are caused by this action, and that they in their turn cause the behaviour we count as voluntary or intentional; they say that beliefs and desires are links in the causal chain that runs from sensory stimuli to 'voluntary' response. These causal intermediaries they take, understandably enough, to be events in the brain or brain-states. Nothing else would credibly fill the role. They do not require there to be just one cerebral event that is the causal intermediary every time anyone acts to drink a cup of tea. Even on a particular occasion there may be no identifiable event or series of events that causes my movement, distinct from the states caused by the clock when I hear it strike half past four, by the teapot when I saw where you put it and so forth. The dissolving, however, of causal intermediaries into this shifting school of cerebral whitebait does not deter them from saying that causal intermediaries are what beliefs and desires are.

There are two differences between this sort of theory and mine. First, since causal intermediaries are states or processes, and for functionalists beliefs and desires are causal intermediaries, it must follow for them that beliefs and desires are states or processes. It is true that they make the concept of a belief or desire relational; a state or process is a belief or desire not because of what it is in itself but because of its relation to stimuli and responsive behaviour. The concept is like that of an uncle or a messenger, not like that of a pattern or a mode of locomotion. But uncles and messengers are human beings, and beliefs and desires, for the functionalist, are states or processes, predicable of the person, or of bodily parts of the person, who believes or desires. On my showing, to attribute a belief or desire to a person is not to predicate anything of the person, whether relational or non-relational, but to offer an explanation.

But do not I, as much as the functionalist, identify beliefs and desires with physical predicates? For me believing and desiring are acting and refraining for reasons and purposes, and acting and refraining are physical. Columbus believed that the Earth was spherical and wanted to go to India *in sailing west*, which was physical enough. It wasn't localized in his brain, but the whole cause of Columbus's action, a functionalist would say, wasn't localized in his brain either. This brings out, however, a second and more fundamental difference.

For functionalists the notion of a belief or desire is causal. It is the notion of something that is related causally to certain antecedents and behaviour. For me it is teleological: it is the notion of a reason or purpose. I hold that the contrast we mark by the terms 'mental' and 'physical' rests on the contrast between teleological and causal explanation. On the face of it, causal explanation and teleological are independent, and indeed apply to different things; we seek causal explanations for changes which occur in a time or after a time and teleological explanations for periods of action or inaction.

Functionalists allow teleological explanations validity up to a point and in certain contexts; they permit and even encourage what D. C. Dennett calls an 'intentional stance' (1981, pp. 6, 237–42). But they hold that teleological explanations must ultimately reduce to explanations in purely causal terms. We can rephrase statements containing verbs of thinking and wanting in ways that make no use of the notions of a reason or a purpose. Jonathan Bennett (1976) develops this strategy. Science provides us with missiles that lock onto a target. If the target moves, the movement affects some part of the missile, perhaps its radar, and this makes the missile change direction, with the result that it eventually hits the target. A philosopher may say that my desiring a cup of tea is like a missile's having a target; I will do what it takes to get a cup of tea; and seeing a tin and thinking it contains teabags is like a missile's registering a movement of the target. Moreover scientists tell us we have eyes because eyes enabled our ancestors to survive and have offspring, and their eyes did that because they were sensitive to light and movement, and therefore registered the movements of dangerous animals like mammoths and the proximity of appropriate sexual partners. A philosopher can say that seeing is the *function* of an eye because it enables its possessor to survive in this way. Larry Wright (1973) and Ruth Millikan (1984) show how to do this.

These considerations may persuade some people to adopt new concepts of perception and belief. It cannot be pretended, however, that they are analyses of existing conceptions. Functionalists no doubt feel that it is part of our ordinary thinking that beliefs and desires are causal intermediaries, but I argued just now that this cannot be shown from our use of phrases like 'because he believed' and 'because he wanted'. Nor does it follow from the fact that we think that human knowledge is causally dependent on stimulation of sense-organs, and influences behaviour: that is not equivalent to thinking that beliefs and desires are causal intermediaries. The notion of a causal intermediary, a link in a chain of causes, hardly goes back before the origins of natural science. In the most primitive societies we find the notion of an ability to get people to behave as you wish; but this is conceived as an art of persuasion, of linguistic skill, working through reasons.

In teleological explanation we explain action and inaction as an exercise of thought, an application of knowledge (real or supposed), a carrying out of a rational desire. The carrying out of a desire is not something really distinct from the desire carried out, and a desire is not really distinct from the belief that makes it rational. Belief, desire and action are not what Hume (*Treatise*, Appendix, p. 636) called 'distinct existences'. Your belief that the glass contains wine does not cause your desire to raise it to your lips, but rather expresses itself in, or takes the form of, that desire. The two are separated by us when we explain your action, when we use connectives like 'for the reason that' and 'in order that'; but the action is explained as an exercise of thought which in itself is indivisible, and an exercise of thought is not a reality distinct from the thought exercised. As grasping the notion of the physical depends on grasping the distinction made by grammar between the going on of a process and the process that goes on, so grasping the notion of the mental depends on grasping the distinction made by grammar between an exercise of thought and the thought of which it is an exercise. An animal without language, on my view, might attribute a perception or a desire to another animal, but could not have any general idea of the mental. This distinction is blurred by scientists who speak of animals as having 'a rudimentary theory of mind' (Hauser et al. 2002, p. 1576).

It is otherwise for functionalists. They need not say that beliefs and desires are really distinct from each other. They can take a holistic view and say that beliefs and desires are interdependent. But they do require a real relation between a belief or desire and any action it explains. For them actions are *effects* of beliefs and desires; for me your reaching for the glass is an *instance* of the belief that wine is there and the desire to drink.

Perhaps some philosophers fear that unless beliefs and desires are causes, explanations in terms of them will be unintelligible. For what, after all, does it mean to say that Othello killed Desdemona *for the reason that* she loved Cassio? What is this relationship which is said to hold between Othello's action and Desdemona's non-existent love? As I said just now, 'reason' does not signify a relation any more than 'cause' in 'Smothering caused Desdemona's death'. There is no such real relation as being the reason for something, but there is such a linguistic act as saying that something is the reason for something.

The fear of unintelligibility may arise from a crude conception of thought: thinking is applying concepts to things, and applying a concept to a thing is modelled, as in Plato's *Cratylus*, on juxtaposing a picture to a thing and saying 'This is a picture of that'. So to think that you are moving for the reason that the plate is dirty and for the purpose of putting it in the sink I should have to picture the relation between a reason or purpose and the action for which it is a reason or purpose. But thinking that you are acting for this reason or purpose is not a matter of applying concepts of a reason or purpose in this simple way. When I think 'He's acting for the reason that the plate is dirty and for the purpose of putting it in the sink', I am not applying the concepts of a reason and a purpose in the straightforward way in which I apply the concept of kissing when I think 'Romeo kissed Juliet'. Rather I am applying the concepts of dirt and a sink in a special way. Perhaps for the reason that the plate in your hand is dirty and, in order that you may reach the sink, I get out of your path to the sink. In this case I make your reason my own and your objective, that the plate should become clean, my own. I attribute an objective to you in helping you to bring it about or trying not to prevent it; whereas if we were playing chess, thinking you have a certain purpose might be acting to frustrate it.

On this view, to believe that someone else has a belief or desire you must not just act for a reason or purpose yourself, but act disinterestedly. Usually it is acting with disinterested benevolence, making what is good for the other person an end in itself to yourself. Occasionally it is acting with disinterested malice, like Iago in *Othello*. Is this disinterested engagement necessary? Don't we often attribute beliefs and desires to others when we are acting self-interestedly? To achieve our goals we have to consider how other people will behave, and it helps to know what they take to be the case and what goals they have. If, when waiting in a queue, I see that the man next to me has a watch, and ask 'What time is it?' I think that he will understand that I want him to tell me the time, and I also think that, for the reason I have asked him, he will do so. So perhaps I attribute disinterested benevolence to him, but am I myself acting benevolently?

In such cases we should certainly *say* that another person has a belief or desire; whether we should really *think* it is another question. If I dial 123 a voice on the telephone will tell me the time, but I do not think that there is a person at the other end who wants to tell me something. I might be treating the man in the queue simply as a speaking clock. We can predict that if people believe certain things they will act in certain ways. If you believe that unless you hand over your wallet I'll cut your throat, you'll probably hand over your wallet. But this may be treating you as a machine so constructed as to do whatever is necessary to continue functioning. The difference between thinking that I am doing what will *cause* you to hand over your wallet and thinking that you are *conscious* of my knife and *afraid* of death, is that in the latter case I either maliciously desire to deprive you of something good (your money or your life) as an end in itself, or I am reluctant to injure you, but carry on in spite of the fact that my action is injurious. If I do not have injuring you either as a positive or as a negative objective I think of you as a kind of wallet-dispensing machine. These considerations will not satisfy philosophers or economists who believe that all action is self-interested and that disinterested benevolence and disinterested malice are equally impossible, but this is not the place to argue the point further. I am here concerned rather with beliefs generally than with beliefs about beliefs.

Another fear philosophers may have is that if teleological explanation cannot be reduced to causal, the action explained must be what they call 'counter-causal', that is, *not* causally determined, *not* a mere continuation of earlier physical processes on the cosmic billiard table. But I have not seen any compelling argument that shows it implies this. If such an argument were produced, most people, I am sure, would prefer to keep explanation in terms of reasons and jettison universal causal determination. Philosophers sometimes argue for universal causal determination on the ground that 'the overwhelming majority of scientists now reject vital and mental forces and accept the causal closure of the physical realm' (Papineau 2009, p. 57). Behind this argument from authority lies the assumption that if our actions are not caused by physical forces, they must be caused by forces that are non-physical. That is to assume universal causal determination of some kind, and begs the question against anyone who holds that some of our behaviour is not causally determined by past history at all.

* * *

The preceding discussion was restricted to belief and desire. But the concept of the mental embraces two other things: bodily sensations like pain, and certain feelings sometimes called 'phenomenological properties' of experience. Some philosophers concentrate on these things. What fascinates them, it might be said, is rather sentience than intelligence. Although this leads them to group bodily sensations and phenomenological qualities together, they are different and I shall deal with them separately.

The paradigm bodily sensation is pain. There are also pleasant sensations of warmth, intoxication and sexual arousal. Hunger and thirst either are bodily sensations or involve them, and Ryle liked to remind people of twinges and tickles, but it is enough here to consider pain and sensations of pleasure.

We talk of feeling a pain, and we also say that pain *is* a feeling, a sensation. Feeling and sensing are modes of awareness, and awareness is a mental phenomenon if anything is. Hence our way of speaking suggests that pain is both something of which we are aware and something mental, and philosophers since Locke have swallowed this suggestion. Locke believed that 'the infinite wise author of our being' has 'annexed' pain to 'great heat' (*Essay* 2.7.3–4); Berkeley (1964b, pp. 175–8) says the two are identical, and brushes aside (see pp. 194–7) the suggestion that we should distinguish sensations from their objects. Among twentieth-century philosophers who take pain to be both an object of awareness and something mental are Wittgenstein (*PI* 154), Davidson (1982d, pp. 211–13) and Saul Kripke (1980, pp. 146–7). Whereas, however, being aware of something is mental, if we take pain as that of which a person in pain is aware, then unlike emotions such as grief it is not mental but bodily. That is why we call it a 'bodily' sensation.

Confusion arises because the concept of pain as something felt is partly psychological. The word means a bodily state of which we are aware as an object of aversion for its own sake. Aversion is something mental, but while some things to which we are averse are mental also, the object of our aversion when we are in pain is not. The concept of pain is like that of a reward. The word 'reward' means something given for a certain reason. The notion of a reason is psychological, but what is given may be purely physical. That what we are averse to when we are in pain is bodily or physical is evident from the way in which we try to rid ourselves of it. We remove thorns that are sticking into us, withdraw from hot metal that that is scorching our skin, take pills for headaches and engage physicians to take physical action to change our bodily state. Local anaesthetics alter, and general anaesthetics stop, our awareness of states of which without anaesthetics we should be aware as objects of violent aversion.

Painful and pleasant bodily sensations have physical causes. Sometimes the cause is easily identified, sometimes it is elusive, but we must suppose that the pleasant sensations of smoking, drinking and sex are caused by tobacco, alcohol, and bodily contact, or we should not seek them as we do; and states brought about by physical action must be physical.

To be aware of a bodily state as painful and as an object of aversion, even if you are totally paralyzed or in a so-called 'locked in' condition, is for your awareness of it to take the form of wanting it to stop, and, if you have an idea of some action that will stop it, as desire for that action. You may, of course, have overriding reasons for refraining from that action, or for submitting to painful treatment. You may even desire a state to continue precisely because you are aware of it as being at one level an object of aversion; you are aware of your awareness of it as an object of delight. To be aware, in contrast, of a bodily state as pleasant is to want it to go on, independently of any consequences, or be averse to its interruption, perhaps sometimes to be averse temporarily to doing anything.

This is what it is to experience pleasant and painful sensations; it is awareness of our present bodily state as good or bad. But besides experiencing sensations we dread and desire them. When I dread pain I am averse to acquiring a bodily state, independently of any consequence that might result from it, and if I desire a pleasant sensation I have acquiring a bodily state as an object of desire independently of any consequence. These feelings of bodily fear and bodily desire differ from the actual experiencing of sensations in being more intellectual; we might imagine an organism that can feel pain and want it to stop without being able to anticipate it; similarly with pleasant sensations. But any organism with sentience, I suggest, must be aware of present states of its body as good or bad, and have getting rid of some states, and preserving or acquiring others, as objectives.

That is enough about bodily sensations; they fit easily into an account which connects psychological phenomena with reasons and purposes. Phenomenological qualities (or *qualia* as philosophers sometimes call them) require more space, since it is unclear precisely what they are. Heil (2003, p. 14) calls them 'properties of conscious experiences', but what are experiences? Non-philosophers use the English noun 'experience' and the verb 'to experience' in a wide variety of ways. Heil says that looking at a ripe tomato is 'undergoing a particular kind of visual experience, one you might naturally describe as an experience of seeing a ripe tomato', and that such experiences differ from 'experiences of seeing experiences of seeing ripe tomatoes', and he goes on 'Let us suppose that your experiences are occurrences in your brain' (p. 223). This usage does not seem to me natural, and his words could not easily be translated in French or classical Greek by the words we usually employ to render 'experience' in those tongues. Frank Jackson (1982, since retracted) appealed to *qualia* in order to deny that all that exists is physical; he argued that *qualia* are real but non-physical. Other philosophers do not deny that all that exists is physical, but say that though phenomenological properties are physical to the extent that they have physical causes, we do not know what those causes are. We must believe, says Colin McGinn (1989), that they are caused by events in the brain; but for us this must always be an act of faith, either because our brains are such that it is physically impossible for us to see how phenomenological properties are produced, or because this is somehow logically impossible, though a clinching philosophical argument to show this has still be to found. Heil thinks that phenomenological properties are 'perfectly ordinary qualities of brains' with which we have what Russell called 'direct acquaintance', qualities 'noticeable, perhaps, only under special circumstances'. 'Assuming', he says, 'we are acquainted non-perceptually with qualities of our experience, and assuming our experiences are neurological goings on, we do seem to have something like "direct acquaintance" with neurological qualities' (2003, pp. 229, 234–5). Heil draws on an article by Thomas Nagel (1979) to explain the notion of a phenomenological quality, and I shall do the same.

If you were born deaf and made to hear by a surgical operation, your friends might ask you 'What is it like to hear?' This does not mean 'What is hearing like?', a question to which you might reply 'It's a way of perceiving things at a distance, like seeing and smelling.' Rather it means 'What does it *feel* like to hear?' That is not something we normally ask people who have enjoyed good hearing all their lives. Similarly if (like the children in Eric Linklater's story *Wind on the Moon*) you had turned yourself into a kangaroo, I might ask you 'What is it like to be a kangaroo?' This means not 'What is a kangaroo like?' (to which 'A wallaby' is a reasonable answer) but 'What does it feel like to be a kangaroo?' If, however, you asked me 'What does it feel like to be a human being?' I should find your question puzzling. Are you being offensive and suggesting that for once I am not behaving like a beast? Nevertheless some philosophers think that just as 'What is it like to hear?' is a question which has an answer when put to someone born deaf, so it has an answer when put to someone whose hearing has always been normal, and 'What is it like to be a human being?' also has an answer. There is something, they say, which it is like (or feels like) to see a piece of red cloth, to taste a pineapple, to belong to the species to which you belong. And this is what is meant by a 'phenomenological property', the *feel* (though it is not a tactile sensation like warmth) of our experiences. A satisfactory account of sentience would have to explain this; it would have to say not only why (like recording equipment) we are sensitive to light and sound but why there is something it feels like to see and hear and be the sort of sentient beings we are.

Whereas bodily sensations exist – there really are bodily states of which we are aware as objects of desire and aversion – phenomenological properties are, I think, illusions conjured up in the way described by Wittgenstein: 'What is *particular* about the way "red" comes, is that it comes while you're philosophising about it, as what is particular about the position of your body when you concentrated on it was concentration' (*BB*, p. 159). In my terms, philosophizing about perceptible qualities produces double vision; and what distinguishes us from light-sensitive paper and phonographs is not 'direct acquaintance with neurological properties' unless that means awareness of bodily states as good or bad.

I do not mean that we cannot be consciously aware of perceptible properties. Often we are unconsciously aware of them. We are aware of the presence of other living organisms, and of objects like rivers, blocks of ice and pianos through the senses, and if that is so, we must be aware of their perceptible properties in a way, but we need not be consciously aware of the colour of an object we see, or of the sound of an object we hear. If I pick up a handkerchief that is lying on the carpet, I probably shouldn't have seen it unless it had been different in colour from the carpet, but I may not be consciously aware of the colour. I should be consciously aware of its colour if I bought it because of its colour. Similarly if I stop because you shout 'Look out!' I am aware of the sound of your voice, but perhaps not consciously, whereas if I approach you at a party because I like the sound of your voice I am conscious of it. And not only can the visible and audible qualities of things be reasons for acting, but we can know they are our reasons. I can know that I have chosen a shirt for its colour or a piano for its timbre. This kind of conscious awareness of qualities occurs when we wonder whether they are good reasons for acting or refraining from action, when we pass practical judgement on our behaviour.

Qualia are not the only products of double vision we may encounter when we think about thinking. Just as we are unwilling to say that the material of an object *is* its causal powers, but want to say that it *has* causal powers, suggesting that the powers of the object really belong to its material, so we are reluctant to say that acting for reasons and purposes *is* believing and wanting. We postulate beliefs and desires which are entities that cause the action – whether 'functional' states identical with physical processes in the modern manner, or non-physical states and processes, as philosophers from Descartes to Russell preferred. And as we attribute causal powers not to planets, clouds or elephants, but to flesh, gold and hydrogen, and ultimately to the ultimate components of matter, so we attribute beliefs and desires not to living organisms, but either to parts of them like brains, or to non-physical entities housed in them that we call 'minds', 'souls' or 'spirits'.

* * *

I said in Chapter 4 that Chomsky considers *animate* and *human* to be grammatical subcategories of nouns. They may sound as if they are rather scientific than grammatical terms, since they signify sorts of object, but we classify things as animate or human not only by their biological make-up but by how we speak of them. 'Human being' (or *Homo sapiens*) is indeed a zoological term; but we conceive human beings as organisms which act for reasons and purposes, so if we use a subject-expression with a teleological construction we *personify* the subject, speak of it *as animate*.[3]

The word 'animate' is usually restricted to animals, but if it is the contrary of 'inanimate', and 'inanimate' means 'without life', then it should stretch to anything we consider alive; it should be coextensive with 'living'. We often say that plants are alive. We say, at least, that they die, and Aristotle attributed to them *psukhê*, the Greek equivalent of the Latin *anima*. Scientists today study micro-organisms like bacteria that were unknown to Aristotle, and James Lovelock has argued that the Earth's atmosphere, oceans and topsoil constitute a kind of macro-organism unknown to any earlier generation. Have we a concept of life which applies to all these things?

Scientists are inclined to define life in terms of such things as being 'highly organized', 'homeostatic', 'growing and developing', being 'adapted', 'taking energy from the environment and changing it from one form to another', 'responding to stimuli', 'self-replication' and 'feedback'. Thompson (2012, pp. 33–4), who takes the first seven of these definitions from Helena Curtis (1979), questions whether they are useful even for scientific purposes. When the J. Craig Venter Institute announced that it had constructed an artificial living cell (May 2010), its construction was claimed to be living on the ground that it was self-replicating. Thompson does not discuss feedback, but it stretches to such inanimate mechanisms as thermostatically controlled heating systems.

We might ask why anyone should want to divide things into two groups by these criteria. The criteria are selected because they are supposedly well defined in the sciences, and make no reference to purpose or goodness, but the hope is that they will enable us to separate things that can be harmed or benefited from things that can't. A living thing is one that can be harmed and benefited, whereas an inanimate object cannot, though it may be made more or less useful or dangerous to living things – a work of art, for instance, may be made more or less pleasing or satisfying. Anything that is sentient can be harmed or benefited, because (if my account of sentience is correct[4]) some of its movements are to obtain a benefit or avoid harm. We sometimes say that plants need light or moisture and seek them. If they *seek* light and moisture, if, that is, some of their movements or developments are for the purpose of obtaining these things, they are certainly alive, and it is hard to see how we can deny that they are sentient. If we are unwilling to say that they *seek* light and moisture, but still say they *need* them, we may be speaking of them not as alive but in the way we speak when we say 'Your car needs oil', – in reality it is you who need oil for its engine. If we nevertheless insist that light and moisture are good for vines, and that uprooting them is bad, I am not sure we are consistent. Saying that some things are good for plants and others bad goes with attributing functions to parts of them like roots, leaves, pistils and stamens. These functions, taking in moisture, photosynthesis and the rest, are things that are necessary if the plant is to grow and produce offspring. But it is hard to see how growth and reproduction benefit the plant, rather than its cultivator or consumer, if none of its functions are discharged in order that there may be growth and reproduction. If nothing that goes on in them goes on *for* their benefit, how can they have interests of their own? We cannot help things that cannot, of their nature, help themselves.

Aristotle thought that there are processes which go on in organisms for their benefit independently of sentience. He took not only the growth of plants but the development of organs in embryos and the digestion of food to be such processes. But this may have been because he could not see how they could be caused by action upon the organism by other things. Recent discoveries of the make-up of the cell, of the genetic code and so forth have made this seem possible, while modern philosophers like Wright (1973) show how we can apply to animals and even to plants a concept of biological function that is independent of any non-causal notions.

Thompson describes himself as following in Aristotle's steps, and his account of life (2012, pp. 76–82, 201–2) certainly resembles Aristotle's. He wishes to distinguish living things from inanimate by the grammar of our descriptions of them. We say things like 'Bobcats breed in spring', using simple, as distinct from continuous, verb-forms, and 'Foxgloves have blossoms of this shape in order to attract such and such insects', using teleological connectives. The second point is Aristotelian (*Physics* 2 199a23–30; *De Anima* 2 412b1–3), and Thompson rejects an account of the connectives in terms of natural selection: 'These propositions are in no sense hypotheses about the past' (p. 79). The first is Aristotelian too. Thompson takes the simple verb-forms to express something as natural. What a thing does, Aristotle says in *Physics* 2, is natural in so far as it has its source within the thing, either in its matter or in its form. It is natural for bobcats to move downwards when pushed out of a window because of the material of which they are composed, and it is natural in a different way for a living thing to do what is good for a thing of that form. Breeding in spring is natural for bobcats in the latter way, and so is bearing bobkittens and not salmon parr. But if Thompson's analysis of life is the same as Aristotle's, he encounters the same difficulty in applying it to foxgloves unless they are sentient.

Plants and what we class as the simplest animals present a problem if we suppose that biological organisms divide without remainder into those that are sentient and those that are not, or that processes that occur in them either *are* for the sake of something or *are not*. The law of excluded middle holds in arithmetic. Every fraction between 1 and 2 either is or is not greater than the square root of 2. But biological continuity is not like that. If, as we think, later species evolve out of earlier, if, for example, horses are descended from animals that were not horses, but every horse is the offspring of two horses, it cannot be the case that all the ancestors of today's horses either were or were not horses. It could be, then, that while some processes in organisms are definitely for the benefit of the organisms, and some definitely not, a process might be neither, and whereas some organisms are definitely sentient and others definitely not, some are neither, and there is no first that is. Perhaps that is how, in Aristotle's words, 'nature proceeds from inanimate to animals little by little in such a way that, because of the continuity, we cannot tell (*lanthanein*) to which those in between belong' *(Historia Animalium* 7–8 588b4–6).

However that may be, the notion of life which is of practical importance is connected with explanation as follows. If we explain any of a thing's behaviour as being for a reason or a purpose, or explain anything which happens in it as occurring for its benefit, we think of it as alive. 'Aristotle thinks plants are alive' describes the form of Aristotle's thought when he thinks that leaves grow in order to protect fruit. If we think that everything a thing does is causally explainable, we think it is a mechanism, natural or artificial. 'Modern biologists think that plants and animals are mechanisms' may describe the form of their thought when they are doing biology. (This use of 'mechanism' belongs rather to philosophy than to ordinary speech, in which 'mechanism' and 'machine' are usually reserved for artefacts with some complexity.) If we are unwilling to accept a teleological explanation of any of a thing's behaviour or anything that goes on in it, we think it is inanimate. It should be observed, however, that it is not always clear whether an explanation is teleological or causal. 'A plant grows leaves because they benefit the plant by protecting its fruit' sounds teleological, but if the thought behind it is that there are leafy plants now because in the past those plants that grew leaves had more descendants than those that didn't, because the leaves protected the fruit, we are offering, in Thompson's phrase, a 'hypothesis about the past'. (Aristotle, in contrast, thought he was explaining the process we see in spring.) As I said earlier, the question whether the same thing can be explained both teleologically and as a mere continuation is still undecided. My point here is simply that just as materiality is expressed by the grammar of causal discourse, so life, sentience and intelligence are expressed by the grammar of teleological discourse.

* * *

If that is right, 'alive', 'sentient' and 'intelligent' or 'rational' do not signify predicates or properties; they are used in phrases like 'speak of as sentient', 'think of as intelligent', to signify forms of thought and speech. In this respect thinking and saying are similar. But there are differences between saying and thinking, and I shall end this chapter by calling attention to some of them.

We say things in languages like English and French, but we do not think things in languages. At first that may sound false. Surely English speakers think in English, and talk of trying to think in French? We have these locutions, certainly, but that is because a good deal of thinking is thinking how to say things. That is particularly true of philosophers: they try out sentences in their heads. And when I think mosquitoes are present, or a woodpecker, I may say under my breath the word in my native tongue for a mosquito or a woodpecker. But we say things in languages because, although saying is not in itself an act like pushing or depicting, there is always some bodily act involved in saying, usually making sounds or visible marks or (like friends of Helen Keller) touching people. Doing this counts as saying something, or constitutes saying something, if it is done in accordance with rules that vary from society to society.

Just as when we say something our speech must have a certain form – it must be saying that something is present, or that something would be good, or that something was done for a purpose – so when we report a thought we express it as having such a form. But there is no special procedure in which we engage, nothing comparable to constructing a sentence, which counts as having a thought of that form. There is indeed something we do. If I think there are mosquitoes I act for that reason (unless I have some better reason for acting otherwise). But this acting does not merely *count* as thinking that there are mosquitoes. There are no conventions, whether limited to a particular group of people or common to everyone, with which I must comply if I am to have this thought. Acting for the reason that mosquitoes are present is precisely what it is to have a thought of this form. There are techniques for avoiding mosquito bites, but no further techniques for thinking there are mosquitoes. Similarly with more complex thoughts, like thinking that someone else has a belief or desire. When I am driving I may see you gesticulating by the road and think you want a lift. I think this if I stop for the reason that you were gesticulating and in order to give you a lift, or if I drive on, shaking my head severely. My action does not merely *count* as thinking this, and if it *constitutes* this teleological thought, that is not by virtue of any convention.

But if there are no conventional rules that give our thoughts the forms they have, how is it that they have these forms? To that there is a double answer. On the one hand, if we are to survive we must have thoughts of certain forms; we must think that things like fruit and crocodiles are or are not present, and have or lack properties. And if we are to live full human lives we must grasp causes and rational motivation and have arts and language. On the other hand, there are in fact conventional rules determining forms of thought, but they are not rules over and above the grammatical rules of particular languages. We recognize and label forms of thought to correspond to grammatical constructions. The rule for saying that something is the case is a rule for expressing the belief that it is; the rule for saying that something would be good or right is a rule for expressing the desire for it. We differentiate as many forms of thought as we have forms of speech, and if it appears that the same forms of thought are expressed in all human languages, that is because once we have recognized forms of thought expressed in our own tongue, we work out how the same forms can be expressed in other languages with perhaps fewer syntactical resources.

We are inclined, Ryle said in an unpublished lecture, to picture thoughts as like small fish darting about in the mind and hard to catch hold of, but still distinct from one another. We may even imagine that as small fish have parts – heads, fins and so on – so thoughts are composed of distinct parts, perhaps concepts and objects to which the concepts are attached, and have strands connecting one thought to another. 'Concepts', say R. M. Sainsbury and Michael Tye (2011, p. 101), 'are vehicles of representation, tools for thinking. They are individuated historically, and can be combined into structures we call *thoughts*.' Some philosophers, I think, have persuaded themselves that they see all this by some internal sense. The truth is that we interact with the world holistically; thought in itself is formless and undifferentiated. It is not divided even into beliefs and desires as the fish in a net might be divided into herrings and mackerel; still less is it divided into applications of specific concepts. These things – beliefs, desires and concepts – appear when thought is expressed in words. Language is like a filter imposed on thought, through which thought is squeezed in different streams; we might even imagine that the apertures of the filter have different shapes, which the streams take as icing sugar takes the shape of the instruments through which it is squeezed. The linguistic filter is a social product; languages exist only in societies. The shapes of the apertures are determined by the history and circumstances of the society whose language it is. Different societies pick out and give names to different features and patterns in people's behaviour, and these interpretative tools are used in conjunction with one another; a society, for example, which employs the concept of snobbery is likely to have a slightly different set of psychological terms from a society that employs the concept Aristotle expressed by *megalopsukhia*. So there is not, in general, the same one-to-one match of mental and moral terms between different languages that we expect to find between scientific terms or words for kinds of animal, vegetable and mineral.

If I am right that metaphysical terms are correlated with linguistic acts, and linguistic acts are distinguished by grammar, we cannot expect societies in which there is no recognition of grammar to have metaphysical vocabularies matching those of societies influenced by Greek philosophy, and we should not be surprised, therefore, if even such very general psychological terms as belief and desire have no exact equivalents in the language of every civilized people. In point of fact our English words 'believe' and 'belief' hardly have exact equivalents even in other European languages like Greek, Latin and French. What follows, of course, is not that thought is some kind of illusion, any more than it follows from the fact that cooks have different icing utensils that icing sugar is an illusion.

When we try to understand the psychological dimension of our being we hanker after the kind of analysis that applies to physical phenomena. Philosophers in the past simply modelled mental processes and states on physical; today they want to reduce them to processes and states of the brain. Language is not a biochemical process like digestion or perspiration, but spoken and written sentences are physical, and their grammatical structure is anchored in perceptible signs. Grammar is a bridge that takes us from matter to mind without requiring us to sign up either to spiritualism or to materialism.

13

Saying

Ancient philosophers asked what thinking is, but the question 'What is it to say something?' seems to have forced itself upon philosophers only in the twentieth century. Saying things includes not only making statements but also counselling, commanding, requesting and expressing wishes – I take it, as I argued in Chapter 7, that asking a question is *requesting* someone to say something, and expressing a wish is saying something would be good or bad. If I may be permitted broad senses of 'assert' and 'order' to match the broad senses in which, in Chapter 12, I used 'belief and desire', so that asserting is saying things that can be believed and ordering is saying things that can be desired, then the saying I want to consider here comprises asserting and ordering.

We assert and order by making sounds and visible signs. Making sounds and signs are physical actions, but asserting and ordering are not: they are institutional actions performed by complying with rules. We construct English sentences according to the rules of English, and this constitutes asserting or ordering in English, just as exchanging rings with someone in a society according to rules of the society can constitute marrying that person and acquiring certain obligations and rights. The philosophical question is: 'What is it that complying with these linguistic rules constitutes?'

I shall first give what I think is a correct answer to this question. It is derived from H. P. Grice (1957 and 1969), but I use his ideas in my own way. He undertook to give an account of the kind of meaning we attribute to words generally, as distinct from the kind we attach to 'natural' signs (morning sickness as an indication of pregnancy, for example). I use his ideas to give an account precisely of indicative and non-indicative saying. I contrast this with how Wittgenstein describes elementary languages. I show how verbs of saying can be understood, not as signifying modes of action, but as forming constructions for a kind of teleological explanation, the interpretation of linguistic behaviour. Finally I point out that this does not require us to postulate innate linguistic universals. People sometimes write today as if any satisfactory account of language must allow for its arising by the blind working of natural selection, without either assistance from variable social customs or any disinterested concern for other people; I do not feel bound by this constraint.

The beginnings of language are probably to be sought outside the human species. It is hard to see any continuity between the dance of bees, by which the location of pollen is communicated to a hive, and human speech; but it is clear that some hunting mammals teach their skills to their young, and that bats have friendships and make requests of one another is well documented (Wilkinson 1990, pp. 64–70). In all human societies people not only teach skills; they also act in order to make others aware of matters of practical importance: the location of food and drink, and the proximity of sources of harm, like quick-sands and snakes. They act to inform each other, and this behaviour is understood. Not only, I mean, does one person realize that another is acting in order to gather fruit or to avoid being bitten: a young boy, for instance, comes to understand that his mother is doing something in order that he, the boy, may pick a fruit or withdraw from a snake.

In this situation the mother acts in order that the child may act, but she may not count on the child's understanding the purpose of her action. Perhaps she takes his head between her hands and turns it to face the fruit; perhaps she lays her hand on his shoulder and pulls him back from the snake. You can adopt various devices to direct someone's attention to something, and not know which will work or why. But once the child understands that his mother has acted in order that he, the child, may notice something or do something, the mother can adopt a tactic to get her child not just to notice or do something, but to do so through understanding that she has acted for that purpose. She can use a device which will work, she hopes, precisely because her son grasps the purpose for which she uses it.

We have here what Grice saw to be the essential requirement for language: acting to affect another person's state of mind, and relying for success on the other person's realizing that you have acted for that purpose. We have not reached language proper, but we are nearer to it than the participants in Wittgenstein's 'language 1':

> Its function is the communication between a builder and his man B. B has to reach A building stones. There are cubes, bricks, slabs, beams, columns. The language consists of the words 'cube', 'brick', 'slab', 'column'. A calls out one of these words, upon which B brings a stone of a certain shape. Let us imagine a society in which this is the only system of language. The child learns this

language from grown-ups by being trained to its use. I am using the word 'trained' in a way strictly analogous to that in which we talk of an animal being trained to do certain things. It is done by means of example, reward, punishment and suchlike. (*BB*, p. 77; there is no substantial change in the version at *PI* 2, discussed in Chapter 7)

Although Wittgenstein uses the words 'function' and 'communication', he might be describing a completely mindless process. We can imagine a machine which picks up the sounds in a room and converts them into stimuli that depress keys on the keyboard of a computer; when someone sneezes near the fireplace, one key is depressed, and the letter 'a' appears on the screen; when someone drops a cup near the window, another key is depressed and the symbol '%' appears. For all Wittgenstein says to the contrary, the emitting of the sounds 'brick', 'slab', etc. by *A* could be like the sneezing or dropping. And we are told in so many words that *B* is trained like an animal. *B* brings a brick because he has learnt by experience that not to do so when the sound 'brick' is heard is attended by 'punishment', that is, by a painful sensation. *B* does not, in Wittgenstein's scenario, understand that *A* has uttered the sound on purpose, much less that *A*'s purpose was to get himself, *B*, to bring a brick.

Wittgenstein seems to be employing the notion of purpose because he tells us to see how words are *used*, and the notion of use is teleological: to use a pen is to move it for a purpose, and to use a gesture is to make it for a purpose. Wittgenstein does not, however, analyse use in teleological terms, any more than other teleological notions he discusses like guiding and deriving (*BB*, pp. 33, 118–25; *PI* 178). He stresses the difference between cases of being guided, but does not say that what holds them together is acting for certain sorts of reason (like turning left for the reason that your guide does). Attending to how a word is used, for Wittgenstein, is considering situations in which its utterance is common practice, noting what the attendant circumstances are and what the usual results. He could not have used teleological connectives to analyse saying, I suspect, because he did not consider explanation in terms of purpose a genuine alternative to causal explanation. No doubt if you asked him whether explanation in terms of purpose is a different kind of explanation from explanation in terms of causal action, he would reply: 'Yes of course; and there are countless kinds of explanation, even countless kinds of explanation in terms of purpose.' But I think that in reality he held a Humean conception of causal explanation. He says:

> If, e.g., to the question, 'why did you paint just this colour when I told you to paint a red patch?' you give the answer 'I have been shown a sample of

this colour and the word "red" was pronounced to me at the same time; and therefore this colour now always comes to my mind when I hear the word "red"', then you have given a cause for your action and not a reason. The proposition that your action has such and such a cause is a hypothesis. The hypothesis is well-founded if one has a number of experiences which, roughly speaking, agree that your action is the regular sequel of certain conditions which we then call causes of the action. ... The difference between the grammars of 'reason' and 'cause' is quite similar to that between the grammars of 'motive' and 'cause'. Of the cause one can say that one can't *know* it but only *conjecture* it. (*BB*, p. 15; this use of 'grammar' is highly idiosyncratic)

As Hume makes clear, his sort of causal explanation applies in just the same way to voluntary actions and to the workings of the fundamental forces of physics:

A man who at noon leaves his purse full of gold on the pavement at Charing Cross, may as well expect that it will fly away like a feather, as that he will find it untouched an hour later. (*Enquiries*, p. 91)

Here is a provisional account of saying that *does* use teleological connectives. To assert that something is the case is to act in order that another person may *believe* that that is the case, and rely for success on that person's divining from your action that it has that purpose. To order or advise someone to do something is to act in order that the person ordered or advised may *want* to do the thing ordered or advised, and rely for success on the person's divining from your action that that is its purpose.

I think this account is fundamentally sound, but it requires some caveats and additions. In the first place, it explains asserting and ordering in terms of belief and desire. As we have seen, philosophers sometimes conceive belief and desire as attitudes we adopt towards propositions, and the account needs to be developed in such a way as to be independent of that questionable idea. Secondly our provisional account says nothing about words or constructions, and seems compatible with the idea that sentences have meaning as wholes without significant structure. We might suppose that a speaker thinks 'The hearer will have learnt that this is what I usually do when I want to implant the belief that there's a snake at hand.'

Doing something in order to affect another person's state of mind in a definite way, and relying for success on that person's divining that you have that purpose, is not a project that would occur to someone who did not belong to a society with a fairly elaborate set of customs. Presumably society and language are both as old as humanity. Few people today would accept Rousseau's surmise, in *A*

Discourse on the Origin of Inequality, that human beings first arose from casual rapes or breeding pairs that had no contact with one another (1952, p. 175), a speculation that probably owes more to Genesis than to Plato's *Republic*. If I say 'There's a snake there', rules of English lexicography enable me to rely on your thinking I want a snake to come into your mind and rules of English grammar enable me to rely on your thinking I want it to play in your thought the part of *thing because of the presence of which*. As different countries have different rules for marrying and transferring property, so different languages have different rules of lexicography and grammar, and if, when I say 'Don't snigger', I count on your thinking I want sniggering to come into your mind as something from which it would be better to refrain, that is not because of the laws of England but because of the rules of English.

Although asserting and ordering are not themselves ways of representing, depiction or imitation could play a part in the development of language. To revert to my primitive village, the son might think that his mother is trying to get drinking into his thoughts because, though she is not drinking, she is imitating a person drinking. He thinks she is trying to get the idea of a fish into his thoughts because she is drawing for him a picture of a fish. These images are forerunners, not of assertions or orders, but of words, of vocabulary items. They might be used by other people in the village. As the need is felt to bring more and more things into people's thoughts, they could be replaced or supplemented by signs which are not likenesses, but which it is customary in the village to display when you want to bring a mode of action or a sort of object into people's thoughts.

Instead of implanting beliefs and desires I speak of bringing things into people's thoughts. But the thoughts into which they come can be classed as beliefs or desires. A slab may come into your thinking as something believed to be present, or as something thought good to bring. If the thinking does not take either form it is, so to speak, aborted; it comes to nothing and disappears. Similarly with actions and predicates: the sitting position may come into my thought as a position Theaetetus *has* or as one it would be *good* for him to acquire; flying from Athens to New York as something he is doing or as something he ought to do. But if someone just says 'flying', while I may prepare myself to think of flying, I do not actually do so, unless I think about the word: 'That's the word for flying.' An imitation of an action lends itself readily to a command, since it seems natural for human beings to copy what others do – a small child will repeat a word it hears or a gesture it sees. And (as road-sign-makers recognize) a mere picture of an object lends itself to a statement. By itself, however, no word or likeness is either; though it may function as both. When an object is such that its presence is primarily a reason for one particular line of action, as a snake is something primarily to be avoided, or milk stuff primarily to be drunk, utterance of a word for it may have both an indicative and an imperative character. If you are shooting you may take the cry 'Rabbit up' (or 'Gavagai': Quine 1960, pp. 26–40) both as a statement that a rabbit is present and as a command to shoot it. But usually when I speak you think I want something to enter your thoughts in one way or the other, and something about my action tells you which. This, when it is customary and conventional, is its grammar.

Saying something, then, is acting in order that something may enter your hearer's thoughts in a certain way, and relying for success on your hearer's gathering that that is your purpose from the linguistic customs of your society. In Chapter 12 I distinguished technical from practical reasons, and said that technical reasons were reasons for thinking action would be effective. That a sign you use is a word for something, and that the way in which you use it is the construction for asserting or ordering, are technical reasons for your action when you speak. I will illustrate this account by two or three deviant cases.

Suppose you are a Hungarian priest who speaks no English, and we have to converse in Latin; we are walking through the woods, I see a snake and I cry *'Cave! columba!'* You may think I have made this sound to get you to realize there is a snake, and you may be right; but though I meant to say that there was a snake, I actually said that there was a dove, because the Latin for a snake is not *columba* but *colubra*. Or suppose I am one of those who are given to gloomy prophecies. I say to you 'Your horse won't win.' I do not speak in order to implant the belief that your horse will not win (or uproot the belief that it will). I know that you are an incurable optimist, and I speak only in order that I may later be able to say 'I told you so.' And I do not even imagine that you will think my purpose in speaking is to change your belief about the race; I know that you will understand my real ulterior purpose. Nevertheless if your horse does not win it will be true that I *did* tell you so. I used the right words and construction, and did so in order that winning might enter your thoughts as something your horse would not do, even if your actual thought should be: 'He's trying to provoke me by saying my horse won't win.' Finally it does not take two people to say something. The ulterior purpose of saying something is to affect someone's state of mind by bringing things into that person's thoughts: we want to affect someone's mood, to cheer or console or grieve; or we want to mystify and confuse or enlighten. Of course we can want to have these effects on ourselves, and draw on our linguistic ability to talk to ourselves and produce them.

Saying, then, is acting in order to affect someone's state of mind, and having as technical reasons rules of grammar and vocabulary. To explain action in this way is to explain it, or, as we sometimes say, to *interpret* it, as linguistic behaviour, as asserting or ordering. Since we describe the speaker as relying on certain rules we use these rules ourselves in our interpretation. In Chapter 4 I distinguished linguistic from practical meaning and the linguistic meaning of a speaker from that of a speech. When we interpret action as linguistic behaviour, as in 'Galileo said that the Earth rotates', we give the linguistic meaning of the action, but since we assume that the speaker is competent, we take it to be the speaker's meaning too. Interpretation can, of course, go further to include practical meaning.

Verbs of saying are transitive and require to be completed by object-expressions, but these are unlike the expressions that complete other transitive verbs like 'push', 'cut', 'imitate' or 'represent'. They embody what are called 'constructions of reported speech'. Examples in English are 'He said that the Earth is round', 'He ordered them to sail west', 'He denied the existence of God', 'He told them where they might put it'. We can even follow a verb of saying by a complete sentence: 'Descartes asked: "What am I?"' (*Oeuvres* 7, p. 28, line 20). The sentence 'What am I?' by itself counts as direct speech, but when it is put immediately after a verb of saying it becomes 'reported' and constitutes an interpretation, not a piece of mimicry, as our readiness to use a translation shows.[1] People writing English today use quotation marks, but that is impossible in spoken English and it is a scribe's convention not required by English grammar. Verbs of saying require these constructions and they do not have to be used in indicative sentences. If I say 'Galileo said that the Earth rotates' I attribute to him action that can be interpreted as saying this; if I say 'Galileo, don't say that the Earth rotates', I advise against action that can be so interpreted.

Verbs of saying, then, introduce interpretations of otherwise unspecified action. To understand them we must take them as parts of interpretative constructions, and that constitutes knowing what saying is. To say is not to interpret, but to use the word 'say' is. We learn to speak in simple sentences before we learn what saying is. We do not have to wait, however, until we are philosophers and can read Grice, in order to learn this. We know it when we have mastered the constructions of reported speech.

We use the same constructions with verbs of thinking, and this too may be called 'interpreting' behaviour; it is interpreting it as intentional. But 'interpret' is used primarily for interpreting behaviour as linguistic. We then explain the behaviour as more intellectual. Thinking that something is spherical, I claimed, is having the shape as a reason, and that is a simple use of the concept of the shape. According to Bernard Gooch (1950, p. 8), earthworms apply a concept of angular shape. Saying that something is angular with the aim that the shape should enter somebody's thought because of rules of grammar and vocabulary is a more sophisticated use of the concept. Equally thinking that Columbus *thought* the Earth was round is a simpler use of the concept than thinking he *said* it was round, even though saying 'He thought it was round' and 'He said it was round' are, as a matter of surface grammar, equally simple uses of the word.

* * *

In Chapter 4 I compared my position on grammar not only with Wittgenstein's but also with Chomsky's; how does my position on saying things compare with Chomsky's? Chomsky does not tackle the question 'What is saying?' directly. He does, however, make remarks which could suggest a mechanistic view of language. Let me quote more fully than I did in Chapter 4 from the beginning of *Syntactic Structures*:

> Syntactic investigation of a given language has as its goal a grammar that can be viewed as a device of some sort for producing the sentences of the language under analysis.
>
> The fundamental aim of the linguistic analysis of a language L [where L is any language, as it might be English or Mandarin Chinese] is to separate the *grammatical* sequences which are the sentences of L from the *ungrammatical* sequences which are not sentences of L, and to study the structure of the grammatical sequences. The grammar of L will thus be a device that generates all the grammatical sequences of L and none of the ungrammatical. (1957, pp. 11–13)

He invites us to imagine:

> a machine that can be in any one of a finite number of states, and ... switches from one state to another by producing a certain symbol (let us say, an English word) ... Each such machine thus defines a certain language; namely the set of sentences that can be produced in this way. ... And we may call the machine itself a *finite state grammar*. (pp. 18–19)

And he says that if we can adopt this conception of language,

> we can view the speaker as being essentially a machine of the type considered. In producing a sentence the speaker begins in an initial state, produces the first

word of the sentence, thereby switching into a second state which limits the choice of the second word, etc. Each state through which he passes represents the grammatical restrictions that limit the choice of the next word at this point in the utterance. (p. 20)

He is emphatic that the grammar of English is not a finite state grammar, and he is not in general in favour of regarding human beings as machines, but he sticks to the idea that the grammar of English is 'a device that generates all the grammatical sentences of English and none of the ungrammatical'.

There might be ways of classifying sentence-components other than the traditional way of dividing them into nouns, verbs, connectives and their subdivisions. There might be relations between them other than those of subject, verb and object. And there are infinitely many ways of putting components together and transforming constructions. Chomsky mentions rules for turning an affirmative sentence into a negative, an indicative into an interrogative, an active into a passive (1957, pp. 61–3; 1972, pp. 29–32). But he does not attach any practical significance to the differences between these sentences; from the grammarian's point of view they are just differently constructed correct sentences. The rules for transformations in English are what he calls 'structure-dependent', that is, they are formulated in terms of earlier or more basic transformations, in terms of noun-phrases and so on; but there are infinitely many possible transformations even specified in terms like these. Why do little children learning their mother tongue pick out and follow rules which in fact yield assertions or orders or absolute denials? This is the problem that leads him to postulate linguistic universals (1965, pp. 18–30). Although he recognizes that his earlier claims about 'innate dispositions' and 'universal grammar' have encountered resistance, we read in 'The faculty of language' (2002, p. 1577) that 'the existence of some such constraints cannot be seriously doubted'.

Chomsky's tentative solution is that human beings are born with a disposition to look for sentence-constituents of certain types, standing in certain relations, and a disposition to try out certain grammatical rules. For instance we might be born looking for items of the noun and verb types, or for items standing in the subject–predicate relationship, or for rules prescribing certain sorts of transformation and a certain order in which they must be applied. We should then be born, whatever our ethnic origins, with a disposition towards the same grammar, which would therefore be a universal grammar, at least for human beings. This disposition would have a physical basis in the brain, inherited genetically. That there should be a physical structure which disposes us towards one possible grammar out of infinitely many should not seem impossible in view of the fact that there are machines that can produce chess moves which defeat expert chess-players.

There are, however, empirical considerations to give us pause. The notions of a noun and a verb seem fundamental in Greek and Latin grammars, and so does that of the subject–predicate relationship. But in Greek and Latin there is the grammatical difference that nouns decline whereas verbs conjugate; in the languages of China and Polynesia they do not, so can we be sure that these notions are fundamental to their speakers? The rules for the transformations Chomsky mentions vary greatly from one group of languages to another. We may agree with him that certain rules for doing them would never occur to a child, but it does not follow that there is some rule that must be grasped by all children.

These are minor worries. Behind them lies the major difficulty I mentioned in Chapter 4. Why should anyone want to produce grammatically correct sentences? If statements, questions, denials and passive statements are simply sentences produced by following certain grammatical rules, why should anyone want to follow those rules? If we say: 'For no reason. People are just born with a tendency to produce sentences that are produced by these rules,' then we are really viewing speakers as machines. What distinguishes people from inanimate objects, as I said in Chapter 12, is precisely that people act for reasons and purposes.

Chomsky postulates this brain structure, I think, because the only alternative he can conceive (1972, pp 13–44) is the theory of language-learning offered by empiricist thinkers like Russell. Empiricists recognize no kind of explanation that is not reducible to causal. My view of language, in contrast to Chomsky's no less than to Wittgenstein's, is teleological. We construct sentences in order to say that certain things are or are not the case, or that doing certain things would be good or bad. We want our friends to be aware of the presence of things which are of practical significance, things beneficial or harmful in familiar ways, and to do certain things and refrain from doing others; and constructing sentences is a means of achieving these objectives.

Once this is admitted, how languages are learnt, and how grammatical rules come to be grasped, is readily understandable. As I suggested, we can bring a sort of object or a way of acting into someone's mind by producing a likeness of it, and our manner of doing this, the accompanying sounds and gestures, will easily make it clear whether we are saying that such an object is present, advising for or against such a way of acting, or both. The likeness is a rudimentary semantic item, the accompanying sounds or gestures a rudimentary construction. All human beings understand that others mean to make statements and give counsels and commands, and they naturally look for constructions determining whether an utterance is indicative or imperative. They also look for features of the performance which will determine whether, if it is indicative, it is affirmative or negative, and if it is imperative, whether it is an order or a prohibition. Not only what is the case now, but also what was the case and what will be the case can have practical significance. Once children realize this, they will look for indications of tense, whether particles or inflections.

In this way we learn the grammar of the simple sentences. It is common ground that complex sentences are constructed out of simple by grammatical rules. But these rules too have a purpose beyond that of producing grammatically correct complexes. Important purposes are explaining causally and explaining in terms of reasons and purposes. All human beings want to learn how to cause or prevent certain outcomes, and also to understand for what reasons and purposes the people around them act. Any normal child comes to desire these sorts of understanding. Desiring them, it is not surprising that the child should spot the syntax by which people give the appropriate explanations.

No doubt we need special structures in the brain to understand sentences, and the more complex the sentences, the more complex the structures in the part of the brain concerned with speech. But syntax varies considerably from language to language, and it seems to me unlikely that the structures required are genetically determined. We need special brain structures for perceptual and muscular skills: for recognizing different sorts of tree by sight and different bird-cries by ear; for reading written words and music; for touch-typing and playing trills. The capacity to acquire these structures is innate: we inherit brains that can acquire them. But they are actually acquired as we develop. It is in such acquired characteristics that we should look for the physical basis of linguistic interpretation, while the particular sorts of construction we seek are determined by practical considerations, the need for technical information, the desire to inform and guide other people in various ways, to get them to tell us things and so forth. Talking grammatically is not an end in itself, but chatting is.

14

Conclusion

Among the ways in which philosophy differs from other disciplines is this. It is not a botanical problem what botany is about, or a historical problem what history is about. But 'What is philosophy about?' is a genuine philosophical question, and, as any professional philosopher who has been asked it will attest, a hard one to answer. And the difficulty extends to specific problems in philosophy. We are puzzled to explain what freedom is, because we are not sure what it is we want to explain. That is not true of all philosophical problems. When Sidgwick asks whether humility or chastity is a virtue (1874, pp. 306–14) we know exactly what he is talking about. But it is true of problems in metaphysics. I have argued that metaphysics is about things expressed by grammar, and I think that accounts for this peculiarity of philosophy.

It is fairly clear what questions in science are about, because they are about things for which we have words, things that can be predicated or quantified. And questions in history are about past events or states of affairs that can be put into words. But if something is expressed not by a word but by a construction, though we must have some idea of it if we understand the construction, we shall not so easily be clear about what it is. We have enough idea of it to be puzzled about it, but we cannot point to examples of it, and our ways of investigating things that are open to ostension are inapplicable to it. Not all philosophy is metaphysics, but metaphysical questions are paradigmatically philosophical, and the special elusiveness of philosophical problems is understandable if they concern things expressed by grammar.

The question 'What is history about?' belongs to the philosophy of history, and questions about the aim and scope of science belong to the philosophy of science. We speak of other departments of philosophy: the philosophy of language, of religion, of mathematics, of logic, of psychology, of art, of economics. The question then arises: is all philosophy the philosophy of something specific, or is there such a thing as philosophy pure and simple? If there is, it ought to have a field of its own. But the only serious candidates for being subjects of this philosophy pure and simple are the things I have been taking as the topics of metaphysics. If there is such a discipline as philosophy *sans phrase* it is metaphysics. But the topics of metaphysics can be assigned to specific branches: change, time and causation to the philosophy of science, thinking to the philosophy of mind and speaking to that of language. Existence and truth might be discussed by philosophers of logic, and goodness by philosophers of morals. If we want to keep metaphysical topics for some branch of philosophy other than all these, it might have to be the philosophy of philosophy. But we do better, I think, to picture these other branches of philosophy as forming a kind of umbrella, triangular segments of a circle radiating out from a centre that in itself has no area, and metaphysics as that centre. The other divisions of philosophy have areas which become more philosophical as they narrow towards that centre.

In Chapter 1 I compared metaphysics to mathematics and also to painting, to walking in desert places and (citing Hume) to shooting woodcock. These are activities that appeal to us as intelligent individuals. The arts and sciences generally can be pursued by us without much conscious regard for others. But besides being individuals, we are social beings. Belonging as we do to families, villages, nations, churches and clubs, we have emotions and aims as members of these societies. We support them against their rivals; we dread exclusion and disgrace; and we have an eye to their rules and customs even in our solitary pursuits. Metaphysics differs from mathematics and shooting woodcock in that its topics have a bearing on our interests as social beings. Metaphysicians are less dispassionate about the topics they consider than mathematicians. Mathematicians are social beings too. As Rousseau says, every artist loves applause, and desire for fame is a social motivation. Mathematicians want it acknowledged that they are right and their adversaries wrong. But the issues on which they divide have nothing to do with the customs of their societies. Whether a metaphysical position is right or wrong may threaten not just the reputation of its defenders but the customs of their society and therefore their very existence as social beings. Jerry Fodor, reviewing a new book on the relation of the physical to the psychological, speaks of:

> the broadly naturalistic consensus that civilised persons increasingly take for granted: the world consists, at a minimum, of lots and lots of medium-sized objects (tables and chairs, you and me) together with their smaller parts. These interact causally in accordance with natural laws in ways that the material sciences have explored with some success. The history of the world is the totality of such interactions. (2012, p. 34)

We challenge this metaphysical consensus at the risk of being judged uncivilized.

We (or, as usual, we Westerners) divide customs into various classes: some are formulated into laws, some not; some are moral, some political, some religious. We also associate customs with beliefs which, whether true or false, provide some kind of rationale for them. In societies, for instance, where women are excluded from political offices, they are believed to be less capable than men of political judgement; in societies with certain funeral rites, there is believed to be a life after death. If the beliefs associated with customs are challenged, the customs themselves are challenged. Our life as social beings consists in living according to our customs; even when we act against them, at least we then act *despite* them. So we defend our customs as we would our lives as individuals; for their sake people actually surrender their lives in war or martyrdom.

This accounts, I think, for the fact that metaphysicians adopt or cling tenaciously to very paradoxical views. I said in Chapter 12 that attributing thoughts to other people involves acting disinterestedly. That probably sounds surprising; but many philosophers hold something odder: that it is impossible for anyone ever to act otherwise than out of individual self-interest. When we are not philosophizing we often think that someone has acted out of completely selfless concern for some other person or even for sentient beings with which we can have no social ties like butterflies or sperm whales. Why insist that this is impossible? It is sometimes said that if any genuine altruist were born, the altruistic gene would soon be eliminated by natural selection (Carter 2005). That is to assume that all altruism, if it occurred, would be causally determined, determined by our genes and physical action on our nervous system, and that if you sacrificed your own interest once you would do so always. This is not something people naturally think, and I suspect that philosophers are inclined to accept that altruism is impossible because modern economic theory assumes that all behaviour is self-interested, and we live in a society in which economics is institutionalized. It provides salaries and influence to a number of people who, in turn, support the financial services industry, various quangos and consultancies, and business companies big enough to be politically visible and to need lobbyists and public relations agencies.

That all behaviour is causally determined is indeed current philosophical orthodoxy. 'The physical world', says Heil (2003, p. 20), 'is evidently causally closed'. But this physicalism is quite a recent phenomenon. Mill was no physicalist; nor was Russell. The growth of the idea that the mental can be reduced to the physical coincides with the growth in importance of science in the Western world. Until well into the nineteenth century science was thought of rather as Plato speaks of it in *Timaeus* 59c–d:

> Someone who, for the sake of recreation, puts aside discussions of eternal things and considers probabilities about things that come to be, will obtain a pleasure that brings no regrets and endows his life with a moderate and judicious kind of play.

Knowledge of physical nature was sought for its own sake by people working on their own and at their own expense: that is how men like Boyle, Humphrey Davis, Watt, Faraday, Clerk Maxwell, Mendel and Helmholtz made their discoveries. Today science is a group activity carried out by teams. There are big buildings devoted to it in universities and elsewhere. It demands enormous expenditure and the money comes from governments and multinational companies, the former hoping to increase their military capacity, the latter their profits. One way and another, science drives a large part of national economies. The industrial revolution was effected by a few small technical innovations, but now we are accustomed rather to a scientized than to an industrialized society. We also look to science for the services for which our forebears used to look to magic: making ourselves sexually attractive, acquiring perfect children, or, on occasion, causing sterility or death. The belief that rationalizes the place of science in our life is that it has all the answers, that it alone can bring us salvation and happiness. It would imperil this belief if there were 'in one corner of the universe, basically *different*, non-physical entities which do not fall under the laws of physics' (Dennett 1969, p. 5). So long as there is a kind of explanation not yet reduced to causal, it is offensive like Naboth's vineyard.

Philosophers who want all human behaviour to be causally explainable mostly maintain a further paradoxical position: that all causal explanation is ultimately of the billiard ball type. They deny that material objects act upon one another and thereby cause changes; apparent changes are just continuations. This denial itself conflicts with ordinary thinking, and if, as I argued, it entails rejecting the concept of matter and viewing the physical world as no different fundamentally from the world of pure mathematics, that is more paradoxical still.

We saw that doubts about whether anything causes anything were first raised in the Islamic and Christian worlds by theologians. Their aim was to honour God by making him the only genuine cause and holding his creative action responsible for everything (Gilson 1937, pp. 39, 54). Malebranche called the doctrine that fire heats, hardens and so on 'the most dangerous error of the philosophy of the ancients'; the idea of a secondary cause, a '*puissance subalterne*', is that of a '*divinité inférieure*', but still a true divinity, and if we think created things have causal powers, we shall worship them (*Recherche de la Vérité* 6.2.2–3). Improbable as it may sound, I suspect that the motivation of modern philosophers, like that of their predecessors, is religious. It is not recognized as such because the religion is not Abrahamic. God is identified not with a person who is distinct from the natural order and the source of it, but with that natural order itself which science reveals or claims to be revealing. It was held by Descartes and other Christian writers that God's existence is not only not derived from anything else, but derived in a way from himself (*Replies, Oeuvres* 7, pp. 238–9), and the physicist Professor Hawking has been reported, at least, as saying that the physical universe has the power to create itself. The passage I quoted from Mackie in Chapter 10 about earlier times causing later shows that he thought the universe has the power to perpetuate itself. Modern philosophers can declare that no ordinary object causes anything because they think (perhaps unconsciously) that whatever happens results directly from the whole system of the natural world. If they recognized matter and causal powers, material objects would become '*divinités inférieures*'. 'I make no research', says Mill, 'into the ultimate or ontological cause of anything... the true cause which is not only followed by, but actually produces, the effect. No such necessity exists for the purposes of the present inquiry, nor will any such doctrine be found in the following pages' (*System of Logic* 3.5.2). Philosophers today who allow only continuation and regular sequence within the physical order probably feel that the physical order itself is the 'ultimate and ontological' cause of everything.

If so, their metaphysics is influenced by a kind of religious belief. But the picture of a world without matter or causation, a world in which things just happen, also has a certain romantic appeal. To realize that you are in such a world, a literally powerless observer, yet staying cheerful and even finding beauty in the spectacle, appears a form of heroism. Man must 'discover his total solitude, his fundamental isolation ... He lives on the boundary of an alien world; a world that is deaf to his music, and as indifferent to his hopes as it is to his sufferings or his crimes' (Monod 1974, p. 170).

In Chapter 1 I said that our world is one of change, time and causation, in which we act on purpose and for reasons. Chapters 8 to 13 deal with these features. Philosophers in antiquity thought it their job to make them clear to us. Much philosophy in modern times has been devoted to depriving our world of these features, and trying to reconcile us to this impoverishment.

The topics of Chapters 5 to 7 are features less of the world than of rather of our thought and speech about it, and that gives them a slightly different feel. They interest us as social beings certainly no less than the topics of Chapters 8 to 13 and perhaps even more. As social beings we want to know whether objective truth is obtainable, when anything is objectively right or wrong and so forth. But non-philosophers incline to a wide range of positions on these questions, there are plenty of amateur pragmatists, absolutists, relativists and subjectivists; and whatever their tastes, customs or religious beliefs, philosophers are not opposed by a universal consensus. They cannot help being influenced, however, by religious beliefs, by the laws and practices of their society, and even by its intellectual fashions. It is obvious that some philosophers have been led by their religious convictions as well as by metaphysical double vision to attribute beliefs and desires to non-material subjects they call 'souls': only a dualistic conception of human nature, they have felt, is consistent with belief in life after death. Colin McGinn (1989), in contrast, has said: 'It is a condition of adequacy on any account of the mind–body relation that it avoids assuming theism.' Modern philosophers are as nervous of doctrines that might imply theism as medieval philosophers were of doctrines that might be inconsistent with it. But another example has been less remarked upon.

In Chapter 7 I argued that thinking good and desiring or having as an objective are the same. I allowed that there are different ways of desiring and different ways in which something can seem good or right, but I still maintained that desiring or wanting is a kind of thinking, and my position, which is substantially Plato's, makes it doubtful whether we can do of our own free will anything that *at the time of acting* we think bad or wrong. Plato (and, I have argued (1988, Chapters 2–3) Socrates and Aristotle too) saw wrong-doing as the result of erroneous thinking. It was natural, therefore, for Plato to hold that the prime and indeed the sole purpose of penal policy should be reform, and for Aristotle to think of corrective justice primarily in terms of restitution or compensation. In our society, in contrast, great emphasis is laid on punishment, on making wrongdoers suffer. Whereas in classical Greece and Rome injuries to citizens (as distinct from treason, and also sacrilege, which was thought to injure society) were a matter for civil actions, with us they are a matter for prosecution by the state. Aristotle analyses anger as desire to make someone else suffer in return for something (*De Anima* 1 403a29–31; *Rhetoric* 2 1378a30–2), and the Stoics classed it under irrational desire (*epithumia*) as a bad sort of passion (Long and Sedley 1987, vol. 2, p. 406). Philosophers today, however, say that anger, or at least 'outrage', is the 'ethical reaction' when someone else is wrongfully injured (Warnock 2001, pp. 150–1, following P. F. Strawson). The justification for punishments like flogging, death and incarceration is that the wrongdoer knew at the time that he or she was doing wrong. This point is made forcefully by Sophocles's Oedipus (*Oedipus Coloneus* 960–87). The psychological theory that rationalizes our customs is that acting and refraining are the work not of some intellectual capacity, but of an executive faculty called 'the will'. It is not enough to arrive at a judgement of how it would be best to behave; nothing will happen unless the will steps in and either causes us to act virtuously upon our judgement or, if we are wicked, causes us to act wilfully against it. It is not surprising, therefore, that many philosophers today think the Platonic view plainly false, as great a paradox as those of which I spoke just now in connection with the topics of Chapters 8 to 13.

Our customs bring pressure on our metaphysics, and our metaphysics, conversely, prompts criticism of our customs and sets ideals for how we should treat one another. Metaphysicians need not fear that their activity has no influence on social life; rather they should worry that it has too much.

Nor should they be self-conscious about the sort of attention to language which was initiated by Wittgenstein, Ryle and Austin, and which characterized philosophy in Britain in the generation after 1945. It was not an aberration. The whole argument of this book has been that the topics of metaphysics are expressed by the grammar of whatever language we speak. Our grasp of them keeps step with our linguistic capacity. The primary forms of speech are simple statements and counsels or commands; if we can speak at all we know what it is for one thing to be true or false of another and what it is for one thing to be good or bad for another. As our linguistic capacity increases and we learn to express temporal relations, to explain in terms of causes and reasons and to report speech, we come to know all there is to be known about the further topics of metaphysics. It remains only to see that we know this.

To those who say that concentration on language trivializes philosophy I reply that (at least to heirs of Greek civilization) nothing is more important than that the world contains conscious beings, and that we ourselves are not just conscious but intelligent. We can think things true or false, good or bad; we can quantify and compare; we can understand human actions, natural phenomena and the facts of pure mathematics. But we have no conception of this mental dimension of our condition apart from our second-order concepts, our concepts of the forms taken by our speech. Greek had only one word, *logos*, to cover both language and reason. The idea of a rational being is that of one that can speak. Any other idea, whether it is that of an intangible sort of ghost or wraith, or of an immensely complex machine or tangle of nerves, will ultimately be found banal and disappointing.

The concepts of truth, existence, goodness, and the other topics of metaphysics are important precisely because, as I have argued, they are second-order. They are the only concepts of intelligence we have. If we treat them like our concepts of the organisms, the chemical substances, the qualities and processes that are studied in natural science, then we may well find ourselves compelled to declare that matter and mind are both illusions and our lives without purpose. But if, as this book claims, they are purely formal, we are free to maintain, despite all that is said to the contrary, that seeking what is good for ourselves, for the society in which we live and for the individuals we care for, is both possible and intelligent.

Notes

Chapter 1

1 See, for example: Adrian Moore (2009, Introduction); Timothy Williamson (2007, p. 19); George Lakoff and Mark Johnson (1999, pp. 128, 133).
2 See Augustus de Morgan (1872), Appendix pp. 495–9.
3 One of Kant's commentators compares the argument of his Deduction of the Categories to a desert landscape; something close to a desert landscape is used for the cover of a paperback edition of Thomas Nagel's *The View from Nowhere* (1986).
4 See Leibniz, *Opuscules et fragments inedits* (1966, pp. 277–91). Chomsky (1965, pp. 5–6) quotes two eighteenth-century writers, C. Ch. du Marsais and James Beattie, who also cherished the idea of a universal grammar, but they had no great influence on philosophy.
5 See p. 59.
6 Unwillingness to define grammar or distinguish it from lexicography can be seen in students of literature too. James Guetti (1993) first suggests that grammar is 'statements about our language', as distinct from statements about reality (p. 5); then, wishing to contrast grammar with language that performs a practical function, he assimilates the distinction between the two to Wittgenstein's distinction between what can only be shown and what can be said (p. 7); and finally he equates grammar with 'the entire learned totality of the possibilities of language' (p. 19).
7 Aristotle's 'words' are nouns and finite verbs (16a1–2). A *sumbolon* was not a likeness but an agreed tally or earnest; a poker chip would be a *sumbolon* for real money.
8 Richard Rorty, to whose collection entitled *The Linguistic Turn* (1967) we owe the phrase, says that without Kant's distinctions 'it is hard to imagine what an analysis might be' (Rorty 1980, p. 172). I hope to show what it might be.
9 People often say informally 'That's the way it is', or 'That's how things are', but Heil boldly declares 'properties are *ways*: ways objects are' as though *being* were something objects *do*.
10 Justinian's closure of the Platonist School at Athens in 529 is sometimes viewed as an instance of Christian bigotry, and perhaps it was; but much of the work there could hardly have been of value to anyone outside the School, and meticulous

11 '… un livre où j'ai voulu que les femmes mesmes pussent entendre quelque chose, et cependant que les plus subtils trouvassent aussi assez de matière pour occuper leur attention.' Letter to Vatier, 22 February 1638 (*Oeuvres* 1, p. 560).
12 *Nightmare Abbey* (1818) Chapter 1. The darkness still prevails. Charles Taylor (1993, p. 239) quotes the words of Heidegger: 'Man speaks insofar as he replies to language by listening to what it says to him. Language makes us a sign, and it is language which first and last conducts us in this way to the being of a thing.' That may be my own view, but it is not how I want to put it.
13   Peruse by night, peruse them too by day
      Those model pages left to us by Greece.

Chapter 2

1 Liddell and Scott (1943) s.v. *sophia*; the same idea appears in early Hebrew writings, e.g. Exodus 31.1–6.
2 Lloyd (1980, p. 266) suggested that the rise of academic study was an inevitable consequence of democracy in the Greek cities of Ionia. In sixth-century BC Ionia, however, disputes in the Greek cities were settled less by debate than by civil war, exacerbated by treachery and atrocity. At Colophon one party sent the other into exile, the exiles were offered hospitality by the people of Smyrna, and when their hosts went out of the town to celebrate a festival, they shut the gates against them and took over the city; and though they later returned their movable possessions, they never restored their homes or land. The democrats of Miletus locked up the wives and children of their opponents in a spacious building and drove in cattle to trample them to death. Ionia must have been less like democratic England or America in its atmosphere than democratic Northern Ireland or Palestine.
3 Aristotle divides Plato's first type into two: explanations in terms of that out of which a thing arises, and explanation in terms of causal action. These two, however, can both be described as 'physical', and Plato's three types of explanation correspond to the three types of problem Aristotle enumerates in *Topics* 1 105b20–21, physical, ethical and logical.
4 Diels 80 A 1, p. 254, lines 13–14 and A 27. Protagoras may not have been a philosopher in 'our' sense, but it is out of his speculations and those of Prodicus and Cratylus that Plato's philosophy of language arises.
5 *Onoma* is a word for a name; both nouns like 'elephant' and verbs like 'to run' can be called 'words for things' – 'elephant' is a word for a sort of animal, 'to run' a word for a mode of locomotion – and in the *Cratylus*, which is a relatively early

work, Plato uses *onoma* for any word which (unlike 'not' or 'the') can be described as a word *for* something.

6   Being incomplete in this way, *ungesättig*, was noticed by Frege as a property of functional expressions in mathematics; see his 'Function and Concept' (1952, pp. 31-2). A. N. Prior and C. J. F. Williams speak of such linguistic items as requiring to be 'wrapped around' others; see, for instance, Williams (1992, pp. 13-14).

7   For example: *Topics* 1 105b23-4; *Metaphysics Z* 1029b13; *Eudemian Ethics* 1 1217b17. The word Aristotle uses for logic is not *logikos* but *analutikos*. In the *Topics* Aristotle retains Plato's word 'dialectic'; see too *De Anima* 1 403a29.

8   *Humana ante oculos foede cum vita jaceret*
        In terris oppressa gravi sub religione. (*De rerum natura* 1 62-2)
Lucretius's word *religio* does not mean the same as our 'religion', but he did have in mind fears associated with beliefs about the gods and about life after death.

Chapter 3

1   Philosophers sometimes say the phrase contains three 'tokens' of the 'type' 'tomorrow'. They also distinguish between words and morphemes. A word is a gesture, sound or inscribable pattern, but a gesture, sound or pattern is a word only when used in a language. It is not correct to say that the *word* 'mallet', for instance, means 'wooden hammer' in English and 'would prefer' in Latin; the *morpheme* 'mallet' is used in English as a word for a kind of hammer, and in Latin as part of a verb for preferring.

2   J. L. Austin (1962a) distinguished acts *of* speaking, acts performed *in* speaking and acts performed *by* speaking. By a 'linguistic act' here I mean an act *of* speaking, but he and others developed his distinction in ways I have criticized, for instance in my 1991, chapter 3.

3   Further on interrogation see p. 109.

4   Though that is not how Baker (2004) uses the phrase.

5   The earlier Wittgenstein *does* in effect distinguish grammar and lexicography. He says that the standing of words in a certain spatial relation in the sentence *says* that the things they designate stand in a certain relation in reality (*Tractatus* 3.1432). That is to say that it is because of its grammar that a sentence like 'London is north of Rome' says something true or false. He does not, however, extend this account to cover negative or imperative sentences.

Chapter 4

1. See Baker (2004), and Katherine Morris's introduction to it.
2. Baker (2004, p. 80), seems to take this example to be not about water-divining but about reaching down into holes.
3. This is a simpler idea than Heil's 'picture theory' mentioned above, p. 14, and in Chapter 13 I accept it up to a point. Charles Taylor (1993, p. 255) detects it in 'currently dominant theories of meaning in the Anglo-Saxon world'. His objection is not (as I say here) that it cannot explain how truth enters language, but (as I agree below, p. 190) that it fails to cover words which get their meaning from social customs and social history.
4. At least in that it has a similar effect on the eye.
5. Witherspoon (2000, pp. 330–2), discussing this argument, says they are using a notion of grammar not significantly different from the notion mentioned earlier of rules to prevent category mistakes.
6. Bennett introduces grammar only in his penultimate chapter.
7. Edward Witherspoon, James Conant in 'Elucidation and nonsense in Frege and the early Wittgenstein' and Cora Diamond in 'Ethics, imagination and the method of Wittgenstein's *Tractatus*'.
8. 'Im Satzzusammenhage', Frege, 1884/1953, p. x. The word 'context' was inserted by Austin.
9. Guetti (1993) avoids this paradox. For him poetry and nonsense-literature are 'grammatical displays' (p. 3), and although he denies that they have 'real' or 'actual' meaning (p. 15), he allows they are intelligible.
10. The English nouns 'dog' and 'chair' are count nouns; by contrast 'water' and 'butter' are mass nouns, and 'lamb' and 'egg' can be used either as count-nouns or as mass-nouns. I take the view that they are distinguished semantically: a count noun is a word for something quantified by counting, a mass noun one for something quantified by measuring. Rundle (1979, pp. 94, 218–30) differentiates them grammatically by whether they have plurals and can be preceded by the indefinite article. These criteria work for English but not for languages without articles or inflections of number.
11. In the Preface to *PI* Wittgenstein acknowledges a debt to P. Sraffa. Sraffa insisted that linguistic rules tell us not what people actually say but what we allow them to say without criticism: 'If the rules of a language can be constructed only by observation, there can never be any nonsense said' (McGuinness 2007, p. 231).
12. They also say 'grammatical constructions have their own conceptual content', but their example of this, 'Harry sneezed the tissue off the desk', is doubtful English, which suggests they do not think that grammatical constructions generally have such content. What, for instance, would they take to be the content of the predicative 'is'?

Chapter 5

1. Francis Bacon, on the strength of *John* 18.33–8, attributed this question to Pontius Pilate, but more probably Pilate asked 'What truth is it, to which you say you have come to bear witness?' Greek was not the first language of Pilate, the accused Jew or, presumably, the evangelist's source.
2. Davidson (1990, p. 68) has a different usage. By 'relative' truth he means, not truth *of* something, but 'truth in an interpretation, valuation or possible world'.
3. So Simon Blackburn, Noam Chomsky and A. C. Grayling in Gordon and Wilkinson 2009.
4. I argue for yet more forms in Chapter 8.
5. Dummett's analysis of asserting in terms of liability to blame or reproach is of a piece with his analysis of ordering in terms of liability to punishment (1973, p. 301). Because Frege (in translation, 1967, p 22; 1952, p. 128) speaks of 'assertoric force', and Austin (1962a, pp. 120, 147) speaks of 'illocutionary force', philosophers sometimes assume that asserting is an illocutionary act, one performed *in* speaking.
6. I have simplified his example, the first premise of which was 'If the accused was not in Berlin at the time of the murder, he did not commit the murder.' The past tense and the negative apodosis are unnecessary complications.
7. On Aristotle's talk of putting together and separating, see Crivelli (2004) pp. 62–71.

Chapter 6

1. We cannot quantify things except under some specification: we can say how many witches or cauldrons there were, but not how many things; so in 'there is (or isn't) a thing which …' it should always be possible to replace 'thing' by some more specific noun.
2. The logic of Plato and Aristotle did not in fact accommodate this combination of predication and quantification; but it would not be contrary to its spirit.

Chapter 7

1. Michael Dummett (1973, pp. 303–5) makes the strange suggestion that what stand to counsels and commands as truth and falsehood to assertions are being obeyed and disobeyed.

Chapter 8

1. For earlier Indian expressions of this idea (and interest in grammar) see Ananda K. Coomaraswamy (1947).
2. McTaggart's argument was adumbrated in *Mind* (1908), and has received, in my opinion, more discussion than it deserves.
3. For documentation see Robin le Poidevin and Murray MacBeath 1993, pp. 2–5, 223–4.
4. 'That series of positions which runs from the far past through the near past to the present, and then from the present through the near future to the far future, or conversely' (1927, section 306). It is not clear, either what these positions are – McTaggart switches to calling them 'events' – or what 'transitive asymmetrical relation' (s.305) is supposed to generate them.
5. Similarly Robin Le Poivedin: 'An event can become increasingly past' (Le Poivedin 1998, p. 3 n. 2).

Chapter 9

1. I follow Edward Hussey (1983) in translating *kineseos ti* as 'an aspect of change' – 'aspect' in its ordinary, not its grammatical sense. Aristotle goes on to define time as the quantifiable aspect of change (219b2–8). His instinct is sound, but he needs to distinguish two ways in which change can be quantified.
2. Aristotle's *Peri ideôn*, fragment 4: One man cannot resemble a second unless there is a third (Ideal) man whom they both resemble.
3. Holding that simultaneity is relative in this way does not, as Quentin Smith alleges (1998, p. 136), require us to accept the Verificationist Theory of Meaning. Smith's own view that simultaneity is absolute rests on a claim that entities like numbers and propositions exist in time.
4. Russell's reductive definitions of change and motion (1903/1969, p. 469) are in terms of times. These 'times' can be represented as points on the time-coordinate in a graph. What they are in reality, independently of physical processes, Russell does not explain.
5. He toyed, apparently, with the idea that they were parts of God.
6. Or changing direction at it. A ball thrown up vertically does not so much pass through the highest point it reaches as change direction at it.
7. This distinction, and the parallel distinction in connection with limb-movement, was overlooked, it seems to me, by C. Danto in his paper 'Basic Actions' (1965), and by Jennifer Hornsby in her book *Actions* (1980).

Chapter 10

1. By 'objects' Hume meant what he also called 'impressions' (forceful or violent sensations) and 'ideas' (ghostly copies of sensations), but readers treat his arguments as if they could be applied to physical realities.
2. As Gilson points out, the crucial move in the reasoning of the Franciscans, as in that of the Enlightenment philosophers, was to make the primary objects of human knowledge our own states of mind. Other medieval anticipations are noted by T. E. Jessop in Luce and Jessop 1964b, vol. 2, p. 63 n.1.
3. I am grateful for these translations to H.-M. Le Cleac'h, author of the 1997 *Lexique Marquesien-Français* and of many translations between European languages and Marquesan.
4. Or rather, I shall insist, in which as speakers *we* relate them.
5. Or rather the next few states; see Taleb 2008, pp. 176–8.

Chapter 11

1. Heil (2003, pp. 97–102) follows Keith Campbell (1976,) in criticising Boscovitch for holding that the world consists simply of powerful points; but it could be held that powerful objects have their powers acting not uniformly throughout them but from points.
2. One might have thought that the question which floors him, 'How do bodies communicate motion by impulse?' has the same defect as 'What time is it at two a.m.?'
3. David Bostock (1994, p. 72) attributes this idea (I think mistakenly) to Aristotle: 'In every change there is something that persists throughout the change, and some characteristic that it acquires or loses during the change.'
4. A barbarism because the first part of the word 'sociology' is Latin and the second Greek.
5. Kant himself speaks of forms of judgement here rather than forms of speech, and operates with a notion of matter as that which remains through change rather than that out of which things arise.

Chapter 12

1. Gorgias in the remarkable essay that forms Diels 82 B 3 uses *phronein*, 'think', and *logos*, 'speech', in a way that invites philosophical analysis; but it was left to Plato and Aristotle to provide it.

2   Thompson (2008, part 2) criticises this analysis and at least flirts with the idea that explanations of the form 'I did *A* because I wanted to do *B*' are equivalent to 'I did *A* in order to do *B*'.

3   This is not how Chomsky (1965) argued; and I do not think it is a grammatical rule that only a noun for a human being can be a subject of a verb of thinking or saying: grammar permits personification.

4   Lovelock and his followers sometimes claim that their planetary organism 'Gaia' is sentient – see Mary Midgley 2007 – but they do not analyse sentience as I do here.

Chapter 13

1   Davidson would say that in 'Descartes asked that' the pronoun 'that' refers 'to an utterance (not to a sentence)' (1990b, p. 105). I think it refers to a *request* to say what he was.

Bibliography

Alexander of Aphrodisias (1887), *De Anima*, ed. I. Bruns. Berlin.
Ammonius (1998), *Ammonius on Aristotle On Interpretation 9 with Boethius: On Aristotle on Interpretation 9*, trans. David Blank and Norman Kretzman, with essays by Richard Sorabji, Norman Kretzman and Mario Mignucci. London: Duckworth.
Aquinas (1950), *Summa Theologiae*. Turin: Marietti.
Aristotle (1960), *Opera*, ed. I. Bekker. Berlin: W. de Gruyter.
Augustine (1951), Loeb *Confessions*, London: Heinemann.
Austin, J. L. (1962a), *How to Do Things with Words*. Oxford: Clarendon Press.
—(1962b), *Sense and Sensibilia*. Oxford: Clarendon Press.
Ayer, A. J. (1936 [1954]), *Language Truth and Logic*. London: Gollancz.
—(1964), *Foundations of Empirical Knowledge*. London: Macmillan.
Baker, Gordon (2004), *Wittgenstein's Method*, with intro. by Katherine Morris. Oxford: Blackwell.
Baker, G. P. and Hacker, P. M. S. (1985), *Wittgenstein: Rules, Grammar and Necessity*. Oxford: Blackwell.
Barnes, Jonathan (1982), *The Presocratic Philosophers*. London: Routledge & Kegan Paul.
Berkeley, George (1964a [1707–8]), *Notebooks*, in Luce and Jessop (eds), *The Works of George Berkeley*, vol. 1. London: Nelson.
—(1964b [1710/1713]), *Principles of Human Knowledge*, and *Three Dialogues*, in Luce and Jessop (eds), *The Works of George Berkeley*, vol. 2. London: Nelson.
Bennett, Jonathan (1976), *Linguistic Behaviour*. Cambridge: Cambridge University Press.
Bhagavad Gita (1974), trans. Geoffrey Parrinder. London: Sheldon Press.
Bird, Alexander (1998), *Philosophy of Science*. London: UCL Press.
Blackburn, Simon (2009), in Gordon and Wilkinson (eds), *The Works of George Berkley*, vol. 2. London: Continuum, pp. 1–13.
—(2010), 'The steps from doing to saying', *Proceedings of the Aristotelian Society*, 110, 1–13.
Boas, F, (1911), 'Handbook of American Indian Languages', *Bureau of American Ethnology*, Bulletin 40, part 1.
Boethius (1957), *The Consolation of Philosophy*, ed. L. Beiler. Turnhout: *Corpus Christianorum*, series Latina 94.
Bostock, David (1994), *Aristotle, Metaphysics Books Z and H*. Oxford: Clarendon Press.
Boyle, Matthew (2011), 'Self-knowledge and Transparency', *Aristotelian Society*, Supplementary Vol. 85, 223–41.
Bradley, F. H. (1902), *Appearance and Reality*. London: Swan Sonnenschein.

Butterfield, Jeremy (1998), 'Seeing the Present', in Le Poidevin (ed.), *Questions of Time and Tense*, Oxford: Clarendon Press, pp. 13–42

Byrne, Alex (2011), 'Self-knowledge and Transparency', *Aristotelian Society*, Supplementary Vol. 85, 201–21.

Campbell, Keith (1976), *Metaphysics: An Introduction*. Encino: Dickenson Publishing.

Cantor, George (1955 [1895]), *Contributions to the Founding of the Theory of Transfinite Numbers*, trans. Philip E. B. Jourdain. New York: Dover.

Carnap, Rudolph (1956), *Meaning and Necessity*. Chicago: University of Chicago Press.

Carroll, Lewis (1939), *Complete Works*. London: Nonesuch.

Carter, Alan (2005), 'Evolution and the Problem of Altruism', *Philosophical Studies*, 123, 213–30.

Charlton, William (1977), 'Nonsense', *British Journal of Aesthetics*, 17, 346–60.

—(1984), 'Feeling for the Fictitious', *British Journal of Aesthetics*, 24, 206–16.

—(1985), 'Greek philosophy and the concept of an academic discipline', in P. Cartledge and F. D. Harvey (eds), *Crux: Essays Presented to G.E.M. de Ste. Croix*. Exeter: Imprint Academic, pp. 47–61.

—(1987), 'Aristotelian Powers', *Phronesis*, 32, 277–98.

—(1988), *Weakness of Will*. Oxford: Blackwell.

—(1991), *The Analytic Ambition*. Oxford: Blackwell.

—(1995), 'Plato's Later Platonism', *Oxford Studies in Ancient Philosophy*, 13, 113–33.

Chomsky, Noam (1957), *Syntactic Structures*. The Hague: Mouton.

—(1965), *Aspects of the Theory of Syntax*. Cambridge, MA: MIT Press.

—(1972), *Problems of Knowledge and Freedom*. London: Fontana.

—(2002), see Hauser, Marc C. *et al.*

—(2009), 'Truth', in Gordon and Wilkinson (eds), *Conversations on Truth*. London: Continuum, pp. 27–38.

Collingwood, R. G. (1939), *An Essay on Metaphysics*. Oxford: Clarendon Press.

Comrie, Bernard (1976), *Aspect*. Cambridge: Cambridge University Press.

Conant, James (2000), 'Elucidation and nonsense in Frege and the early Wittgenstein', in Crary and Read (eds), *The New Wittgenstein*. London: Routledge, pp. 174–217.

Coomaraswamy, Ananda K. (2008 [1947]), *Time and Eternity*. New Delhi: Munshiram.

Crary, Alice and Read, Rupert (eds) (2000), *The New Wittgenstein*. London: Routledge.

Crivelli, Paolo (2004), *Aristotle on Truth*. Cambridge, Cambridge University Press.

Crump, Ray (2009), 'The Flower' in *Cambridge Literary Review* 1(1), 126–7.

Curtis, Helena (1979), *Biology*. New York: Worth.

Danto, C. (1965), 'Basic Actions', *American Philosophical Quarterly* 2, 241–8.

Davidson, Donald (1982a [91963]), 'Actions, reasons and causes', reprinted in *Essays on Actions and Events*. Oxford: Clarendon Press, pp. 3–19.

—(1982b [1967]), 'The logical form of action sentences', reprinted in *Essays on Actions and Events*. Oxford: Clarendon Press, pp. 105–22.

—(1982c [1967]), 'Causal relations', reprinted in *Essays on Action and Events*. Oxford: Clarendon Press, pp. 149–62.

—(1982d [1970]), 'Mental events', reprinted in *Essays on Action and Events*. Oxford: Clarendon Press, pp. 207–25.

—(1990a [1973]), 'In defence of convention T', reprinted in *Inquiries into Truth and Interpretation*. Oxford: Clarendon Press, pp. 65–75.

—(1990b [1968]), 'On saying that', reprinted in *Inquiries into Truth and Interpretation*. Oxford: Clarendon Press, pp. 93–108.

Dennett, D. C. (1969), *Content and Consciousness*. London: Routledge & Kegan Paul.

—(1981), *Brainstorms*. Brighton: Harvester.

Descartes, R. (1964–74), *Oeuvres*, Adam and Tannery (eds). Paris: Vrin.

Diamond, Cora (2000), 'Ethics, imagination and the method of Wittgenstein's *Tractatus*', in Crary and Read (eds), *The New Wittgenstein*. London: Routledge, pp. 149–73.

Diels, Hermann (1966), *Die Fragmente der Vorsokratiker*, revised by Walther Kranz. Dublin/Zurich: Weidmann.

Dordillon, R. I. (1931), *Langue des Iles Marquises*. Paris: Institut d'ethnologie.

Dummett, Michael (1958–9), 'Truth', *Proceedings of the Aristotelian Society*, 59, 141–62.

—(1973), *Frege, Philosophy of Language*. London: Duckworth.

[Eckhart] (1988), *Meister Eckhart*, ed. Ursula Fleming. Glasgow: Collins.

Evans, Gareth (1982), *The Varieties of Reference*, ed. John McDowell. Oxford: Clarendon Press.

Fodor, Jerry (2012), Review of *Incomplete Nature* by T. Deacon, *The London Review of Books*, 24 May.

Frege, Gottlob (1952), *Translations* (1879–1919), ed. P. Geach and M. Black. Oxford: Blackwell.

—(1953), *The Foundations of Arithmetic (1884)*, trans. J. L. Austin. Oxford: Blackwell.

—(1967 [1918]), 'The Thought', trans. A. M. and Marcelle Quinton, reprinted in P. F. Strawson (ed.), *Philosophical Logic*. London: Oxford University Press, pp. 17–38.

Galton, Anthony (ed.) (1987), *Temporal Logics and their Applications*. London: Academic Press.

Gaskin, Richard (ed.) (2001), *Grammar in Early Twentieth-Century Philosophy*. London and New York: Routledge.

Gettier, E. (1963), 'Is knowledge justified true belief?', *Analysis*, 23, pp. 121–3.

Gildersleeve, B. L. and Gonzalez Lodge (1908), *Gildersleeve's Latin Grammar*. London: Macmillan.

Gilson, Etienne (1937), *The Unity of Philosophical Experience*. London: Sheed and Ward.

Goldman, Alvin (1971), 'The Individuation of Action', *Journal of Philosophy*, 68, 761–74.

Gordon, M. and Wilkinson, C. (eds) (2009), *Conversations on Truth*. London: Continuum.

Gotthelf, A. (ed.) (1986), *Aristotle on Nature and Living Things*. Bristol: Bristol Classical Press.

Gooch, Bernard (1950), *The Strange World of Nature*. London: Lutterworth Press.

Grayling, A. C. (2009), in Gordon and Wilkinson (eds), *Conversations on Truth*. London: Continuum, pp. 74–88.

Grice, H. P. (1957), 'Meaning', *Philosophical Review,* 66, 377–88.
—(1969), 'Utterer's meaning and intentions', *Philosophical Review,* 78, 147–77.
Guetti, James (1993), *Wittgenstein and the Grammar of Literary Experience.* Athens, GA: University of Athens Press.
Haas, W. (1972–3), 'Meanings and rules', *Aristotelian Society Proceedings,* 135–55.
Haldane, John (2011), 'Is every action morally significant?', *Philosophy,* 86, 1–27.
Hare, R. M. (1970), 'Meaning and Speech Acts', *Philosophical Review,* 79, 3–21.
Harré, R. (1970), *The Principles of Scientific Thinking.* London: Macmillan.
Hauser, Marc C., Chomsky, Noam and Tecumseh Fitch, W. (2002), 'The Faculty of Language: what is it, who has it, and how did it evolve?', *Science,* 298.
Heil, John (2003), *From an Ontological Point of View.* Oxford: Clarendon Press.
Hippocrates (1923), *Ancient Medicine,* Loeb Hippocrates, vol. 1. London: Heinemann.
Hobbes, T. (1651), *Leviathan,* ed. Michael Oakeshott. Oxford: Blackwell.
Hornsby, Jennifer (1980), *Actions.* London: Routledge & Kegan Paul.
Horwich, Paul (2000), *Truth.* Oxford: Blackwell.
Hume, David (1888 [1739-40]), *A Treatise of Human Nature,* in *Hume's Treatise,* ed. L. A. Selby-Bigge. Oxford: Clarendon Press, 1888.
—(1951), *Abstract of the Treatise (1740),* in *Hume, Theory of Knowledge,* ed. D. C. Yalden-Thomson. London: Nelson.
—(1902 [1748/1751]), *An Enquiry Concerning the Human Understanding* and *An Enquiry Concerning the Principles of Morals,* in *Hume's Enquiries,* ed. L. A. Selby-Bigge. Oxford: Clarendon Press.
—(1963 [1742-52]), *Essays.* London: Oxford University Press.
Hussey, Edward (1983), *Aristotle's Physics, Books III and IV.* Oxford: Clarendon Press.
Hutcheson, Francis (1725), *Inquiry Concerning Moral Good and Evil,* in *Inquiry into the Original of Our Ideas of Beauty and Virtue.*
Isocrates (1929), *Antidosis,* in Loeb *Isocrates'* vol. 2. London: Heinemann.
Jackson, Frank (1982), 'Epiphenomenal Qualia', *Philosophical Quarterly,* 32, 127–36.
James, William (1916), *Pragmatism (1907).* New York: Longmans.
Kant (1956 [1787]), *Kritik der reinen Vernunft.* Hamburg: Felix Meiner.
—(1965 [1783]), *Prolegomena.* Hamburg: Felix Meiner.
Kenny, Anthony (1963), *Action, Emotion and Will.* London: Routledge & Kegan Paul.
Knox, R. A. (1958), *Literary Distractions.* London: Sheed and Ward.
Kriegel, Uriah (2012), *American Philosophical Quarterly* 50, 1–22.
Kripke, Saul (1980), *Naming and Necessity.* Oxford: Blackwell.
Lakoff, George, and Johnson, Mark (1999), *Philosophy in the Flesh.* New York: Basic Books.
Le Cleac'h, H.-M. (1997), *Lexique Marquesien–Français.* Papeete: Association 'Eo Enata.
Le Poidevin, R. (ed.) (1998), *'Questions of Time and Tense'.* Oxford: Clarendon Press.
Le Poidevin, R. and MacBeath, Murray (eds) (1993), *'The Philosophy of Time'.* Oxford: Oxford University Press.

Leibniz, Gottfried (1996), *Opuscules et fragments inedits*, ed. L. Couturat. Hildesheim: Olms.
Lewis, David (1986), *On the Plurality of Worlds*. Oxford: Blackwell.
Liddell, H. G. and Scott, R. (1940), *A Greek-English Lexicon*, 9th edn. Oxford: Clarendon Press.
Lloyd, G. E. R. (1980), *Magic, Reason and Experience*. Cambridge: Cambridge University Press.
—(1983), *Science, Folklore and Ideology*. Cambridge: Cambridge University Press.
Locke, John (1700), *An Essay Concerning Human Understanding*, 4th edn.
Long, A. A. and Sedley, D. N. (1987), *The Hellenistic Philosophers*, 2 vols. Cambridge: Cambridge University Press.
Lowe, E. J. (1998), 'Tense and Persistence', in Le Poidevin (ed.), *Questions of Time and Tense*. Oxford: Clarendon Press, pp. 43–59.
Luce, A. A. and Jessop, T. E. (eds) (1964a), *The Works of George Berkeley*, vol. 1. London: Nelson.
—(1964b), *The Works of George Berkeley*, vol. 2. London: Nelson.
Lucretius (1949), *De Rerum Natura*, ed. Cyril Bailey. Oxford: Clarendon Press.
Malebranche, N., (1976 [1677–8]) *Éclaircissements* to *Recherche de la Vérité*, *Œuvres complètes de Malebranche*, ed. A. Robinet. Paris: J. Vrin.
Malotki, E. (1983), *Hopi Time*. Berlin: Mouton.
Mansion, J. E. (ed.) (1961), *Harrap's Shorter French and English Dictionary*. London: Harrap.
Maritain, Jacques (1948 [1939]), *A Preface to Metaphysics*. London: Sheed and Ward.
McGinn, Colin (1989), 'Can we solve the mind–body problem?', *Mind*, 98, 349–66.
McGuinness, B. F. (ed.) (1982), *Wittgenstein and his Times*. Oxford: Blackwell.
—(2007), 'What Wittgenstein owed to Sraffa', in G. Chiodi and L. Ditta (eds) *Sraffa or an Alternative Economics*. Basingstoke: Palgrave Macmillan, pp. 227–35.
Mackie, J. L. (1974), *The Cement of the Universe*. Oxford: Clarendon Press.
—(1977), *Ethics: Inventing Right and Wrong*. London: Penguin Books.
McTaggart, J. E. (1927), *The Nature of Existence*. Cambridge: Cambridge University Press.
Mellor, Hugh (1981), *Real Time*. Cambridge: Cambridge University Press.
—(1986), 'Tense's tenseless truth conditions', *Analysis*, 46, 167–72.
Mendelsohn, Richard (2001), 'Frege and the grammar of truth', in Gaskin (ed.), *Grammar in Early Twentieth-Century Philosophy*. London and New York: Routledge, pp. 28–53
Merricks, Trenton (2009), 'Propositional Attitudes', *Proceedings of the Aristotelian Society*, 109, 207–32.
Midgley, M. (ed.) (2007), *Earthly Realism, The Meaning of Gaia*. Exeter: Societas.
Mill, J. S. (1967 [1843]), *A System of Logic*. London: Longmans.
Millikan, Ruth (1984), *Language, Thought and other Biological Categories*. Cambridge, MA: M.I.T. Press.
Monod, Jacques (1974), *Chance and Necessity*, trans. Austyn Wainhouse. London: Fontana.

Moore, Adrian (2009), *The Evolution of Modern Metaphysics*. Cambridge: Cambridge University Press.
Moore, G. E. (1903), *Principia Ethica*. Cambridge: Cambridge University Press.
—(1922 [1903]), 'The refutation of idealism', *Mind*, 12, reprinted in *Philosophical Studies*. London: Routledge & Kegan Paul, pp. 1–30.
Morgan, Augustus de (1872), *A Budget of Paradoxes*. London: Longmans.
Morris, Katherine (2004), 'Introduction', in Baker, Gordon (2004), *Wittgenstein's Method*. Oxford: Blackwell, pp. 1–18.
Nagel, Thomas (1979 [1974]), 'What is it like to be a bat?', reprinted in *Mortal Questions*. Cambridge: Cambridge University Press.
—(1986), *The View from Nowhere*. Oxford: Oxford University Press.
Newton, Isaac (1687), *Naturalis Philosophiae Principia Mathematica*.
Newton-Smith, W. H. (1980), *The Structure of Time*. London: Routedge & Kegan Paul.
Nussbaum, Martha C. (1996), 'Poetry and the Passions: Two Stoic views', in J. Brunschwig and M. C. Nussbaum (eds), *Passions and Perceptions: Studies in Hellenistic Philosophy of Mind*. Cambridge: Cambridge University Press.
Ockham, William of (1951), *Summa Logicae*, ed. Philotheus Boehner. New York: Franciscan Institute.
—(1988 [1974]), *Ockham's Theory of Terms*, ed. and trans. by Michael J. Loux. South Bend, Indiana: St. Augustine's Press.
Oliver, Alex (2001), 'A few remarks on logical form', in Gaskin (ed.) (2001), *Grammar in Early Twentieth-Century Philosophy*. London and New York: Routledge, pp. 142–62.
Olsen, Richard (1978), 'Science, scientism and antiscience in Hellenic Athens: a new Whig interpretation', *History of Science*, 16, 179–99.
Papineau, David (2009), 'Causal closure of the physical and naturalism', in Brian P. MacLaughlin *et al.* (eds), *The Oxford Handbook of Philosophy of Mind*. Oxford: Clarendon Press.
Plato (1578), *Opera*. Geneva: Stephanus.
Plutarch (1957), *Gryllus*, Loeb Moralia, vol. 12. London: Heinemann.
Porphyry (1961), *Introduction to the Categories*, ed. I. Bekker, in *Aristotelis Opera*, vol. 4: Berlin: W. de Gruyter.
Putnam, Hilary (1973), 'Meaning and Reference', *Journal of Philosophy*, 70/19, 699–711.
Quine, W. V. O. (1960), *Word and Object*. Cambridge, MA: MIT Press.
Roby, John (1903), *A Grammar of the Latin Language*. London: Macmillan.
Rorty, Richard (1967), *The Linguistic Turn*. Chicago: University of Chicago Press.
—(1988 [1980]), *Philosophy and the Mirror of Nature*. Oxford: Blackwell.
Rousseau, Jean-Jacques (1952 [1754]), *A discourse on the Origin of Inequality*, in *The Social Contract and Discourses*, trans. G. D. H. Cole. London: Dent.
Rundle, Bede (1979), *Grammar in Philosophy*. Oxford: Clarendon Press.
Russell, Bertrand (1912), *The Problems of Philosophy*. London: Oxford University Press.
—(1921), *The Analysis of Mind*. London: Allen and Unwin.

—(1964) Russell, *The Principles of Mathematics (1903)*, 2nd edn. London: Allen and Unwin.
Ryle, G. (1971a [1960]), 'Letters and syllables in Plato', reprinted in *Collected Papers*. London: Hutchinson, vol. 1, pp. 54–71.
—(1971b [1938]), 'Categories', reprinted in *Collected Papers*. London: Hutchinson, vol. 2, pp. 170–84.
Sainsbury, R. M. and Tye, Michael (2011), 'Concepts', *Aristotelian Society*, Supplementary Vol. 85, 101–24.
Sambursky, S. (1956), *The Physical World of the Greeks*, trans. M. Gradus. London: Routledge & Kegan Paul.
Sautoy, Marcus du (2008), *A Mathematician's Journey Through Symmetry*. London: Fourth Estate.
Sextus Empiricus (1961), Loeb, *Outlines of Pyrrhonism* and *Against the Physicists*, vols 1 and 3. London: Heinemann.
Shaftesbury, Anthony, Earl of (1699), *An Inquiry Concerning Virtue and Merit*.
Shoemaker, S. (1969), 'Time without change', *Journal of Philosophy*, 66, 363–81.
Sidgwick, H. (1874), *Methods of Ethics*. London: Macmillan.
Smith, Adam (1759), *The Theory of Moral Sentiments*.
Smith, Quentin (1998), 'Absolute Simultaneity and the Infinity of Time', in Le Poidevin (ed.), *Questions of Time and Tense*. Oxford: Clarendon Press, pp. 135–83.
Stevenson, C. L. (1944), *Ethics and Language*. New Haven, CT: Yale University Press.
Strang, Colin (1974), 'Plato and the Instant', *Aristotelian Society*, Supplementary Vol. 48, 63–79.
Strawson, P. F. (ed.) (1967), *Philosophical Logic*. Oxford: Oxford University Press.
—(1974), *Subject and Predicate in Logic and Grammar*. London: Methuen.
Taleb, Nassim Nicholas (2008), *The Black Swan*. London: Penguin.
Tarski, Alfred (1944), 'The semantic concept of truth', *Philosophy and Phenomenological Research*, 4, 341–75.
Taylor, Charles (1993 [1980]), 'Theories of Meaning' in *Human Agency and Language, Philosophical Papers 1*. Cambridge: Cambridge University Press.
Thompson, Michael (2012), *Life and Action*. Cambridge, MA: Harvard University Press.
Vendler, Zeno (1957), 'Verbs and Times', *Philosophical Review*, 66, 143–60.
Warnock, Mary (1998), *An Intelligent Person's Guide to Ethics*. London: Duckworth.
White, Alan (1987), *Methods of Metaphysics*. London: Croom Helm.
[Whorf, Benjamin Lee] (1991), *Language, Thought and Reality, Selected Writings of Benjamin Lee Whorf*, ed. John B. Carroll. Cambridge, MA: MIT Press.
Wilkinson, G. F. (1990), 'Food sharing in vampire bats', *Scientific American*, vol. 262 (2), pp. 64–70.
Williams, C. J. F. (1989), *What is identity?*. Oxford: Oxford University Press.
—(1992), *Being, Identity and Truth*. Oxford: Clarendon Press.
Williamson, Timothy (2007), *The Philosophy of Philosophy*. Oxford: Blackwell.
Witherspoon, Edward (2000), 'Conceptions of nonsense in Carnap and Wittgenstein', in Crary and Read (eds), *The New Wittgenstein*. London: Routledge, pp. 315–49.

Wittgenstein, Ludwig (1955 [1921]), *Tractatus Logico-Philosophicus*. London: Routledge & Kegan Paul.
—(1958 [1933–5]), *Blue and Brown Books*. Oxford: Blackwell.
—(1958 [1945–9]), *Philosophical Investigations*. Oxford: Blackwell.
—(1978), *Philosophical Grammar*. Berkeley, CA: University of California Press.
Wright, L. (1973), 'Functions', *Philosophical Review,* 82, 139–68.

Index

absolute and relative, in grammar 41, 70, 74, 102
absolute time and space 136–7, 148, 218
accidence 39
action 140
Al Ashari 142
Alexander of Aphrodisias 160, 162
Ammonius 125
Anaxagoras 34
Anaximander 21
Anaximines 21
anger 210–11
Anytus 34–5
Aquinas 105
Archytas 24
Aristophanes 24, 28
Aristotle 2, 18, 19, Chapter 2 *passim*, 47, 52, 79, 86, 96, 190, 210, 217
   on categories 44–5, 51, 54, 97
   causation 153
   change 117, 129, 131
   existence 78, 90–1
   explanation 27, 142, 145, 214
   goodness 105–6
   language 11
   life 169, 185–8
   matter 158
   relations 75–6
   time 120–1, 123, 125–6, 127, 218
aspect 5, 7, 124–5, 140, 218
asserting 69, 74, 81–3, 193, 196
attitudes, propositional 85–6, 174–5, 196
Augustine 6, 52, 120–1, 135, 214
Austin, J. L. 83, 211, 215, 216, 217
Ayer, A. J. 2, 10, 47, 50, 71, 101, 153

Bacon, Francis 217
Baker, G. P. 50, 51, 55–7, 59, 64, 215, 216.
Barnes, Jonathan 21, 34
Beattie, James 213
being, and becoming 7, 30, 77, 118–19, 145–6, 162
   and existing 78
belief 5, 12, 33, 84, 85, 119, 169–81, 185, 189, 190–1, 196–7, 207–9
Bennett, Jonathan 59, 177–8, 216
Berkeley, George 47, 141, 148, 157, 162, 181.
Bhagavad Gita 120
Bird, Alexander 164
Blackburn, Simon 70, 110, 217
Boas, F. 123
Boethius 47, 120
Boscovich, R. J. 158
Bostock, David 219
Boyle, Matthew 172
Bradley, F. H. 75, 152
Butterfield, Jeremy 125
Byrne, Alex 172

Campbell, Keith 219
Cantor, Georg 138
Carnap, Rudolph 51
Carroll, Lewis 61, 107
Carter, Alan 207
categorematic and syncategorematic terms 7, 38, 76–7
categories
   ontological 13, 44–5, 51, 166
   category mistakes 51, 61
causation 4, 5, Chapter 10 *passim*
   causal agents, action, conditions 143–4, 151, 172–3
   causal explanation 27–8, 214
   causal powers 159–62
   see also functionalism
change 117–19, 142–3, 145–6
Chomsky, Noam 8, 11, 39, 44, 45–6, 54, 62–7, 91, 185, 200–3, 213, 217, 220.
Cobbett, William 8
cognitive science 14, 34
Collingwood, R. G. 2, 142
comparison 16, 39, 76–7, 94
Comrie, Bernard 128, 140

Conant, James 61, 216
conditional sentences 12, 16, 41, 80, 111, 145
constructions, grammatical 4–6, Chapter 3 *passim* 216
   language without 7, 59
contemporaneity 133, 153
   and tense 122, 123
   see also simultaneity
context, and truth 73
   context principle 59–62, 216
continuation 142, 152, 179, 180, 188, 208–9
Coomaraswamy, A. K. 218.
counting and measuring 89, 134
counter-causal 180
Craig Venter Institute 186
Cratylus 28, 214
Crivelli, Paolo 125, 217
Curtis, Helena 186
customs 2, 33, 106–7, 194, 196, 206–7, 210–11, 216

Danto, C. 218.
Davidson, Donald 70, 118, 154, 172, 181, 217, 220
'deflationary' theories 70–1, 110
Democritus 34
demonstratives 8, 30, 92, 93
denial 41, 73–4, 79–80, 86, 104, 201, 202.
Dennett, Daniel 177, 208
Descartes, Rene 7, 18, 47, 48, 142, 152, 157–8, 162, 163, 171, 175, 176, 185, 209
desire 4, 7, 33, 110–14, 119, 143, 149, 151, Chapter 12 *passim*, 196–7, 210 *see also* objectives
Diamond, Cora 216
dispositions 170, 174, 201
disquotation 17, 70, 82
distance 77, 131, 134
Dordillon, R. I. 123
double vision 136–7, 153, 161, 184–5, 210
Dummett, Michael 69, 70, 83, 217

Eckhart, Meister 120
Empedocles 22, 34
endoxa 52
eternity 120

Eudoxus 24
Evans, Gareth 172
existence 4, 5, 15, 77, 78, 89–90, 93, 94, 96–8, 127, 133, 135, 206
explanation, 27 *see also* causal, teleological
expressing 5–6, 11, 41–2, 50

Fitch, W. Tecumseh 11, 91
Fodor, Jerry 206
Franciscan theologians 142, 219
Frege, Gottlob 10, 92
   on assertion and negation 74, 79–86
   context 59–60, 216
   force 217
   functions 215
   number 27, 91
   questions 109
   sense and reference 41
   thoughts 2, 71–3, 175
   'tone' 58
   truth 69, 82–3
'Frege–analytic' 17
fundamental forces 151, 162, 196
functionalism 173, 176–9

Galton, Anthony 7, 128
Gaskin, Richard 7
Gettier, Edmund 12
Gilbert, W. S. 8, 118
Gildersleeve, B. L., and Gonzalez Lodge 65
Gilson, Etienne 142, 165, 208
Goldbach, Christian 3
Goldman, Alvin 118
Gooch, Bernard 200
Gorgias 35, 219
goodness 4, 43, 155, Chapter 7 *passim*, 206
grammar 7, 8–9, 28–9, Chapter 3 *passim*, 66, 191
   surface and depth grammar 14, 43, 44, 59, 101, 110, 200
grammarians 9, 37, 44–5, 50, 56, 65, 93, 119, 155, 165
gravitational force 162
Grayling, Anthony 217
Gregory of Nyssa 214
Grice, H. P. 193, 194, 199
Grotius 100

Guetti, James 213, 216

Haas, William 64
Hacker, P. M. S. 51, 55–7
Haldane, John 104
Hare, R. M. 101, 104, 109
Harré, Rom 158, 164
Hauser, Marc C. 11, 91, 179
having 77–8
Hawking, Stephen 209
Hegel, G. W. F. 18
Heidegger, Martin 78, 214
Heil, John 13–14, 183, 207, 213, 216, 219
Heraclitus 21
Hippocrates 160
Hobbes, Thomas 100, 111–12
Horace 19
Horwich, Paul 70
hulê 158
Hume, David
 on causation 141–2, 147, 148, 152, 154, 173, 195–6
 existence 89–90
 goodness 100
 'impressions and ideas' 47, 50, 151, 219
 metaphysics 1–2, 18, 206
 pleasure 113
 power 160, 164
Hussey, Edward 218
Hutcheson, Francis 47

identity 77
indicative and non-indicative 4, 10, 41, 51, 60, 70, 73, 80, 82–4, 91, 105, 108, 110, 117, 142, 193, 198, 199, 201, 203
inflecting 9, 29–30, 39, 44, 64–5
instants 52, 120, 127, 130, 135–6, 138, 139, 165
interpreting 5, 190, 193, 199–200
Isocrates 35

Jackson, Frank 183
James, William 69
Johnson, Mark 14–16, 34, 65–6, 69, 128, 129, 144, 213
Johnson, Samuel 6

Kant, Immanuel 10, 11, 18, 47, 67, 90, 100, 106, 166, 213, 219

Kenny, Anthony 112, 113
Knox, R. A. 6
Kriegel, Uriah 175
Kripke, Saul 181

Lakoff, George 14–16, 34, 65–6, 69, 128, 129, 144, 213
language, philosophy of 8
 and thinking 84, 188–91
Le Cleac'h, H.-M. 219
Le Poidevin, Robin 125, 218
Leibniz, G. W. 7
Lewis, David 125
lexicography 8, Chapter 3 *passim*
life 65, 169, 185–8
linguistic acts 4, 39–40, 45, 55–6, 60, 64, 66, 75, 77, 108, 109, 179, 190, 215
linguistic and practical meaning, purpose 42, 57–9, 62–3, 83, 199
'linguistic turn' 10, 17, 213
linguistics 8, 11
Lloyd, G. E. R. 21, 214
Locke, John
 on causation 142, 148, 153, 154
 change 117
 existence 89
 goodness 99–100, 106
 introspecting 47, 49–50, 53, 171, 175
 pain 181
 powers 158, 160–1
 substance 162, 165–6
logic, material logic 51
logical syntax 50–1
logikos, logos 29, 211, 215, 219
Long, A. A. 210
Lovelock, James 185, 220
Lowe, E. G. 124
Lucretius 34, 215

MacBeath, Murray 218
Mackie, J. L. 101, 153, 209
Malebranche, Nicholas 141, 148, 208–9
Malotki, Ekkehart 123
Maritain, Jacques 78
Marsais, R. 213
mathematics 3, 27–8, 32, 72, 86, 92, 114, 120, 124–5, 171, 206, 208
McGinn, Colin 183, 210
McGuinness, B. F. 216

McTaggart, J. E. 89, 121, 125, 150, 218
megalopsukhia 190
Mellor, Hugh 121–2
Mendelsohn, Richard 69
Merricks, Trenton 175
metaphysics 1–3, 18, 205–6
Midgley, Mary 220
Mill, J. S. 47, 163, 164, 207, 209
Millikan, Ruth 178
Monod, Jacques 209
Moore, Adrian 213
Moore, G. E., 47, 55, 100, 171–2
Morgan, Augustus de 213

Nagel, Thomas 183, 213
necessity 12, 28, 81, 141, 154, 164–5
negations, 81 *see also* denial
Newton, Isaac 136–7, 148, 152
Newton-Smith, W. H. 133
nonsense 38, 61–2, 63, 216
nouns 9, 40, 42, 44, 185, 202, 213, 214, 217
    abstract 40, 75, 94, 97
    count and mass 60, 63, 216
    and finite verbs 28–9, 31, 123–4
number 2, 3, 9–10, 27, 90–2, 98, 125, 218
    in grammar 7, 9, 29, 31, 216
Nussbaum, Martha C. 112

objective truth, rightness 5, 71, 84, 103, 155, 210
objectives 99, 105–8, 110–14, 119, 173, 174, 179–80, 182–3
Ockham, William of 38, 76, 92
Oliver, Alex 7
Olsen, Richard 34
Orwell, George, 18, 29
Oxford English Dictionary, Shorter 8, 52

Papineau, David 181
Parmenides 22, 29, 35
Peacock, Thomas Love 18
perfect tense-forms 123, 128, 140
phenomenological properties 181, 183–4
philosophia 21, 33
philosophy Chapter 2 *passim*, 205–6
physicality, the physical 4, 10, 27, 71, 114, 162, 166, 167, 177–9, 209
    physicalism 169, 206–7

Plato 18, 19, Chapter 2 *passim*
    on bodies 152, 157–60
    categories 13, 44
    change 118–19
    existence and quantification 78, 90, 94, 98, 217
    explanation 27–8
    eternity 120
    grammar 28–9, 214–15
    parts of psyche 107
    pictures 56
    politics 32–3
    relative terms 29, 75–7
    science 34, 208
    thinking 31, 84, 169, 219
    truth 29–30, 69, 72, 73–4, 79, 109
    wrong-doing 210
Plutarch 33
polite forms 42
Pope, Alexander 6
Porphyry 47
possibility 12, 28, 81, 98, 132
practical and linguistic meaning 42, 57–62, 199
practical necessity and possibility 28, 81
practical orientation 110
practical rationality 107
practical and technical reasons 170, 198
pragmatism 69
predicates 73–5, 76, 91–2
    negative 79
predication
    by analogy 90
    forms of 77, 79, 92, 119
    and quantification 4, 40, 90, 91, 94–7
predicative 'is' 78, 217
preventing 143, 150–1
Prior, A. N. 128, 215
processes 115, 127–30
Prodicus 28, 35, 214
proper names 38, 41, 60, 92
Protagoras 28, 35, 69, 214
Proust, Marcel 162
psukhê 185
psychological aspect, terms 5, 169, 190, 191
Puffendorf, Samuel 100
Putnam, Hilary 95, 176
Pyrrhonians 142

qualia 2, 183
quantification 4, 40, 43, Chapter 6 *passim*
   of change 131–2
questions 109
Quine, W. V. O. 74, 198

reasons, and belief Chapter 12 *passim*
   technical and practical 170, 198
'redundancy' theories *see* 'deflationary'
reflexives 50, 77
relations 44, 75–8, 108
   between thoughts and action 177, 179
   causal 153–5
   spatial 77, 134, 215
   temporal 5, 81, 121–4
research 2–3, 17, 23–4, 34
rhetoric 42, 58
Rorty, Richard 213
Rousseau, Jean-Jacques 196–7, 206
Rundle, Bede 7, 94, 123, 216
Russell, Bertrand 18
   on 'acquaintance' and objects of 47, 50, 71, 151, 153, 183
   change 117, 119, 120, 125, 138–9, 146, 165, 218
   and Chomsky 202
   desire 112
   physicalism 112, 185, 207
   relations 76
   see also nonsense
Ryle, Gilbert 51, 61–2, 90, 118, 181, 190, 211

Sainsbury, R. M. 71, 190
Sambursky, S. 34
Sapir, Edward, and Whorf, Benjamin Lee 9–10
Sartre, Jean-Paul 78
Sautoy, Marcus du 3
saying 57–8, 62, Chapter 13 *passim*
scepticism 5, 69, 107, 120, 142, 155
Sedley, D. N. 210
sensations, bodily 106, 181–3
sense and reference 41
sentences
   need to define 66, 202–3
   without grammar 59
Sextus Empiricus 142, 153

Shaftesbury, Antony Earl of 99
Shoemaker, S. 133–4
Sidgwick, Henry 205
similarity 76
Simplicius 16
simultaneity 130–1
skill 14, 140, 143, 159, 170, 203
Smith, Adam 47, 99–100
Smith, Quentin 218
society 60, 77, 80, 106–7, 112–13, 163, 189, 190, 196–7, 206–8, 210
Socrates 23–4, 25, 28, 31, 34, 210
sophia 21, 214
Sophocles 211
Speusippus 24
Sraffa, P. 216
Stevenson, C. L. 101
Stoppard, Tom 11
Strang, Colin 130
Strawson, P. F. 79, 211
Suarez, Francisco 100
sumplokê (weaving together) 44, 56, 86
syncategorematic terms 7, 38, 76, 77
syntax 8, 39, 203
   logical syntax 50
   see also grammar

Taleb, Nassim Nicholas 219
Tarski, Alfred 70
Taylor, Charles 214, 216
teleological explanation 62, 174–5, 177–83, 185, 187–8, 195–6, 202
tense 5, 120–6
Thales 21
'that' clauses 51, 72, 75, 199
Thompson, Michael 124, 128, 146, 186–8, 220
thought Chapter 12 *passim*
   and language 84, 188–91, 211–12
   Fregean thoughts 71–3
   thoughts instantiated by actions 179
time 4–5, 14–15, 135
   empty 133–4, 135
   practical significance of 147
   and preventing 150–1
   reality of 120–2, 125
   stretches of 130
   travel and locations in 137–8
Todd, H. J.: *Todd's Johnson* 8

token and type 215
tone 58
transitive and intransitive 5, 49–50, 145–6, 155, 199, 218
truth Chapter 5 *passim*
   absolute and relative 70, 74
   deflationary theories of 71–2, 110
   in existential statements 93–4
   and rightness 110
Tye, Michael 71, 190

uniform motion 148, 152, 153
universals 12, 30, 74
   linguistic 67, 194, 201
use, of words and sentences 58–9, 60, 195

Vazquez, Gabriel 100
Vendler, Zeno 7, 129, 146
verbs, finite 29, 213
verificationism 218
voice, active and passive 5, 124, 145
volition 175

Warnock, Mary 100, 211
White, Alan 2
White, Gilbert 23–4
Whorf, Benjamin Lee 9–10, 123
Wilkinson, G. S. 194
will, faculty of 211
Williams, C. J. F. 77, 215
Williamson, Timothy 12–13, 14, 16–17, 28, 70, 213
Witherspoon, Edward 51, 60, 216
Wittgenstein, Ludwig 11, 14, 15, 45–64 *passim*, 71, 72, 101, 161, 181, 211, 213, 215
   on categories 54
   explanation 195–6
   his use of 'grammar' 7, 48, 50, 51–2, 59
   nonsense 61, 63–4, 216
   orders 108, 194–5
   sense-data 54, 153, 184
Wright, Larry 178, 187

Xenophanes 21, 22
Xenophon 31

www.ingramcontent.com/pod-product-compliance
Lightning Source LLC
Chambersburg PA
CBHW050138240426
43673CB00043B/1710